The Myth Against Myth

A Study of Yeats's
Imagination in Old Age

Daniel Albright

The Myth Against Myth

A Study of Yeats's
Imagination in Old Age

LONDON
OXFORD UNIVERSITY PRESS
1972

Oxford University Press, Ely House, London W.1

GLASGOW   NEW YORK   TORONTO   MELBOURNE   WELLINGTON
CAPE TOWN   IBADAN   NAIROBI   DAR ES SALAAM   LUSAKA   ADDIS ABABA
DELHI   BOMBAY   CALCUTTA   MADRAS   KARACHI   LAHORE   DACCA
KUALA LUMPUR   SINGAPORE   HONG KONG   TOKYO

ISBN O 19 212188 X

© Oxford University Press 1972

*Printed in Great Britain
by W & J Mackay Limited, Chatham*

to Richard Ellmann

Contents

Acknowledgements

I WISH to thank Michael Yeats and The Macmillan Company, both in England and America, for permission to quote from the copyrighted poetry and prose of William Butler Yeats; and Faber and Faber Limited for permission to quote from Wallace Stevens' 'Sunday Morning' and two of the Cantos of Ezra Pound.

One ought to make a full confession here, for the only original sin is plagiarism. But I can list only a few names of those to whom I am deeply grateful: first, Richard Ellmann; Mrs. Leone Albright, a woman of great maternal and maieutic cleverness; two people whose households made New Haven habitable for me when I wrote this book, Mrs. Anne Marks and Mrs. Ione Riquelme; and my fine research assistants, Mr. David Cook, Miss Debbie Biemiller, and Miss Karin Larson.

Preface

THE Western sensibility does not dissociate, it only ramifies.
Yeats, Eliot, and many others have considered that the direction
of our literary evolution was downhill, from Dantescan vividness
of vision, unity of personality, to Miltonic coldness to modern
fragmentation; but the fragmentation seems an adequate response, for the increasing complexity of our civilization requires
increasingly subtle analysis, the finest dissection of capillaries.
The business of the modern poet is the tessellation of fragments,
and it is through this act that he finds, or creates, his sensibility.

This book is a study of Yeats's image of the human mind, his
painstaking construction of his own personality by means of
poetry. To some extent, Yeats tried to translate his intimate,
public self directly into an objective, verbal image; but although
he included his friends in his poetry, even distant people, they
all remain stylizations or shadows, and Yeats was left alone with
the form-trace of his own life as his only satisfactory myth. Yeats
hardly touched his wife in his poetry; Yeats's friends are often
more powerful in death than in life—Robert Gregory, Florence
Farr, MacGregor Mathers, executed Irish revolutionaries; even
Maud Gonne, the great love of Yeats's life, is inhuman, the
Rose of the World when young, a bronze sculpture when old.
After *The Countess Cathleen*, rich human interaction is very limited in Yeats's art; his plays are parabolic, while his lyric voice is
involuted, generalized ('all men's speech'), evolving from hyper-
dulia to retrospection.

The method Yeats used to forge his soul did not involve anything that we commonly call autobiography. Homely incident
is wholly irrelevant; Yeats disliked nothing more than the kind
of art which reduces to tape-recorded dialogue and hidden

cameras—the naturalistic art which he associated with Stendhal's mirror. Yeats's real autobiography is called *A Vision*—and that book is an attempt to let Western civilization, or the mind of the race itself, write its own autobiography; at that period in his life Yeats tried to find in the structure of history the structure of his own personality. If the first book of *A Vision* teaches anything it teaches that the highest development of personality, the human zenith, the full moon, occurs between Keats and Blake; so it is to the great branching-out of early romanticism that we must turn to discover what Yeats was trying to recreate in himself.

It seems that English poetry after the seventeenth century was increasingly unable to deal with the growing diffuseness of human personalities. Up till the end of the Renaissance it was easy to classify people according to moral or familial or occupational or physiological categories; and, because the categorization is secure, the individuation, the human uniqueness, of any character can be established on a firm ground. As late as the eighteenth century Pope could use such structures as the ruling passions to generate personalities from comfortably knowable premises. But in Pope's satires the ultimate degradation is to be no one at all; and this insecurity of personality, this sense that the self can remain unformed, or deliquesce, shows the new anxiety that is slowly emerging. For comparison, Donne ridicules through the principle of analogical descent; his satires are full of apes, puppet shows, wax gardens, and other types of low simulacra. Pope suggests, on the other hand, that the objects of his satire may not attain any form at all: Sporus is immature androgynous, a child of dirt, a mass of parts that do not fit together; Dulness lives among maggots, embryos, inchoate things; Atossa is scarce once herself, by turns all womankind; in fact, women have no characters at all. And Swift reveals, in those most terrifying poems 'A Beautiful Young Nymph Going to Bed' and 'The Progress of Beauty', that individuation may reduce to a mass of prostheses, beneath which the human dissolves into excrementious formlessness. After Pope and Swift, Samual Johnson tries to cling to individuality as well as he can: he says again and again in the curious manual on epitaph-writing which concludes the *Life* of Pope that an epitaph must show the traits that manifest the uniqueness of its subject; and admirably fulfills his precepts in his poem on Robert Levett. But

Gray and Collins drift out into isolated emotions, not full men but shards of personality, fear, superstition, night-meditations, a mythy distant poetical character.

It is clear that some of the romantic poets tried to fuse the fragments of an overevolved human consciousness into a single inclusive mind, the Zoas reconciled or the Ravine of Arve; and that this process of poetic discovery was at the same time the discovery of the poet's self. Therefore the expanded mind of the poet holds in a matrix all perceived objects, the whole world, in which the vast interactions of wind, waves, land masses, and subterranean caverns are emblems for the workings of the mind which contains them. 'I am a portion of all I behold' is the motto of such disparate romantic works as 'Childe Harold's Pilgrimage' (Canto III) and Whitman's 'There was a Child Went Forth'; but if the poet cannot see anything which is not himself it will not be easy for him to integrate his ordinary social identity into this enormous selfhood. For example, the Spenser of the *Amoretti* for all his graceful conventionality, is the historical Irishman whose behaviour is consistent with what we know of his biography and poetical reminiscences, such as 'Colin Clout's Come Home Again'; he writes poems to a woman who does not seem under his imaginative control, a woman whose rejection or acceptance seems more determined by her own temperament than by the formal exigencies of his sonnet sequence; he speaks of problems which are Edmund Spenser's and no one else's, such as trying to finish the *Faerie Queene* while carrying on a love affair.

The Keats of the great odes, on the other hand, may have a more vivid personality, but a biographer could not learn any useful facts from the poetry; Keats was a medical student from a poor home, extremely short, tubercular, but all this is invisible; to live a day-to-day life inside a body of a certain height counts for nothing to a romantic poet. Keats, by expressing all men's desires, made the contours of his personality unforgettable; but, as he himself understood in 'The Fall of Hyperion', he could only achieve this by writing a poetry incompatible with the humanitarian instinct, simply because his vision could not subsume contemporary London, or his friends, or even that pervasive vague woman Fanny Brawne. Blake solved the social problem with his usual forthrightness by presenting the names of his contemporary

persecutors in *Jerusalem* as if they were still more creatures of
his epistemological fantasy; but Shelley found perhaps the most
daring solution in the most romantic of all romantic love poems,
the 'Epipsychidion'. If the mind of Shelley contains volcanoes
and seas, is in fact the world, then he can deal with his friends
cosmically, one world to another; his girl friends become the
sun, the moon, a comet, governing 'This world of love, this *me*'.
His human interaction has been abstracted into gravitational
physics; he has successfully replaced the tensions between man
and woman with purely mathematical tension, independent of
the given man or the given woman but embodying the complexity
of their interrelationship. These beautifully insoluble forces of
human contact (prefigured in the fourth act of *Prometheus Un-
bound*) allow Shelley to maintain his strict universality, genera-
lity, while presenting the private universe of his personal experience; 'Adonais' fills in the cosmos a little further, as his dead
friend Keats becomes a star exercising an attractive force of its
own.

   These are the poets who most persistently influenced Yeats;
and indeed Yeats uses the gravitational ploy himself in his superb love poem, 'Chosen', in which the woman and her lover
again turn into the earth and the sun. But Yeats's solution to the
problem of constructing a self-in-poetry could not be Shelley's;
Shelley's millenium did not admit of political or personal fulfilment, as far as we can see, but Yeats's did, although not
without further evolution of vision. 'Alastor' and 'The Wanderings of Oisin' frame the great era of romantic voyages; the hero
of Alastor found the sublimity of death, while Oisin, compelled
to live, raged against the pusillaminity of life. So Shelley died
young and Yeats survived into old age; and the length of his
days offered to Yeats a metaphor for his artifact-self that would
not have occurred to Shelley. Yeats's mind does not expand into
space, that is, perceived phenomena, a humanized nature; instead it expands into time, embracing personal and racial
memory. According to the 'Introduction to *The Words upon the
Window-pane*' each man sees the form of history as the form of his
own life, so that his life repeats in miniature the development of
Western civilization. From this proceeds Yeats's personal in-
timacy with cyclical history in *A Vision*; and when he says in
'The Second Coming' that the centre cannot hold, he is talking

about a state of mind, almost a mental breakdown, as much as about post-war society; and when he prophesies a second coming, he is prophesying his own rebirth. A few years later, at the age of sixty, in 'The Tower' Yeats says, 'Now shall I make my soul'; and I am principally concerned here with Yeats reborn, preterist, contracted from a monstrous romantic mind to a rough thing, man-sized but fierce, objectified, staring as we all do at a romantic world with new-born modern eyes.

1

Flesh Made Word

―――⊃○⊙○⊂―――

'The Tower'

IN 1923 Yeats won the Nobel prize, and during his sojourn in Stockholm he kept a diary; near the beginning he writes of the process of lyric composition:

Every now and then, when something has stirred my imagination, I begin talking to myself. I speak in my own person and dramatize myself, very much as I have seen a mad old woman do upon the Dublin quays, and sometimes detect myself speaking and moving as if I were still young, or walking perhaps like an old man with fumbling steps. Occasionally, I write out what I have said in verse, and generally for no better reason than because I remember that I have written no verse for a long time. I do not think of my soliloquies as having different literary qualities. They stir my interest, by their appropriateness to the men I imagine myself to be, or by their accurate description of some emotional circumstance, more than by any aesthetic value. When I begin to write I have no object but to find for them some natural speech, rhythm and syntax, and to set it out in some pattern, so seeming old that it may seem all men's speech, and though the labour is very great, I seem to have used no faculty peculiar to myself, certainly no special gift. I print the poem and never hear about it again, until I find the book years after with a page dog-eared by some young man, or marked by some young girl with a violet, and when I have seen that I am a little ashamed, as though somebody were to attribute to me a delicacy of feeling I should but do not possess.[1]

No one would guess that Yeats's lyrics arose from such disorderly mania, such fumbling postures; nor would anyone guess that Yeats felt so remote from his finished compositions, as if the laborious pressure which fused his babbling into a perfect diamond came from somewhere beyond the poet's own comprehension. Part of the doctrine expressed in this passage is common in Yeats's earlier thinking; for instance, in his *Reveries over Childhood and Youth*, published in 1914, Yeats mentions that a lyric poet must be able to assume 'one out of half a dozen traditional poses, and be lover or saint, sage or sensualist, or mere mocker of all life';[2] but nowhere before *The Bounty of Sweden* does Yeats look so dispassionately at the jumbled sources from which poetry springs, or record with such honesty the peculiar half-embarrassment which is the poet's lot in ordinary life. Throughout the passage Yeats seems to be thinking of his heroic and love lyrics; at least it is hard to imagine a girl pressing a violet in, say, 'The Phases of the Moon'; but at this period in his life Yeats was becoming increasingly experimental in his personae, even beginning to write a few poems which sound almost as if they had originated in some old-womanish self-muttering. The 1923 'The Gift of Harun Al-Rashid' shows Yeats covering his face with the gauziest of fictions; but that poem, although its conclusion is quite human, suffers too much from the expository *malaise* of *A Vision* to reveal much of the inchoate self-dramatization from which it, too, presumably sprang. It is not until 'The Tower', written about two years after *The Bounty of Sweden*, that we can see Yeats, sixty years old, detecting himself speaking and walking 'like an old man with fumbling steps'—and wondering what he is doing, and why he is doing it, and perhaps noting the similarity between that imaginary old man's walk and his own gait.

Yeats records in his 1930 Diary a fragment of a conversation: 'Presently I said to my wife: "Now that my vitality grows less I should set up as sage."'[3] This is a sample of the musing which underlies 'The Tower', but in the poem itself everything is dramatized, objective, subtly masked. The poem begins with a great oratorical breast-beating expostulation:

> What shall I do with this absurdity—
> O heart, O troubled heart—this caricature,
> Decrepit age that has been tied to me
> As to a dog's tail?
>   Never had I more
> Excited, passionate, fantastical
> Imagination, nor an ear and eye
> That more expected the impossible—

No, not in boyhood when with rod and fly,
Or the humbler worm, I climbed Ben Bulben's back
And had the livelong summer day to spend.[4]

The word 'caricature' sets the tone of the opening: old age may be a caricature, but the poet has further caricatured old age as a clattering tin can, curiously separable from the poet's dog's-body; and that excessively heart-felt invocation to his heart ('O heart, O troubled heart') has more than a tinge of lyric parody. This is followed by a more positive declaration of the passion which still inheres in the poet's imagination, as if he were pre-paring himself for a heroic denunciation of old age—exactly as Blake did in a passage that Yeats quoted in 1897:

'I have been very near the gates of death,' Blake wrote in one of his last letters, 'and have returned very weak and an old man, feeble and tottering, but not in spirit and life, not in the real man, the imagination, which liveth for ever. In that I am stronger and stronger as this foolish body decays.'[5]

That is one solution possible for an ageing poet, and, although Yeats veers away from it before he reaches it, the potentiality for that sort of statement remains in the poem.

The tone shifts abruptly as the thought of his imagination's excitability brings up a memory of his imagination in boyhood; the three-line idyll of the boy Yeats fishing on Ben Bulben has the curious feeling of an old man's half-satire on an old man's memories of childhood, summed up in the phrase 'humbler worm' and all its connotations of Wordsworthian fake sentimentality, a deliberately overblown affection for natural minutiae. The logic of this transition is also odd, since the boy's 'fantastical/Imagina-tion' seems to expect nothing more impossible than a fish; but there is a suggestion of the unified animism of childhood in the phrase 'Ben Bulben's back', and the 'livelong summer day' seems to recede back into a youth's dream of an endless summer. If there is any serious import to this first memory, it is that youth is the proper time for poetry and imagination (as in 'Sailing to Byzantium'); and Yeats did not disdain to quote Wordsworth with complete gravity in *Per Amica Silentia Lunae*:

Our daily thought was certainly but the line of foam at the shallow edge of a vast luminous sea; Henry More's *Anima Mundi*, Wordsworth's 'immortal sea which brought us hither', and near whose edge the children sport, and in that sea there were some who swam or sailed, explorers who perhaps knew all its shores.[6]

Yeats's faith in the immediate impact of a child's perceptions can be seen in an introduction he wrote for Rabindranath Tagore's *Gitanjali*:

An innocence, a simplicity that one does not find elsewhere in literature makes the birds and the leaves seem as near to him as they are near to children, and the changes of the seasons great events as before our thoughts had arisen between them and us.[7]

Yeats concludes from his memory of his childhood that something is missing in his old age, even if his imagination is as fantastical as ever; he must choose, tentatively, between a life of abstract speculation and the poet's life, and if he chooses the latter he must let himself be mocked by his old body; the assumption behind those alternatives is that poetry is somehow an act of the body and the body's desires, and that assumption will be borne out by the rest of the poem.

> It seems that I must bid the Muse go pack,
> Choose Plato and Plotinus for a friend
> Until imagination, ear and eye
> Can be content with argument and deal
> In abstract things; or be derided by
> A sort of battered kettle at the heel.

Thought can usurp our imaginations and even our physical senses ('ear and eye'), just as it rises between the adult and his perception of the seasons in the passage from the *Gitanjali* introduction quoted above. This descent into abstraction is surely a last resort for a poet, especially for a poet with Yeats's intense hatred of abstractions; but it is all treated with good humour, almost too gently to be the gallows humour of old age. The kind of quiet togated discussion suggested by the thought of having Plato and Plotinus as one's friends is surely not under serious consideration; one can imagine a bored Yeats replying, 'Yes, Socrates . . . indeed, Socrates . . . to be sure, Socrates' forever in some Platonic dialogue. There is a passage in 'A Packet for Ezra Pound' which may be relevant to that Muse and her suitcase:

But Muses resemble women who creep out at night and give themselves to unknown sailors and return to talk of Chinese porcelain . . . the Muses sometimes form in those low haunts their most lasting attachments.[8]

It must be emphasized that physical lustfulness underlies the creations of poets, because this is important to the rest of the poem; and Yeats will not cut himself free of the battered kettle at his heel, no matter what he threatens here.

Yeats's mask retains its straight-faced near-whimsy, but it is not hard to see the potentiality for the rage of Part II: 'Did all old men and women . . . rage/As I do now against old age?' How can a passionless ravaged body sustain the passionate imagination of a poet? Blake declared that the imagination grew stronger as the body decayed; but if bodily vigour is necessary for poetry, Yeats cannot make Blake's declaration; and Yeats knows the case-histories of other poets, and how old age has affected them:

A poet, when he is growing old, will ask himself if he cannot keep his mask and his vision without new bitterness, new disappointment. Could he if he would, knowing how frail his vigour from youth up, copy Landor who lived loving and hating, ridiculous and unconquered, into extreme old age, all lost but the favour of his Muses?

> The Mother of the Muses, we are taught,
> Is Memory; she has left me; they remain,
> And shake my shoulder, urging me to sing.

Surely, he may think, now that I have found vision and mask I need not suffer any longer. He will buy perhaps some small old house, where, like Ariosto, he can dig his garden, and think that in the return of birds and leaves, or moon and sun, and in the evening flight of the rooks he may discover rhythm and pattern like those in sleep and so never awake out of vision. Then he will remember Wordsworth withering into eighty years, honoured and empty-witted, and climb to some waste room and find, forgotten there by youth, some bitter crust.[9]

If Yeats mocks Wordsworth, Wordsworth's fate may return to mock him; and Yeats's tower, as we know from 'Blood and the Moon', has a waste room at the top, lying in wait. Ariosto is a possible persona, too, for Yeats in this poem: Ariosto's harmony with astronomical rhythms, his quiet contentment with natural life, is reminiscent of more than one passage in Part III.

But Landor resembles Yeats here more than any of the others do, with his ridiculously savage emotions, his stripped body—a genuine wild old wicked man; but there is one important difference. The Muses prod Landor in vain, because he has lost his memories, and he has nothing left to sing about; while Yeats retains everything in his mind, and his memories can be channelled into the rest of 'The Tower', indeed can gush through all the poems of the last years of his life. According to 'The Tower', memory is not only the theme for poetry, it is virtually the substance and achievement of life itself.

Part II of 'The Tower' begins with a tremendous summoning of images and memories from the landscape of Thoor Ballylee:

> I pace upon the battlements and stare
> On the foundations of a house, or where
> Tree, like a sooty finger, starts from the earth;
> And send imagination forth
> Under the day's declining beam, and call
> Images and memories
> From ruin or from ancient trees,
> For I would ask a question of them all.

The human imagination has started the great act of creation which extends from here to the middle of Part III. In Yeats's thought, images and symbols have a way of unfurling until they include and evoke the widest range of human experience:

A meditation on sunlight, for instance, affects the nature throughout, producing all the effects which follow from the symbolical nature of the sun. Hate must, in the same way, create sterility, producing many effects which would follow from meditation on a symbol. Such a symbol would produce not merely hate but associated effects. An emotion produces a symbol—sensual emotion dreams of water, for instance—just as a symbol produces emotion.[10]

By summoning the images of the old, Yeats is summoning his own rage against old age; and by summoning old poets he is gathering up his own creative energy, preparing himself for the world-creation of Part III.

The organization of Part II is clearly spatial, proceeding from Mrs. French, who lived 'Beyond that ridge', to Mary

Hynes, 'somewhere upon that rocky place', then nearer still to Hanrahan, 'somewhere in the neighbouring cottages', and finally to the ancient occupants of the tower itself. There is a kind of defiant randomness about the sequence which may forever resist complete elucidation, but it is generally true that all the characters tread on the interface between fantasy and history; and in all the incidents the human imagination somehow alters the surface of physical reality to suit its will. In every incident there is a victimizing of some sort, and it slowly becomes clear that the artist is both the 'heart's victim and its torturer.'[11] The incidents progress in imaginative power from Mrs. French to the dead poet Raftery to the living (and superior) poet Yeats to the Great Memory itself.

Mrs. French and the insolent farmer are the first pair of torturer and victim; the moral of this little tale is that the minor whims, even grisly ones, can find some route to expression in physical reality. Here there is no miracle of artistry, nor any direct imposition of human will—only the almost telepathic oneness of purpose between the serving-man and Mrs. French; as Donald Torchiana says,[12] Mrs. French is gifted with her serving-man's inner ear, as well as the clipped ears of the farmer. The silver candlestick, the dark mahogany and the wine do indeed suggest the dignified beauty of eighteenth-century aristocracy, but I also find a hint of a mediumistic state in that description, a suggestion that Mrs. French—almost by birthright—is in touch with the powers of the Great Memory, as well as the powers of her servant's shears. In any case, the farmer's sin against Mrs. French is a sin against her century's custom and ceremony, and retribution comes quickly and precisely, without the slightest effort of Mrs. French herself.

Yeats next considers Mary Hynes and the relationship between Raftery's song and her own body:

> Some few remembered still when I was young
> A peasant girl commended by a song,
> Who'd lived somewhere upon that rocky place,
> And praised the colour of her face,
> And had the greater joy in praising her,
> Remembering that, if walked she there,
> Farmers jostled at the fair
> So great a glory did the song confer.

The colour of Mary's face—'so white that it looked blue, and she had two little blushes on her cheeks'[13]—seems to be none of her own doing, only part of the glory that the song conferred. Raftery's sense of her beauty was the result of arbitrary choice or hearsay or supernatural insight ('those that are blind have a way of seeing things, and have the power to know more, and to feel more',[14] as a man told Yeats in *The Celtic Twilight*), since Raftery was blind; but his blindness only serves to prove that it is the song that creates the woman, and not vice versa.* If the farmers jostled only to see a half-imaginary girl who would have lived and died in unremembered peasanthood without Raftery, there are also signs that Raftery himself is beginning to be absorbed into a kind of fable. He is identified with the fabulous Homer later in the poem, and Yeats wrote of his blindness:

Some think that Raftery was half blind, and say, 'I saw Raftery, a dark man, but he had sight enough to see her,' or the like, but some think he was wholly blind, as he may have been at the end of his life. Fable makes all things perfect in their kind, and her blind people must never look on the world and the sun.[15]

Although Raftery did not die a century before 'The Tower' was written, he is already being transmogrified by the racial memory of Ireland into a legend. Memory has a certain aesthetic shaping power to it, even as Raftery's art or Mrs. French's whims; and memory's alchemy is slowly emerging as the dominant theme of the poem.

I mentioned before the effortlessness of Mrs. French's realization of her desire; Yeats in *The Celtic Twilight* quotes some reports of the extreme facility, the utter spontaneity, of Raftery's verses:

'He was the greatest poet in Ireland, and he'd make a song about that bush if he chanced to stand under it. There was a bush he stood under

---

* Yeats wrote in *The King's Threshold* (*Collected Plays*, p. 127) that poets create the value of money, create heroism, create war, create kings:

    Seanchan.   Well, if you are a poet,
   Cry out that the King's money would not buy,
   Nor the high circle consecrate his head,
   If poets had never christened gold, and even
   The moon's poor daughter, that most whey-faced metal,
   Precious; cry out that not a man alive
   Would ride among the arrows with high heart,
   Or scatter with an open hand, had not
   Our heady craft commended wasteful virtues.

from the rain, and he made verses praising it, and then when the water came through he made verses dispraising it.[16]

Raftery seems able to subsume all external reality into his songs; but what is more amazing is that the bush could answer back:

. . . an old pensioner at Kiltartan says, 'He was standing under a bush one time, and he talked to it, and it answered him back in Irish. Some say it was the bush that spoke, but it must have been an enchanted voice in it, and it gave him the knowledge of all the things of the world. The bush withered up afterwards, and it is to be seen on the roadside now between this and Rahasine.'[17]

For a moment, the bush seemed animated by Raftery's power; all this points to the interdependence between poetry and the natural world which is the theme of the Mary Hynes story. Yeats copies down an English translation of Raftery's song in several places in his prose works; and that song foreshadows in a distorted way some of the elements of 'The Tower':

> O star of light and O sun in harvest,
> O amber hair, O my share of the world, . . .
>
> She is the sun in the heavens who wounded my heart.[18]

Mary Hynes becomes, in the focusing mirror of Raftery's song, the whole universe, 'Aye, sun and moon and star, all.' This concentration of the universe within a human body is the inverse of what Yeats does in Part III, the extruding of the universe from the human soul.

Raftery's song also gives a clue about the music that drove astray the wits of the man who drowned in the Cloone bog:

> There is sweet air on the side of the hill
> When you are looking down upon Ballylee;
> When you are walking in the valley picking nuts and blackberries,
> There is music of the birds in it and music of the Sidhe.[19]

In the original story of the drowning, there was no mention that the man was 'maddened by those rhymes'; indeed, Yeats at first offers his readers a choice of explanations: 'And certain men, being maddened by those rhymes,/Or else by toasting her a score of times . . .'; but I think that this supposed alternative has no more significance than any other imaginative blending of hypnotic songs with drunkenness, such as 'drunken with singing as with wine'.[20] In Raftery's song, Mary's presence evokes music from the air, natural and supernatural music, 'music of the birds . . . and music of the Sidhe'; but Yeats declares that the music is nothing less human than Raftery's own song. Yeats shifts all power from Mary to Raftery; and later Yeats makes it certain that the choice of that particular peasant girl was quite arbitrary, almost ridiculous: 'mocking Muses chose the country wench'. Again, the Muses form their most lasting attachments in low haunts.

That word 'wench' may suggest that Mary's life was not as chaste as would befit such an idealized figure, and there are one or two clues in *The Celtic Twilight* which seem to substantiate this rumour:

These poor countrymen and countrywomen in their beliefs, and in their emotions, are many years nearer to that old Greek world, that set beauty beside the fountain of things, than are our men of learning. She 'had seen too much of the world'; but these old men and women, when they tell of her, blame another and not her, and though they can be hard, they grow gentle as the old men of Troy grew gentle when Helen passed by on the walls.[21]

Like Helen, Mary seems to be a well-travelled girl; and I feel that beneath Yeats's glittering fantasia of moonlight and sun-light, beneath Raftery's bewitching music, it is physical desire that drove Raftery into song and drove, second-hand, his lis-teners into the Cloone bog. In 1906, Yeats wrote that Homer's art sprang from the physical desires that were balked by Homer's blindness:

WHY THE BLIND MAN IN ANCIENT TIMES WAS MADE A POET

A description in the *Iliad* or the *Odyssey*, unlike one in the *Aeneid* or in most modern writers, is the swift and natural observation of a man as he is shaped by life. It is a refinement of the primary hungers and has the least possible of what is merely scholarly or exceptional . . . .
In primitive times the blind man became a poet, as he became a fiddler in our villages, because he had to be driven out of activities all his nature cried for, before he could be contented with the praise of life. And often it is Villon or Verlaine, with impediments plain to all, who sings of life with the ancient simplicity.[22]

It is frustrated lust which is the source of Raftery's power, the power that deforms the physical world into all that magical chaos of light and darkness, that gives glory to Mary's face, that jostles the farmers at the fair, that pushes a man into the great bog. Indeed the whole human race is victimized by Homer's blindness, by the vision of beauty that his blindness created:

> Strange, but the man who made the song was blind;
> Yet, now I have considered it, I find
> That nothing strange; the tragedy began
> With Homer that was a blind man,
> And Helen has all living hearts betrayed.
> O may the moon and sunlight seem
> One inextricable beam,
> For if I triumph I must make men mad.

'Only an aching heart/ Conceives a changeless work of art';[23] the sublimations of a blind poet may have betrayed us all, or caused a man's drowning; but, as Part III shows, we cannot survive without those poets and their world-creating songs; even Homer's Helen, whether she usurps our love for real women or not, may at least serve the purpose of the Greek statues in *On the Boiler*, of providing for 'the sexual instinct of Europe its goal, its fixed type'.[24] The various interacting causative chains between the desire which caused the work of art and the desire that that work of art arouses in its audience and the relationships between the subject and the object of art are no more extricable than Yeats's inextricable beam of moonlight and sunlight. That mingled beam seems to refer in this poem primarily to the interrelation of lunar imagination and ordinary reality ('they mistook the brightness of the moon/ For the prosaic light of day'); but Yeats had thought of that image many years before, although it meant different things to him at different times in his life:

Old writers had an admirable symbolism that attributed certain energies to the influence of the sun, and certain others to the lunar influence. To lunar influence belong all thoughts and emotions that were created by the community, by the common people, by nobody knows who, and to the sun all that came from the high disciplined or individual kingly mind. I myself imagine a marriage of the sun and moon in the arts I take most pleasure in; and now bride and bridegroom but exchange, as it were, full cups of gold and silver, and now they are one in a mystical embrace. . . . Was it not Aeschylus who said he but served up dishes from the banquet of Homer?—but Homer himself found the great banquet on an earthen floor and under a broken roof.[25]

Again, poetry, the lunar imagination, comes from simple earthy folk life, just as Homer sat on an earthen floor and Raftery canonized the bushes near the 'neighbouring cottages' of Thoor Ballylee.

In one line, 'For if I triumph I must make men mad', Yeats identifies himself with Raftery, or at least takes Raftery as a model of poetic success. I think that Yeats means that he wants to have the power to desolidify the world, un-Locke it, return it to a primitive undifferentiated mental substance in which sunlight and moonlight are interchangeable, in which objects are as transmutable as Hanrahan's pack of cards—to make the world as vivid and volatile as it seems in the polymorphous perversity of infancy. In Yeats's later years he discovered that he could, to some extent, actually impose his will on the texture of external reality, and he discovered that to his sorrow; I hear a ghostly echo of 'if I triumph I must make men mad' in 'The Man and the Echo':

> Did that play of mine send out
> Certain men the English shot?
> Did words of mine put too great strain
> On that woman's reeling brain?[26]

When Yeats enumerates the list of the 'images and memories' who have answered his summons, Mary Hynes is not present at all, and the last apparition of the whole sequence to appear is 'The man drowned in a bog's mire'; perhaps he got more of Yeats's sympathy than any of the others.

Mary Hynes died young—'Dust hath closed Helen's Eye',[27] as Yeats titled the section of *The Celtic Twilight* which tells the story of Mary and Raftery; so he could not ask Mary his question about old age. There is nothing in that essay to suggest what Raftery's own answer would be; but in a 1906 issue of the *Samhain* Yeats quotes a poem he calls 'Raftery's poem about himself':

> I am Raftery the poet,
> Full of hope and love;
> With eyes without light;
> With gentleness without misery.

> Going west on my journey
> With the light of my heart;
> Weak and tired
> To the end of my road.
>
> I am now,
> And my face to a wall,
> Playing music
> To empty pockets.[28]

There is no sense in this poem of Hanrahan's or Yeats's rage against ageing; Raftery is 'Full of hope and love . . . With gentleness without misery'; but the final image of Raftery facing the wall, 'Playing music/ To empty pockets', suggests a kind of exhausted desolation. He has nothing left except the light of his heart, the inner light which guides the blind; but if his power of song has not wholly left him it has at least diminished below the beggar's effective threshold of hearing. Surely Raftery belongs in the company of Hanrahan and the bankrupt master and the others, for he has wisdom concerning the emptiness of old age; but Raftery is 'Weak and tired', lacks Hanrahan's profane fury, and is fittingly dismissed, allowed to return to his rest, his eyes 'impatient to be gone'.

After Yeats has intertwined the moonlight and the sunlight, praying for Raftery's lunatic power, he arouses from his memory a poet that he created himself, a poet even more decrepit and beggarly than Raftery:

> And I myself created Hanrahan
> And drove him drunk or sober through the dawn
> From somewhere in the neighbouring cottages.
> Caught by an old man's juggleries
> He stumbled, tumbled, fumbled to and fro
> And had but broken knees for hire
> And horrible splendour of desire;
> I thought it all out twenty years ago. . . .

In comparison, Raftery was a very pure sort of artist, cut off from direct participation in worldly affairs because of his blindness, converting the universe into a passionate disinterested song until he found that he could deprave the sun and the moon. I have shown, I believe, that underneath all that aimless music there lay insatiate human desire; but it is sublimated, hidden, while Hanrahan is all lust and broken knees, his poetry devoted to nothing more miraculous than seduction (which is perhaps miraculous enough). Raftery's art is very primitive and druidic, the kind of magic art that appealed to Yeats when he was young; a passage from his 1901 essay 'Magic' sounds almost as if it had been written with Raftery in mind:

Men who are imaginative writers to-day may well have preferred to influence the imagination of others more directly in past times. Instead of learning their craft with paper and a pen they may have sat for hours imagining themselves to be stocks and stones and beasts of the wood, till the images were so vivid that the passers-by became but a part of the imagination of the dreamer, and wept or laughed or ran away as he would have them. Have not poetry and music arisen, as it seems, out of the sounds the enchanters made to help their imagination to enchant, to charm, to bind with a spell themselves and the passers-by?[29]

I do not mean that this type of art lost its hold on Yeats's imagination; indeed Part III of 'The Tower' shows Yeats himself exercising that pure synthetic power in which physical nature and passers-by are absorbed indifferently into the poet's vision; I mean only that Raftery's enchantments are more characteristic of Yeats's youthful dreams than is the stripped-down, hungry art of Hanrahan. If Yeats felt close to Raftery, he feels closer still to Hanrahan, his child and his father; and one can hear Hanrahan's voice speaking in more than a few of the *Last Poems*.* When Hanrahan stumbles, tumbles, fumbles on his broken knees, one may think of Yeats 'walking perhaps like an old man with fumbling steps' as he dramatizes himself in *The Bounty of Sweden*; and Yeats and Hanrahan seem to be so closely attuned to each other that Yeats forgets the goal of Hanrahan's hounds at about the same instant that Hanrahan's own memory was blotted out: 'O towards I have forgotten what—enough!'

Yeats himself wrote very eloquently about his great empathy with his imagined poet: 'I had finished *The Secret Rose*, and felt how it had separated my imagination from life, sending my Red Hanrahan, who should have trodden the same roads with my-

---

* 'The Wild Old Wicked Man', for instance, presents a Hanrahan-like poet, still awe-struck before the manifestation of God—the 'stream of lightning'—but still contriving seduction songs.

self, into some undiscoverable country.'[30] However, in the stanza
which introduces Hanrahan, Yeats's position is more analogous
to the old juggler's than to Hanrahan's: it is simultaneously
Yeats and the old juggler who drive Hanrahan 'drunk or sober
through the dawn'; the old juggler is the Raftery-type magician,
while Hanrahan is more like the man drowned in the great bog
at Cloone. In the Hanrahan stories, world-transforming magic
occurs beyond the range of poetry: Hanrahan is an almost passive victim of the card tricks of a shadowy old man; it is Echtge
who has the power to transform darkness into daylight, not Hanrahan; Hanrahan merely observes the mist and the rose-petals
congeal into a vision of lovers—not only does Hanrahan not
create the vision, but he does not even understand what it is
until Dervorgilla explains it. Hanrahan as a poet seems to pre-
cipitate magical events, but they are never in his control; there
is only one place in all the Hanrahan stories where Hanrahan
does anything spell-binding, bewitching, enchanting, or even
charming:

He stood up with her then, and led her out by the hand, and some of the
young men were vexed, and some began mocking at his ragged coat
and his broken boots. But he took no notice and Oona took no notice,
but they looked at one another as if all the world belonged to themselves alone. . . . in place of dancing he began to sing, and as he sang
he held her hand, and his voice grew louder, and the mocking of the
young men stopped, and the fiddle stopped, and there was nothing
heard but his voice that had in it the sound of the wind. . . . any one
that saw her would have thought she was ready to follow him there and
then from the west to the east of the world. . . . Oona's mother was
crying, and she said, 'He has put an enchantment on Oona. Can we not
get the men to put him out of the house?'[31]

The naïve peasant girl is swept off her feet by the glib beggar—
that is nearly the best that Hanrahan can do as a poet and as a
seducer.

　　Hanrahan's art is not always tendentious and woman-chasing,
but he is no advocate of *ars gratia artis*; typically, Hanrahan's
poetry springs not from subliminated desire but from blatant
lust. Only in this one incident—from 'The Twisting of the Rope'
—do we see Hanrahan actually in action, but in most of the
stories there is a faint background of seduced women hovering
in the distance, although Hanrahan refuses to be a Leporello to

his own catalogue. Hanrahan is a poet of the naked essentials of the human condition,* and his art is the art of paring-down rather than the art of transmutation; he stays close to the natural world either in theme ('Red Hanrahan's Curse') or in ultimate intent ('The Happy Townland'); Yeats's shift from Raftery to Hanrahan is almost the first example in Yeats's poetry of the shift in his conception of art from (to take extreme examples) 'To Ireland in the Coming Times' and 'The Circus Animals' Desertion'.

It is very curious that when Hanrahan quotes an early version of the first stanza of 'The Happy Townland' at Oona, even though he paints that paradise for the earthiest of intentions, one of Oona's thwarted admirers calls out, '"It is not to the Country of the Young you will be going if you go with him, but to Mayo of the bogs"'[32]—as if even that minor excursion into transcendence must be undercut. But Hanrahan's reply is stranger yet:

. . . 'It is very near us that country is, it is on every side; it may be on the bare hill behind it is, or it may be in the heart of the wood.' And he said out very loud and clear, 'In the heart of the wood; O, Death will never find us in the heart of the wood. And will you come with me there, Oona?' he said.[33]

He claims, more or less seriously, that true love has the power to elevate Mayo of the bogs into the Country of the Young, although his assertion of immortality is perhaps more effective as a good line than as a genuine poetic vision; but what is chiefly interesting about this speech is that the eternal summer, the eternal dancing of the 'high hollow townland', is no more distant than the common hills of our world. The descent and relocation of paradise become increasingly literal in Yeats's imagination, culminating in the pan-sexual paradise of 'News for the Delphic Oracle'.

The meaning of the story of Hanrahan and the old juggler is not simple, and the reader of 'The Tower' is not helped by the fact that Yeats breaks off his narrative at the point when the story becomes puzzling:

* Yeats wrote in his notes to *The Wind among the Reeds* that 'Hanrahan is the simplicity of an imagination too changeable to gather permanent possessions' (*The Variorum Edition of the Poems of W. B. Yeats*, eds. Peter Allt and Russell K. Alspach, p. 803), his art the art of the celebrant who can offer nothing.

Good fellows shuffled cards in an old bawn;
And when that ancient ruffian's turn was on
He so bewitched the cards under his thumb
That all but the one card became
A pack of hounds and not a pack of cards,
And that he changed into a hare.
Hanrahan rose in frenzy there
And followed up those baying creatures towards—

O towards I have forgotten what—enough!

He followed those baying creatures towards a house illuminated from within by daylight in which the Sidhe-queen Echtge sat enthroned, with four old women holding a cauldron, a stone, a spear, and a sword.* The old women announce that their symbols are emblematic of pleasure, power, courage, and knowledge, all correspondences which recall the old juggler's card-suit formula, '"Spades and Diamonds, Courage and Power; Clubs and Hearts, Knowledge and Pleasure."' Hanrahan is terrified out of his mind and says nothing; the old women reproach him for his cowardice, very much as Gurnemanz reproaches Parsifal for not asking any questions about the Cup and the Spear (Pleasure and Courage in Yeats's symbolism) in Wagner's *Parsifal*;† and Hanrahan's seeming lack of curiosity prevents some mysterious restoration of the spirit-ruler (also as in *Parsifal*): '. . . the last said, "His wits are gone from him." And then they all said, "Echtge, daughter of the Silver Hand, must stay in her sleep. It is a pity, it is a great pity."'[34] Some beneficial *rapprochement* of earth and the supernatural is evidently thwarted by Hanrahan's timidity; nevertheless I believe that the Hanrahan stories can be read as allegory of the artist's relations with nature and supernature, and that Hanrahan is correct in rejecting, for whatever reason, any direct contact with the Sidhe.

---

* These four objects are defined as the treasure-hoard of some half-forgotten giant kings of ancient Ireland in 'Baile and Aillinn' (*Collected Poems*, p. 464). According to Joseph Hone (*W. B. Yeats 1865–1939*, p. 157), when Yeats and Maud Gonne visited Westminster Abbey they identified the Stone of Destiny there with the stone mentioned among the four talismans of the Tuatha de Danaan; Maud asked Yeats, ' "Have you no magic to get the spirit of the stone to Ireland . . .?" ' but Yeats found his art in that case as powerless as Hanrahan's.

† Yeats wrote that Wagner 'draws his symbols—as in "Parsifal"—from things that have been in the very blood of Europe for centuries' (from an interview in *The World*, 1903, quoted by Donald Torchiana, *W. B. Yeats & Georgian Ireland*, p. 300).

In many of the stories in *The Celtic Twilight* and *The Secret Rose*, various attempts to reach out to the world beyond our life result in a consummation in death; for instance, the old man in 'The Heart of the Spring' who seeks to join his life to that of the Sidhe by hearing the music that occurs for one instant in the heart of the spring is found dead, although at the moment of his death a thrush, who seems to have wandered into the story out of *The Shadowy Waters*, begins to sing. In 'The Queen and the Fool' there is even more sinister evidence that contact with Echtge is not Hanrahan's proper goal in life:

I have heard one Hearne, a witch-doctor, who is on the border of Clare and Galway, say that in 'every household' of Faery 'there is a queen and a fool,' and that if you are 'touched' by either you never recover, though you may from the touch of any other in Faery.[35]

Hanrahan is dumbfounded enough by what little contact he does have with Echtge. He would have been best advised never to follow the baying hounds at all, although his half-conscious willingness to approach any sort of experience, human or super-human, may have been attractive to Yeats. I suggest that 'Red Hanrahan' is 'To the Rose upon the Rood of Time' set to prose: Hanrahan must come near to perfect timeless beauty, but he must shove it away before it gets too near. It seems that he does for-feit all that the four old women offer him, pleasure, power, cour-age, and knowledge. He certainly demonstrates in the stories that he lacks them all: he is restless, dissatisfied, and frustrated, never happy until the day of his death; he does not have enough power to undo the barricades of a dedicated Irish mother; we see Hanrahan afraid in three of the six stories; and Hanrahan, al-though a Virgil scholar, does not once understand anything that befalls him, is outwitted with equal ease by mortal and immortal.

Yet, paradoxically, part of his poetic power comes from his disappointment, certainly from his rage; Yeats wrote in *Per Amica Silentia Lunae*:

The poet finds and makes his mask in disappointment, the hero in defeat. The desire that is satisfied is not a great desire, nor has the shoulder used all its might that an unbreakable gate has never strained.[36]

If a poet's muscles are built isotonically, then Hanrahan should be the greatest of them all, for his desires always take him beyond the limit of his physical strength, his understanding, and his intelligence. I conclude that Hanrahan, in life, does not need Echtge or her four talismans; on the other hand, she seems to need him, and her summons perhaps has the ambiguous moral value of the many 'Belle Dame sans Merci' stories told in 'Kidnappers'—the vaguely malevolent illustrations of Blake's axiom that eternity is in love with the production of time. The story 'The Death of Hanrahan' suggests that Hanrahan in death will attain consummation with one of the Sidhe, probably Echtge, but there are many clues that the artist should not try to by-pass life in order to find that consummation, that he should instead work up through common things towards the supernatural; Echtge does not approach him directly, in her full majesty, but in the embodiment of the old hag Winny; and her four emblems also descend into common household objects:

'. . . the light was shining on the big pot that was hanging from a hook, and on the flat stone where Winny used to bake a cake now and again, and on the long rusty knife she used to be cutting the roots of the heather with, and on the long blackthorn stick he had brought into the house himself. And when he saw those four things, some memory came into Hanrahan's mind, and strength came back to him, and he rose sitting up in the bed, and he said very loud and clear, 'The Cauldron, the Stone, the Sword, the Spear. What are they? Who do they belong to? And I have asked the question this time.'[37]

The battered Parsifal has at last found his voice, and everything is immediately revealed; the supernatural is hidden in our ordinary life, and we only have to ask the right questions to find the proper *via positiva*. Similarly, it turns out that in all of Hanrahan's many love affairs, he was searching for Echtge without knowing it; the earthy hag Winny—in fact, her face is 'grey like crumbled earth'—says, '"You will go looking for me no more upon the breasts of women."' The artist must deal with the concrete reality he sees around him; the Rose must leave space for the 'common things that crave'; yet the poet may hope that he will find that infinite beauty after death.

I can offer one last parallel between Hanrahan's experience of dying and Yeats's own visions of the supernatural. Just before Hanrahan's discovery of Winny's identity, the fire flares in a blaze of revelation: '. . . the light where it was nearest to him filled with sparks of yet brighter light, and he saw that these were the points of swords turned towards his heart.'[38] Twenty years later Yeats wrote:

. . . I even wonder if there may not be some secret communion, some whispering in the dark between Daimon and sweetheart. . . .

I sometimes fence for half an hour at the day's end, and when I close my eyes upon the pillow I see a foil playing before me, the button to my face. We meet always in the deep of the mind, whatever our work, wherever our reverie carries us, that other Will.[39]

The Hanrahan stories are somewhat obscure, but they perhaps provide a fairly coherent allegory of the materials and goal of the artist as Wild Old Wicked Man. This allegory is both clarified and perplexed by the 1897 version, in which the story of the pack of hounds and Echtge does not appear at all. In its place, as the opening story of the sequence, there is something called 'The Book of the Great Dhoul and Hanrahan the Red', which Yeats entirely discarded. In that story, one of the Sidhe, named Cleena of the Wave, is invoked by Hanrahan repeatedly, by means of a book of magic, until she falls in love with him, and adopts a mortal body in order to remain with him. But Hanrahan has just lost a teaching job as a result of a peccadillo with a woman, and is disenchanted with the whole sex; he refuses her ('out of pride,/ Cowardice, some silly over-subtle thought'), and she curses him:

'. . . you have looked so often upon the dust that when the Rose has blossomed there you think it but a pinch of coloured dust; but now I lay upon you a curse, and you shall see the Rose everywhere, in the noggin, in woman's eye, in drifting phantoms, and seek to come to it in vain; it shall waken a fire in your heart, and in your feet, and in your hands.'[40]

Perhaps Yeats rejected this version because Hanrahan's rejection of the Sidhe is more meaningful if he is rejecting Echtge's inhuman 'long pale face' than if he is rejecting Cleena's warm mortal body; there is no reason why the artist may not cohabit with the Muse as long as he makes sure she keeps company in low haunts.

One peculiar passage in the story 'Red Hanrahan's Curse', which Yeats left relatively unrevised, whether through carelessness or intention, may indicate that the story of Hanrahan and Cleena had not entirely lost its hold on Yeats's imagination:

The girl stopped her crying, and she said, 'Owen Hanrahan, I often heard you have had sorrow and persecution, and that you know all the troubles of the world since the time you refused your love to the queen-woman in Slieve Echtge; and that she never left you in quiet since. . . .'⁴¹

Hanrahan does not exactly refuse Echtge his love in the version of 1907; he merely neglects to ask the right questions. And there is nothing about a curse in 'Red Hanrahan', the story added in 1907, although there is a definite suggestion that Echtge some-how blighted his life; the curse does not appear until the end of 'The Twisting of the Rope'. If Hanrahan does not find fulfil-ment in love, the reason may be that he is searching for Echtge on the breasts of women; but he does not seem to understand his predicament with any clarity until the last story. Perhaps the two introductory stories fused in Yeats's imagination, and Hanrahan's failure to ask any questions became tantamount to a spurning of Echtge's love; but what Yeats took of the Hanrahan legend into 'The Tower' suggests that Yeats was more interested in Hanrahan's perpetually balked exploration of physical reality than in any sort of phantom Rose impeding his sight of our world.

Near the end of Part II of 'The Tower' Yeats hustles all of his apparitions off-stage except Hanrahan; Hanrahan has some wisdom about women which Yeats needs to hear, or to create, and Hanrahan is Yeats's prime focus of hatred of old age:

> The poet, Owen Hanrahan, under a bush of may,
> Calls down a curse on his own head because it withers grey;
> Then on the speckled eagle-cock of Ballygawley Hill
> Because it is the oldest thing that knows of cark and ill;. . . .
> Then curses he old Paddy Bruen of the Well of Bride
> Because no hair is on his head and drowsiness inside. . . .
> And then old Shemus Cullinan, shepherd of the Green Lands,
> Because he holds two crutches between his crooked hands; . . .
> But he calls down a blessing on the blossom of the may
> Because it comes in beauty, and in beauty blows away.⁴²

This is known as Hanrahan's curse upon old age, but in fact Hanrahan does not once curse old age; he curses several old doddering men, a pike, a yew, an eagle, and even his own head, but he does not curse old age. This poem deals in very concrete symptoms of ageing, even as 'The Tower' itself ends amid concrete symptoms; and it is Hanrahan's specificity, his lack of abstraction, which gives the curse its power—enough power to burn down Hanrahan's house, as it turns out. I take it as the final difference between Raftery's art and Hanrahan's that Raftery's song could drive men Pied-Piper-fashion into a bog, while Hanrahan's curse could only make men chase after him waving heavy sticks. Hanrahan is not only a victim of the old juggler's magic, he is also a victim of his own poetry.

Before considering what Hanrahan learned in the grave I must treat the last and nearest of Yeats's apparitions:

> I must recall a man that neither love
> Nor music nor an enemy's clipped ear
> Could, he was so harried, cheer;
> A figure that has grown so fabulous
> There's not a neighbour left to say
> When he finished his dog's day:
> An ancient bankrupt master of this house.

The assumption behind this stanza is that men create that which answers their needs: Hanrahan needed love, so he created seduction songs to find that love; Raftery, the ninety-nine per cent pure artist, was gratified aesthetically by his own music; and Mrs. French sent out the proper signals to satisfy her desire for revenge. But the ancient nineteenth-century owner of Thoor Ballylee had desires which exceeded any possibility for gratification; and it is clear that the four central characters are being arranged in order of increasing neediness, and increasing inability to satisfy those needs, increasing frustration. Mrs. French had attained a state of magnificence and harmony, and needed only trivial satisfaction; Raftery was a beggar, and blind, who, although he was cheered by his music, died with neither money nor an audience; Hanrahan, cheated of contentment, wandered joylessly through many women's bodies. The ancient bankrupt master was no artist, although he had opportunities to display his ingenuity by avoiding creditors (as recorded in Yeats's notes to the poem); he seems to have passed beyond the point where art is of human utility. Although he is a historical character, he is growing 'fabulous', receding into the racial memory, just as Raftery did; the events of his life have become so blurred that

'There's not a neighbour left to say/ When he finished his dog's day'. Although he could create nothing to benefit himself, he seems to be able to focus the all-creating power of the racial memory; he stands on the threshold between history and fantasy, and behind him there arise images, seen in infinite regression as if between two mirrors, of all the heroic occupants of the tower over the ruin of which he presided:

> Before that ruin came, for centuries,
> Rough men-at-arms, cross-gartered to the knees
> Or shod in iron, climbed the narrow stairs,
> And certain men-at-arms there were
> Whose images, in the Great Memory stored,
> Come with loud cry and panting breast
> To break upon a sleeper's rest
> While their great wooden dice beat on the board.

As the ancient bankrupt master fades into fable, the old soldiers become substantial and solid, disturb Yeats's rest.

I detect a prophecy in this stanza, the same prophecy as those in 'The Gyres' and 'Under Ben Bulben': all that is worn-out, primary, will fade away, and the old antithetical race of man, crying out, panting, becoming corporeal as Yeats listens, will be restored. Certainly these men are part of the racial pride that Yeats bequeathes at the beginning of Part III. It is the poet's function to make real those images in the Great Memory:

> Sing the lords and ladies gay
> That were beaten into the clay
> Through seven heroic centuries;
> Cast your mind on other days
> That we in coming days may be
> Still the indomitable Irishry.[43]

In the play *Calvary*, the Roman soldiers gamble for Christ's cloak with dice, and they comment that Christ is not the 'God of dice'; those soldiers, like the rough men-at-arms, must wait for the new era and its non-deterministic gods. However, Yeats needs to explore his personal world, the realm of his rage and his memories, before he is ready to join the men-at-arms in a tour of the exterior consciousness of the Great Memory; so the men-at-arms are dismissed with the other images, leaving only Yeats's rage and memory expert, Hanrahan.

Old lecher with a love on every wind,
Bring up out of that deep considering mind
All that you have discovered in the grave,
For it is certain that you have
Reckoned up every unforeknown, unseeing
Plunge, lured by a softening eye,
Or by a touch or a sigh,
Into the labyrinth of another's being . . .

Hanrahan in life was the artist of life itself, caught up in experiential reality, lurching recklessly towards any place that his desires pulled him. His memories are 'mighty' only because of the fullness of his life and the strength of his passion; and in the grave he may know the answer to the question, What does an artist's imagination do when his body is withered and empty?— the question that bothered Yeats in Part I.

In effect, Yeats answers his own question by thinking out a sequel to the Hanrahan stories; and he finds that Hanrahan after death is busy sorting out his memories of women, making them formalized and aesthetic; he is re-arranging the chaotic but intense impressions in his memories into a pattern. The blind plunges of his sexual intercourse are 'unforeknown, unseeing' because he merely experienced his women, haphazardly and without thought; but in the grave, free of 'Body and its stupidity', he can arrange his memories into 'one clear view'.[44] The word 'labyrinth', a periphrasis so superb that it becomes almost a *mot trouvé* (I think also of 'declivities' in 'Parting'), suggests a secret order that Hanrahan's continual reckoning may at last discover.* Yeats himself does exactly the same thing at the end of Part III, as if Hanrahan had shown him the solution to his problem: Yeats takes his 'memories of love,/ Memories of the words of women', along with a few other elements, and composes aesthetically from those elements his 'superhuman/ Mirror-resembling dream'.

However, Hanrahan, even in the grave, is not pure intellect,

---

* In his essay 'The Tragic Theatre' Yeats describes how romantic love discards the individuated human female in favour of an unearthly paradigm of her beauty, a 'labyrinth of its lines' (*Essays and Introductions*, p. 244). And in 'William Blake and his Illustrations to the *Divine Comedy*' Yeats describes how the distorted images of the 'vegetable glass of nature' point the way into 'some divine labyrinth' (*Essays and Introductions*, p. 117).

and can still be embarrassed, victimized, by the memories which
constitute in death his entire existence:

> Does the imagination dwell the most
> Upon a woman won or a woman lost?
> If on the lost, admit you turned aside
> From a great labyrinth out of pride,
> Cowardice, some silly over-subtle thought
> Or anything called conscience once;
> And that if memory recur, the sun's
> Under eclipse and the day blotted out.

Some students of Yeats believe that the 'woman lost' is Echtge,
but I cannot persuade myself that Yeats has any particular woman
in mind.* It is true that Hanrahan turned aside from Echtge because of 'Cowardice' (but certainly not because of pride, 'some
silly over-subtle thought/ Or anything called conscience once');
and it is true that Echtge literally did eclipse Hanrahan's sun
and blot out his day; but I believe that the intent of the stanza is
to dwell on Hanrahan's state of mind in cogitating about
spurned and spurning women, a state of mind that is part of the
universal male experience, rather than on the specific women.
Even in death we are obsessed with our lost women, our retreat from human life, our scruples, and our divided desires. The
moral is that man must not turn against his own desires, balk
or censor himself—or the 'horrible splendour of desire', the
bristly magnificence that his lust has created, will be self-
destroyed.

This stage of the Dreaming Back, the stage of memory and
obsession, will come to us all after death:

We carry to *Anima Mundi* our memory, and that memory is for a time
our external world; and all passionate moments recur again and again,
for passion desires its own recurrence more than any event, and whatever there is of corresponding complacency or remorse is our beginning
of judgment; nor do we remember only the events of life, for thoughts
bred of longing and of fear, all those parasitic vegetables that have
slipped through our fingers, come again like a rope's end to smite us
upon the face . . .[45]

In *The Only Jealousy of Emer*, the Ghost of Cuchulain retreats

* Of course, Maud Gonne was probably not far from his mind when he considered
the relevance of Hanrahan's information to his own life.

from supernatural consummation with Fand because he is obsessed by his memories of women:

> *Woman of the Sidhe.*
>   What pulled your hands about your feet,
>   Pulled down your head upon your knees,
>   And hid your face?
> *Ghost of Cuchulain.* Old memories:
>   A woman in her happy youth
>   Before her man had broken troth,
>   Dead men and women. Memories
>   Have pulled my head upon my knees.[46]

And Diarmuid and Dervorgilla are sundered in death by the
memory of their traitorous love in *The Dreaming of the Bones*:

> *Young Girl.* Although they have no blood, or living
>   nerves, . . .
>   Their manner of life were blessed could their lips
>   A moment meet; but when he has bent his head
>   Close to her head, or hand would slip in hand,
>   The memory of their crime flows up between
>   And drives them apart.[47]

Yeats believed that remorse was at least as futile and destructive in life as in death:

> Although the summer sunlight gild
> Cloudy leafage of the sky,
> Or wintry moonlight sink the field
> In storm-scattered intricacy,
> I cannot look thereon,
> Responsibility so weighs me down.[48]

As in the *Gitanjali* introduction, thought interferes with our perception of nature, comes between us and the beauty of the world,
the moonlight and the sunlight. But in the light of Part III, the
sun's eclipse has more sinister connotations: if the bitter soul
that creates the universe, 'sun and moon and star, all', turns its
power against itself, becomes lost in the mazes of its own brooding, then the great creative act will falter, and the sun may dis-
solve in the involutions of the mind's self-torture; and obsessive

memory may be the uncreating word that blots out the prosaic
light of day.*

Yeats's great testament in Part III begins with an image suggesting a return to the origin of things, a steady movement up-
stream, back to dawn:

> It is time that I wrote my will;
> I choose upstanding men
> That climb the streams until
> The fountain leap, and at dawn
> Drop their cast at the side
> Of dripping stone . . .

No one seems to have read these lines without noting the resemblance in metre and theme to 'The Fisherman'; and that
poem is surely one of the creations which Yeats bequeaths in
this will; in that poem Yeats imagines a fisherman

> Climbing up to a place
> Where stone is dark under froth,
> And the down-turn of his wrist
> When the flies drop in the stream;
> A man who does not exist,
> A man who is but a dream . . .[49]

It is a poet's prerogative to create his legatees as well as his
bequests; the world of 'The Tower' is no honest Ireland, but a
fiction, a creation of the human imagination, 'Images and memories' wholly under Yeats's control. By Part III everything is
getting sucked into the human mind, and it is not surprising
that the opening is entirely synthetic, composed only of the re-
sonating sounds of well-known poems; Yeats is gathering mo-
mentum from his own previous poetry, working towards the
most inclusive statement about the power of the imagination
that he ever made. The next lines remind us that the strong,

---

* In *Where There is Nothing* Paul Ruttledge believes that the sun and the moon
are themselves part of the world of sensual illusion, and therefore must be extinguished along with thought and memory if 'measureless eternal life' is to be attained:

We must get rid of everything that is not measureless eternal life. We must put
out hope as I put out this candle. And memory as I put out this candle. And thought,
the waster of Life, as I put out this candle. And at last we must put out the light of
the Sun and of the Moon, and all the light of the World and the World itself.

(W. B. Yeats, *The Variorum Edition of the Plays*, ed. Russell K. Alspach, pp. 1139–40).

loose trimetre of 'The Fisherman' is also the metre of 'Easter 1916'; and the theme of self-sacrifice given for a despised state sounds exactly like the theme of 'An Irish Airman Foresees his Death':

> I declare
> They shall inherit my pride,
> The pride of people that were
> Bound neither to Cause nor to State,
> Neither to slaves that were spat on,
> Nor to the tyrants that spat,
> The people of Burke and of Grattan
> That gave, though free to refuse . . .

This pride in the accomplishments of the Irish aristocracy will soon broaden into the pride in which all men of imagination can share, for accomplishing the work of God. Burke appears in these lines as an exemplar of distinguished Irish nationalistic thought, of course, but Yeats treasured most in Burke's writings his metaphor of the organic development of the state:

> And haughtier-headed Burke that proved the
> State a tree
> That this unconquerable labyrinth of the
> birds, century after century,
> Cast but dead leaves to mathematical
> equality . . .[50]

I mention this because the whole universe is turning organic in 'The Tower'; and Burke has wisdom about the secret order built into the artifice of the state, the 'labyrinth of the birds'— just as Hanrahan had something to tell about another organic labyrinth. Haughtier-headed Burke's pride (which was part of Burke's bequest to Yeats) finally spills out in one great bequest over the whole landscape:

> Pride, like that of the morn,
> When the headlong light is loose,
> Or that of the fabulous horn,
> Or that of the sudden shower
> When all streams are dry,
> Or that of the hour
> When the swan must fix his eye
> Upon a fading gleam,

> Float out upon a long
> Last reach of glittering stream
> And there sing his last song.

The metaphoric time of day is established as dawn at first, (the fishermen drop their cast at dawn, too), although Part II was set in evening twilight; Yeats has indeed found the power to scramble solar light that he prayed for at the end of the Raftery stanzas. The beautiful images of bottled-up things at last flooded out, with light, fruit,* and water—all the environmental necessities of man, foreshadowing the creative acts of the next lines—yield to the swan. The descent from the dawn, the cornucopia, and the clouds down to the swan, the descent from the headlong light to the fading gleam, adumbrates the descent from the first stanza of Part III to the last, where Yeats retreats from world-creator to student of his own body.

The swan episode is yet another recapitulation of a previous poem, although in this case the poem is not one of Yeats's own, but Sturge Moore's 'The Dying Swan', as Yeats admits in the notes to 'The Tower'. Moore's poem contains an image, 'brim, brim o'er/ With love', which may have been connected in Yeats's mind with the images of spilling-over which precede the swan, although Yeats's swan brims o'er with pride and not with love; Moore's swan also sails into the 'sun's heart', which may relate to Yeats's earlier light imagery. Yeats perhaps attributes too much to Moore's influence, for Yeats used the swan's cry in his 1904 *The King's Threshold* as a metaphor for the voices of the artists whose songs will create the future of the race:

> *Youngest Pupil.* O silver trumpets, be you lifted up
> And cry to the great race that is to come.
> Long-throated swans upon the waves of time,
> Sing loudly, for beyond the wall of the world
> That race may hear our music and awake.[51]

This passage shows how effortlessly Yeats can pull his own image from the image of the swan, proceed in 'The Tower' from the swan's song to the world-creation of the poet. The swan's song is, as everyone knows, a legendary cry anticipating death; and to Yeats it meant evidently that death itself can be rendered

---

* The image of the cornucopia is borrowed from 'A Prayer for my Daughter', which is another of the poems to which Yeats is indebted in this vast synthesis.

aesthetic, song-like, through the proud artistic power of the old
man; the last song that Yeats writes for his fishermen is the
coldest and most passionate of them all. I believe that the swan
of 'The Tower' relates to all of the dead singing birds that
warble everywhere in his work: the transmuted souls in *The
Shadowy Waters*, the golden bird in 'Sailing to Byzantium', the
kindred cowards in 'Cuchulain Comforted'. Man is somehow
freed from the wreck of his body if he can learn to transform it all
into song—or he is freed from his pain if not from his body, as
the student Yeats learns at the end of the poem. I do not think
that it is too much to say that the swan's song creates its death.

> And I declare my faith:
> I mock Plotinus' thought
> And cry in Plato's teeth,
> Death and life were not
> Till man made up the whole,
> Made lock, stock and barrel
> Out of his bitter soul,
> Aye, sun and moon and star, all . . .

Yeats had been waiting at least twenty years to say that. In 1904
he wrote,

I have read in a fabulous book that Adam had but to imagine a bird, and
it was born into life, and that he created all things out of himself by
nothing more important than an unflagging fancy; and heroes who can
make a ship out of a shaving have but little less of the divine preroga-
tives.[52]

Yeats also found that, with a little careful whittling, he could
force Berkeley's thought into a similar configuration:

Berkeley wrote in his *Commonplace Book*: 'The Spirit—the active
thing—that which is soul, and God—is the will alone'; and then, remembering the mask that he must never lay aside, added: 'The concrete of the will and understanding I must call mind, not person, lest
offence be given, there being but one volition acknowledged to be God.'[53]

If it is true that *esse est percipi*, then Berkeley's doctrine about the
seven days of creation might be used as evidence that human perception is a kind of creation: 'Berkeley thought the Seven Days
not the creation of sun and moon, beast and man, but their entrance into time, or into human perception . . .'[54] But those

critics who rely on Berkeley to explain 'The Tower' cannot ignore the fundamental differences between Yeats's thought and
Berkeley's merely by pointing to Yeats's disappointment with
Berkeley's orthodoxy after the *Commonplace Book*. Yeats knew
that Berkeley would never have agreed with 'The Tower':

If photographs that I saw handed round in Paris thirty years ago can be
repeated and mental images photographed, the distinction that Berkeley drew between what man created and what God creates will have
broken down.[55]

Yeats states conclusively that the Berkeley of the *Commonplace
Book* did not think that human perception created the universe:
'Berkeley in the *Commonplace Book* thought that "we perceive"
and are passive whereas God creates in perceiving. He creates
what we perceive.'[56]

The thesis that man creates all things seems to be derived
more from Blake than from Berkeley. Yeats often quoted Blake's
line 'God Himself only acts or is in existing beings or men';[57]
and Blake's great vision at the end of *Jerusalem* is perhaps the
earliest of all the drafts of Yeats's lines—in Blake's epic, the
'Four Living Creatures' constituting the resurrected human
race

> conversed together in Visionary forms
>   dramatic which bright
> Redounded from their Tongues in thunderous majesty,
>   in Visions
> In new Expanses, creating exemplars of Memory and
>   of Intellect
> Creating Space, Creating Time according to the
>   wonders Divine
> Of Human Imagination, throughout all the Three
>   Regions immense
> Of Childhood, Manhood & Old Age & the all tre-
>   mendous unfathomable Non Ens
> Of Death was seen in regenerations terrific or
>   complacent varying
> According to the subject of discourse & every
>   Word & Every Character
> Was Human . . .[58]

But neither Berkeley nor Blake can explain the most interesting question associated with Yeats's lines: Why is the

human soul bitter in its creating act? That description is perfectly consonant with the themes of the rest of the poem, because all the creation that we have seen sprang from bitterness:
blind poets, presumably including Raftery, sing out in frustration because they do not have the outlets for their desires that
ordinary men have; Hanrahan created his curse out of sheer
fury, and his love-songs because of his often-balked lust; even
the old owner of the tower outwitted his creditors out of bank-
ruptcy and destitution; and the swan sings because it is faced
with the bitterness of death. In Sturge Moore's poem it is
clearer than in Yeats's that pain has a creative function in the
swan's death:

> O silver trumpet, pour
> Love for defiance back
> On him who smote! . . .
> O wondrous-gifted Pain, teach thou
> The god to love, let him learn how.[59]

The bitterness of the soul in its creation of 'sun and moon and
star, all' serves to clinch the identification of that creative act
with the creative acts of the poets described earlier in the poem;
if mankind creates the universe, 'poets and painters and musicians . . . are continually making and unmaking mankind',[60]
as Yeats wrote as early as 1900.

There is one established legend of creation, as well, which
specifically claims that the universe was made out of the creator's
bitterness, Valentinus' Gnostic explanation of creation. According to Valentinus, the world was made by a rather imbecilic de-
miurge, whose mother Acamoth (or Achamoth), although a
spirit herself, was cut off from God and the spirit-world. The
church-father Irenaeus, who did not report heresies in a manner
likely to attract converts, wrote of Acamoth:

All . . . things owed their beginning to her terror and sorrow. For
from her tears all that is of a liquid nature was formed; from her smile
all that is lucent; and from her grief and perplexity all the corporeal
elements of the world. For at one time, as they affirm, she would weep
and lament on account of being left alone in the midst of darkness and
vacuity; while, at another time, reflecting on the light which had forsaken her, she would be filled with joy, and laugh; then, again, she
would be struck with terror; or, at other times, would sink into con-
sternation and bewilderment.[61]

The Rosicrucianism which Yeats studied so intensively in his intellectually scandalous youth owed much to Gnostic thought, and Yeats might have come across Acamoth's creation there; and Swift (of all people), whom Yeats studied intensely in his respectable middle age, quotes in Latin the second sentence of the cited passage at the end of section 10 of *A Tale of a Tub*. All things flow from Acamoth's primitive loneliness, but Acamoth is neither gratified by what she has created (indeed she created nothing but her own excrement, the fact which so amused Swift) nor exhausted from her efforts. She is too spiritual, too inhuman to serve as a proper model; she also creates out of weakness, as if Oscar Wilde had made up the story, while Yeats's mankind creates his physical environment out of his necessitous strength, to satiate partially his insatiable desires and needs. 'The desire that is satisfied is not a great desire', but the desire that is satisfied by the sun and moon and stars is at least a magnificent one. Man's soul was bitter because his need for a universe was frustrated until he made it himself; but the planets and stars now constellate themselves into an image of his pride. If man is bitter now, it is only because the universe is still not enough to satisfy him; or because he is victimized by the space and time he has himself created.

This doctrine never appears with such intensity again in Yeats's writings, although it is an important theme in several of the famous poems in *The Winding Stair*; every time the creation motif appears it becomes more blatantly physical, culminating in a passage from 'Vacillation':

> From man's blood-sodden heart are sprung
> Those branches of the night and day
> Where the gaudy moon is hung.
> What's the meaning of all song?
> 'Let all things pass away.'[62]

Here the moon, because it is the fruit of a contaminated tree, seems imperilled by the fickle race that manured it—the episode is reminiscent of one of Grimm's fairy tales, called 'The Moon', in which townspeople climb an oak tree and snip off pieces of the moon, quarter by quarter. It is a long descent from the bitter soul to the blood-sodden heart, and the moon itself has changed from a source of pride to a fragile tinsel cut-out.

In Yeats's prose, the creation theme becomes intertwined in the 1930s with his studies of Indian religion, into which he tried to synthesize the wisdom of the romantic poets:

In pure personality, seedless *Samādhi*, there is nothing but that bare 'I am' which is Brahma. The initiate, all old Karma exhausted, is 'the Human Form Divine' of Blake, that Unity of Being Dante compared to a perfectly proportioned human body; henceforth he is self-creating. But the Universal Self is a fountain, not a cistern, the Supreme Good must perpetually give itself. The world is necessary to the Self, must receive 'the excess of its delights,' and in this Self all delivered selves are present, ordering all things, from the Pole Star to the passing wind. They are indeed those spirits Shelley imagined in his *Adonais* as visiting the inspired and the innocent.[63]

The Self which orders all things is the composite Self of the human race, the *Anima Hominis*; seedless *Samādhi* is the mental state in which the external world collapses into 'unimpeded personality', 'that bare "I am"', in which all objects vanish in the 'complete light' of the divine Self. From this inauspicious development Yeats's creation theory proceeds at last to the thesis that each man builds the structure of human history according to the events of his life, a pale distortion of 'The Tower' which appears in *Wheels and Butterflies*:

Swift seemed to shape his narrative upon some clairvoyant vision of his own life, for he saw civilisation pass from comparative happiness and youthful vigour to an old age of violence and self-contempt, whereas Vico saw it begin in penury like himself and end as he himself would end in a long inactive peace.[64]

There are as many explanations of history as there are human beings—a relativism which tends to reduce all historical structure down to idiosyncratic delusion, for mankind creates only a theory for interpreting reality, not reality itself. Finally, Yeats believed, in *On the Boiler*, that explanations of reality were interchangeable, one almost as good as another, and certainty only the illusion that one had uncovered the innermost ivory ball:

But if I would escape from patter I must touch upon things too deep for my intellect and my knowledge, and besides I want to make my readers understand that explanations of the world lie one inside another, each complete in itself, like those perforated Chinese ivory balls.[65]

The world is at last outside of us, alien, a puzzle incapable of solution.

After bequeathing the man-created universe, Yeats also declares his faith in man's ability to create his own afterlife:

> And further add to that
> That, being dead, we rise,
> Dream and so create
> Translunar Paradise.

This is clearly the climax of the poem; the loose trimetre of the beginning of Part III, full of strong accents scattered amid clusters of weak syllables, has at last stiffened into clenched iambs; I believe that this is the finest example in Yeats's poetry of his self-declared technique for manipulating his rhythms:

When I began to rehearse a play I had the defects of my early poetry; I insisted upon obvious all-pervading rhythm. Later on I found myself saying that only in those lines or words where the beauty of the passage came to its climax, must rhythm be obvious.[66]

Everything in Part III is so incantatory, so consciously 'poetic'; yet the diction is informal, sometimes quite colloquial. Does it mean anything that when man makes up the whole of life and death, he composes it into the shape of a rifle, 'lock, stock and barrel'? Is it a subtle clue that old men are ravaged by the world that man has created, or is it simply a colloquial idiom used without thought of its origin? The texture of the passage sounds strong and serious, as if there were no irony present, yet there are these slight incongruities.

I think it is fairly well established that Yeats accepted the ontological difference between the mind's constructs and ambient reality; the year after he wrote 'The Tower' he spent several months bickering with Sturge Moore about the status of an imaginary cat that Ruskin once threw through a window. Yeats took the adamantly Berkeleian position that Ruskin's cat and a housecat are equally real, composed of the same substance; yet Yeats knew that the cats differed radically in continuity:

If you say the fact that we think of one image as 'phantasmal' decides the matter, we are in great perplexity to decide what we mean by 'phantasmal.' Certainly the 'phantasmal' image is the more isolated, just as 'Ruskin's cat' is isolated—it does not seem to have kittens— but is one bead by itself less real than a bead upon a string?[67]

A man can create a bead, but he cannot tie that bead permanently into the fabric of reality; why, if mankind wove the fabric, do those beads drop so quickly out of sight? 'The Tower', taken as a whole, also does not assert that man creates the universe; so it seems reasonable to assume that the declaration of human omnipotence is made only so that the poet can make a strategic withdrawal. Man gives value to the universe, as the rest of Part III goes on to prove, and that valuation may be tantamount to creation, in Berkeley's epistemology or anyone else's; even to Locke, a basket of fruit, without a human race to perceive it, would be nothing more than a set of tasteless grey slabs. The assertion 'Death and life were not/ Till man made up the whole' may be intended to be only a partial truth, for if that is the whole truth mankind created a great deal of needless suffering for itself; and the 'Translunar Paradise', in the light of Yeats's other writings, definitely has a built-in tendency to decay. Yeats on occasion recorded incidents of the mind's power to create its own afterlife:

. . . as Cornelius Agrippa writes: 'We may dream ourselves to be consumed in flame and persecuted by daemons,' and certain spirits have complained that they would be hard put to it to arouse those who died, believing they could not awake till a trumpet shrilled. A ghost in a Japanese play is set afire by a fantastic scruple, and though a Buddhist priest explains that the fire would go out of itself if the ghost but ceased to believe in it, it cannot cease to believe. . . . Years ago I was present when a woman consulted Madame Blavatsky for a friend who saw her newly-dead husband nightly as a decaying corpse and smelt the odour of the grave. 'When he was dying,' said Madame Blavatsky, 'he thought the grave the end, and now that he is dead cannot throw off that imagination.'[68]

These grisly obsessions, more like Hanrahan's self-destructive fixations on lost women than like any sort of 'Translunar Paradise', are almost as close as one can come in Yeats's writings to the mind-created afterlife so ringingly described in 'The Tower'.

After his Genesis I, Yeats begins the long painful process of extricating himself and his creations from the alleged glory of the human race:

> I have prepared my peace
> With learned Italian things
> And the proud stones of Greece,

Poet's imaginings
And memories of love,
Memories of the words of women,
All those things whereof
Man makes a superhuman
Mirror-resembling dream.

Yeats here is making no creation *ex nihilo*; he is composing 'Images and memories', aesthetic objects, into a more inclusive aesthetic pattern; the building-blocks of his dreams are themselves artifacts. He first absorbs into his contemplation Italian learning and Greek architecture, synecdoches of all human grandeur and creation, which form the bridge between this section and the previous one; but he has turned to those creations which are indisputably created by man. Then Yeats begins to arrange his own imaginings (note that the phrase is 'Poet's imaginings', not 'Poets' imaginings'), surely including Hanrahan and probably the other characters of Part II, into the existential transcript of his life; but the most emphasized elements of this composition are 'memories of love', just as Hanrahan himself spent his afterlife organizing his scrap-book into cold coherence.

The doctrine in this passage is probably influenced by Schopenhauer's theory[69] that memory turns the events of our lives into cold sequential patterns which release us from the emotions which originally accompanied the events:

. . . it happens that, especially when we are more than usually disturbed by some want, the sudden recollection of past and distant scenes flits across our minds like a lost paradise. The imagination recalls merely what was objective, not what was merely subjective, and we imagine that that something objective stood before us then just as pure and undisturbed by any relation to the will as its image now stands in the imagination; but the relation of objects to our will caused us just as much affliction then as it does now. We can withdraw from all suffering just as well through present as through distant objects, whenever we raise ourselves to a purely objective contemplation of them, and are thus able to produce the illusion that only those objects are present, not we ourselves. Then, as pure subject of knowing, delivered from the miserable self, we become entirely one with those objects, and foreign as our want is to them, it is at such moments just as foreign to us. Then the world as representation alone remains; the world as will has disappeared.[70]

I have quoted this passage at length because it explains exactly my feeling about the word 'superhuman'; once arranged by the memory, events in our lives seem to have an existence independent of our own existence, 'delivered from the miserable self', and we can contemplate our lives dispassionately, without suffering. The dream is superhuman only because it is aesthetic, objectified, and therefore independent of the dreamer, in the same sense that any work of art, including 'The Tower', is superhuman. Therefore the 'superhuman/ Mirror-resembling dream' is not identical with the 'sun and moon and star' above; it is only a composition arranged from the elements of one man's personal experience, not a theory of cosmology. The dream of the poet's past life resembles a mirror because Yeats can see nothing except himself in it; that dream is his interior environment (as the 'sun and moon and star' comprise his external environment), and the lineaments of that dream are fitted perfectly to the contours of Yeats's thought.

The 'Mirror-resembling dream' corresponds to Yeats's day-to-day memories as a portrait bust would correspond to his face; and in support of this view—that memory preserves a permanent form which transcends life, is superhuman—I can adduce a little poem which appears in *The Wild Swans at Coole*, called 'Memory'; the women with charm, or a lovely face, are wholly evanescent, unmemorable, when compared to the permanent contour-form made in Yeats's memory by the woman whom he loved but could not keep:*

> One had a lovely face,
> And two or three had charm,
> But charm and face were in vain
> Because the mountain grass
> Cannot but keep the form
> Where the mountain hare has lain.[71]

In these final sections of 'The Tower', Yeats focuses all his attention on his inner world; whether man has created the outer world or not, an old man is its victim, and must spend his energies on that narrow segment of reality which is still under his control. Yeats dismisses the outer world to concentrate on his

---

* I support this interpretation of 'Memory' by citing the first draft of the fourth line, which read 'I could not change for the grass' (Jon Stallworthy, *Between the Lines*, p. 205).

memories of women and his art in the same way that he dismissed Raftery in Part II to listen to Hanrahan; Raftery's art
had the same sort of impersonal witchcraft that Yeats employed
at the beginning of Part III to construct the universe, while Hanrahan's art was the art of bodily desires and the formalization
of memory. Yeats does not repudiate the racial creation, but it
does fade from sight; that kind of art is a suitable aspiration or
achievement for a young race, or a young man (as Yeats says of
his story of the juggler's magic, 'I thought it all out twenty
years ago'); but that sort of creative ejaculation is spent, even
the rhythmic impetus of Part III is shuddering to a halt, and an
old poet must content himself with the themes of his own heart,
as Yeats remarks over ten years later in 'The Circus Animals'
Desertion'. All men in death will be occupied in arranging their
memories into patterns, just like the dead Hanrahan of Part II
and the old Yeats of Part III; in death we are all artists:

. . . even the most wise dead can but arrange their memories as we
arrange pieces upon a chessboard, and obey remembered words alone

. . . Then gradually they perceive, although they are still but living
in their memories, harmonies, symbols, and patterns, as though all
were being refashioned by an artist, and they are moved by emotions,
sweet for no imagined good but in themselves, like those of children
dancing in a ring . . .[72]

Dancing children, like the dead, are capable of 'pure aimless joy',
disinterested, without any utilitarian object, therefore aesthetic:

Indeed, when he [Tagore] is speaking of children . . . one is not certain that he is not also speaking of the saints: 'They build their houses
with sand, and they play with empty shells. With withered leaves they
weave their boats and smilingly float them on the vast deep. Children
have their play on the seashore of worlds. They know not how to swim,
they know not how to cast nets. Pearl-fishers dive for pearls, merchants
sail in their ships, while children gather pebbles and scatter them
again.'[73]

I will take that picture of children constructing boats out of
withered leaves as a transition to the next stanza of 'The Tower':

> As at the loophole there
> The daws chatter and scream,
> And drop twigs layer upon layer.

When they have mounted up,
The mother bird will rest
On their hollow top,
And so warm her wild nest.

Those twigs have no more intrinsic value than the withered leaves described above; but the mother bird has them arranged into a habitable environment, and is content with such purely formal creation. I think that the twigs refer primarily to the Italian things, proud stones, poet's imaginings, and so on, mentioned in the previous stanza, although this point is not undisputed by critics. There is one bit of internal evidence in the poem's structure which supports this thesis: Parts I and III are written almost entirely in *a b a b* quatrains, and every stanzaic break in Part III, except this one, falls at the end of a quatrain; but in this instance the episode of the daws is linked by the dream-scream rhyme to the 'Mirror-resembling dream' section directly preceding it, perhaps suggesting faintly that the mirror-resembling dream and the daw's nest are the tenor and vehicle of the simile beginning with 'As at the loophole there'. Insofar as the twigs represent the artifacts and memories of Yeats's life, they indicate how externalized, superhuman, the artifacts and memories have become; and the parable illustrates the complex relationship between the mirror-resembling dream and Yeats himself. Without an intellect to find the proper over-all design, the imaginings and memories would be as disconnected and meaningless as stray twigs; once arranged, the memories have a purposive form independent of their creator, yet they seem to be 'hollow', valueless, if the creator passes away—the nest needs a mother bird to warm its hollow top.

But Part III is specifically a will, and Yeats can bequeath his 'nest'—his poems and his biography—to posterity, his own fishermen (who reappear suddenly in the next stanza); and that posterity can provide the human warmth necessary to make his works meaningful, even after Yeats's death; a nest can be used by any number of generations of birds. Indeed, since the fishermen are so clearly artifacts of Yeats's imagination, it may be said that Yeats is hatching his posterity in his own nest. Insofar as the daws' twigs refer to man's entire environment, both internal and external, the parable shows how far reality has stiffened and been dehumanized since man made up the whole of life and death in the middle of the previous stanza; mankind in the parable only arranges his physical world into a comfortable easy chair, and there is no suggestion that the twigs grew on a tree fertilized by the blood of jackdaws. In any case, Yeats is trying to express something of what his life and works will mean to the human race after his own death; and he certainly believed that his ghostly shape would still inhere in his works; when he looked into his mirror-resembling dream, what did he see but his own face?

> The dead living in their memories are, I am persuaded, the source of all that we call instinct, and it is their love and their desire, all un-knowing, that make us drive beyond our reason, or in defiance of our interest it may be; and it is the dream martens that, all unknowing, are master-masons to the living martens building about church windows their elaborate nests . . .[74]

It is curious how the nest rises 'layer upon layer', as if it were a metonymy for the tower itself, which was not built by Yeats himself, only occupied by him—just as the race of daws built the nest, not the mother bird herself. The mirror-resembling dream is not wholly composed of elements created by Yeats, either; somewhere near its base are 'learned Italian things/ And the proud stones of Greece'. All these symbols spill into each other without any logical separation; Yeats paces upon the battlements of the tower or stares down on his mirror-resem-bling dream, and the daws' nest synthesizes these external and internal actions into an interpenetrating whole.

If Yeats has laid down his imaginings and memories into a tower-shaped edifice, then Yeats himself is the ancient bankrupt master of that tower; and we see why the old debtor of Part III was the last and innermost of the series of apparitions. The clearest identification between the daws' nest and the tower is the fact that the nest has a 'hollow top'; the tower also had a waste room on top, and Yeats found symbolic significance in that: 'Is every modern nation like the tower,/ Half dead at the top?'[75] When the mother bird has successfully warmed the wild nest, and the superhuman dream at last resembles a mirror, then it would seem that the work of arrangement is complete; but 'The Tower' takes up a new theme at its end. The mirror-resembling dream answers the problems raised in Part II, the problems of Hanrahan's fixed memories; but the questions of Part I have been only partly answered. The memories have been given order; but what about the battered kettle at the heel? Yeats reintroduces the symptoms of old age when, after a short affirmation of his bequest to the fishermen, he points out that he was himself made of the same metal as the fishermen before being broken by the 'sedentary trade' of poetry; Yeats's poetry did not cause old men to chase him, Hanrahan-fashion, with sticks (although his divorce speech almost did), but Yeats is a victim of his craft nonetheless:

> I leave both faith and pride
> To young upstanding men
> Climbing the mountain-side,
> That bursting under dawn
> They may drop a fly;
> Being of that metal made
> Till it was broken by
> This sedentary trade.

The fishermen enter the poem again, I think, because the problem of Yeats's relationship to his posterity is an important aspect of the wild nest simile. Yeats used to be made of the same stuff as the fishermen; but the fishermen, according to 'The Fishermen', do not exist, are only dreams; again, a poet's youth is the time for miraculous dream-like vitality, pride, faith, while in old age a poet must be content with his broken metal, his body's scrap-iron. Even in Yeats's identification of himself as a fisherman grown old, he is extricating himself from the world of the young fisherman much more definitely than in the earlier sections of Part III: they remain young and mythical, he remains old and all-too-human. But in the concluding section of the poem Yeats attains a remarkable secular transfiguration:

> Now shall I make my soul,
> Compelling it to study
> In a learned school
> Till the wreck of body,
> Slow decay of blood,
> Testy delirium
> Or dull decrepitude,
> Or what worse evil come—
> The death of friends, or death
> Of every brilliant eye

That made a catch in the breath—
Seem but the clouds of the sky
When the horizon fades;
Or a bird's sleepy cry
Among the deepening shades.

If Yeats cannot forge in the smithy of his soul the uncreated conscience of his race, as he might have wished in youth, he can at least attempt the more limited and personal objective of forging his soul in the wreck of his body. He tries to make his soul through the process of objectifying old age and death; the passage from Schopenhauer cited above provides, I think, the key to this as well as to the objectification of memory: 'We can withdraw from all suffering just as well through present as through distant objects whenever we raise ourselves to a purely objective contemplation of them . . .'. Through an act of will we can look at our present condition with the same aesthetic remoteness, with the same cold eyes, with which we regard the events of the past that lie in our memories; and in that suppression of personal emotion all suffering associated with old age and death will vanish. Yeats does not himself transcend the physical world, for he is still standing on terrestrial soil, looking up at the clouds which objectify the 'evils' in his life; but the wreck of body and the death of friends have become transcendental, painless, through the same process of formal composition that made Yeats's imaginings and memories a 'superhuman' dream. Everything about the poem's conclusion suggests that the evils are being arranged aesthetically, not only because they are sorted out into neat trimetre quatrains, but also because they are turning into clouds, formal elements of pictorial composition; the learned school might easily be an art school, like the mosaic-arrangement classes in 'Sailing to Byzantium', or at least a course in art appreciation. Old age and death are immutable evils, and no amount of assertion about the creative power of poetry can remove them. But through proper intellectual discipline the wreck of body will be no battered kettle but itself a theme for artistic vision and poetry; and the existence of 'The Tower' itself proves that proposition. Or were the bitter souls that made the sun and moon only old men who sought to make some baubles in the sky to bequeath to their offspring?

In any case, Yeats can manufacture nothing more celestial

than the clouds of the sky, and those unexpected correlatives
deserve explanation. A little-known essay published in 1901
casts some illumination on Yeats's associations with cloud symbolism; after quoting three stanzas from Raftery's song about
Mary Hynes (including 'O star of light', which shows how much
of 'The Tower' was fused in Yeats's imagination even in 1901),
Yeats writes,

This song, though Gaelic poetry has fallen from its old greatness, has
come out of the same dreams as the songs and legends, as vague, it may
be, as the clouds of evening and of dawn, that became in Homer's mind
the memory and the prophecy of all the sorrows that have beset and
shall beset the journey of beauty in the world.[76]

This dovetails perfectly with the last sentence of the 1900 essay,
'"Dust hath closed Helen's Eye"':

It may be that in a few years Fable, who changes mortalities to immortalities in her cauldron, will have changed Mary Hynes and Raftery
to perfect symbols of the sorrow of beauty and of the magnificence
and penury of dreams.[77]

Fable changes mortalities to immortalities, so Mary Hynes becomes a symbol of the sorrow of beauty, as she changes from
dead flesh to immortal memory; but clouds also symbolize the
sorrow of beauty, and therefore presumably represent the same
transition, from beautiful dying flesh to changeless memory;
clouds objectify sorrow, show the conversion of sorrow from
pain to cold memory or colder prophecy.* If the clouds are the
memory and prophecy of the sorrows that beset the journey of
beauty, surely they can also be the memory of the sorrows that
beset the decay of heroic metal broken by sedentary trade; art
changes mortalities into immortalities, and therefore can change
dull decrepitude into 'the clouds of the sky'. This argument
strongly ties together Parts II and III of the poem, for it was
Raftery's 'fable' that changed Mary from girl to symbol, and
Raftery symbolizes the 'magnificence and penury of dreams';

---

* Yeats associated clouds with old age, and freedom from old age, as early as
John Sherman: 'Grey clouds covering the town with flying shadows rushed by like
the old and dishevelled eagles that Maeldune saw hurrying towards the waters of
life' (W. B. Yeats, *John Sherman & Dhoya*, ed. Richard J. Finneran, pp. 78–9).
Maeldune's eagles were flying towards rejuvenation, and the clouds in 'The Tower'
may symbolize something of a secular resurrection.

magnificence and penury are the engendering contraries of 'The Tower', as seen in Raftery himself, and in the contrast between the two halves of Part III, the magnificent creation and the penurious descent into decrepitude. It may be said that 'The Tower', like Plato's love, is the child of plenty and poverty.

I said before that the last section of 'The Tower' was a kind of mundane transfiguration, and there is a passage in *Discoveries*, written almost twenty years before the poem, which shows the supernatural analogue of this transfiguration; in this passage Yeats is watching stormy clouds around a tower near Urbino:

Away south upon another mountain a mediaeval tower, with no building near nor any sign of life, rose into the clouds. I saw suddenly in the mind's eye an old man, erect and a little gaunt, standing in the door of the tower, while about him broke a windy light. He was the poet who had at last, because he had done so much for the word's sake, come to share in the dignity of the saint. He had hidden nothing of himself, but he had taken care of 'that dignity . . . the perfection of form . . . this lofty and severe quality . . . this virtue.' And though he had but sought it for the word's sake, or for a woman's praise, it had come at last into his body and his mind. Certainly as he stood there he knew how from behind that laborious mood, that pose, that genius, no flower of himself but all himself, looked out as from behind a mask that other Who alone of all men, the countrypeople say, is not a hair's-breadth more nor less than six feet high. He has in his ears well-instructed voices, and seeming-solid sights are before his eyes, and not, as we say of many a one, speaking in metaphor, but as this were Delphi or Eleusis, and the substance and the voice come to him among his memories which are of women's faces . . .[78]

The tower's poet has the dignity of a saint, and has himself become the mask of Christ (who, according to Aran legend, stood exactly six feet tall); but leaving aside that religious orthodoxy, we can see that the poet has attained in old age the perfect objectification of himself: he has become impersonal, stiffened into a pose, a mask, and his genius is 'no flower of himself but all himself'—he has become one with his achievement. But even in this super-earnest 1907 prose, there are faint traces of Hanrahan's motivating lechery: the poet sought perfection of form either 'for the word's sake, or for a woman's praise'; and when the angelic voices whisper in his ears, they blend into 'his

memories which are of women's faces'—even in this high-flown
early version, the poet builds his tower out of 'memories of love,/
Memories of the words of women'.

But 'The Tower' ends, not among the clouds of the sky, but a
little closer to earth, in the ground melody of a bird's cry, an
alternative objectification of the wreck of body and the death of
friends. There are two birds in this poem: first, the swan, which
expresses its death in a song; and second, the mother daw, which
hatches her young on the edifice of the past itself. The bird that
ends the poem is left unspecified, but it could be either the swan
or the daw. The swan's song originally sounded defiant, since it
seemed to rouse Yeats to mock Plotinus' thought and cry in
Plato's teeth; but at the end the cry has been purged of all defiance, is sleepy, spontaneous, artless. The hour of the swan's
death was coupled through zeugma with the dawn, the cornucopia, and the sudden shower, as if the hour of the swan's death
were as fruitful as the famous void in *Per Amica Silentia Lunae*
which was associated with the hymen of the soul.[79] I can detect
no such passage into magnificence at the end of 'The Tower'; but
if the wreck of body is only a bird's cry, then all that pain has
passed away through the same process of lyric objectification
which the swan used to create its almost joyous death. But the
sleepy cry could also be a languorous cry of physical contentment, like the cry of a mother bird sitting on the nest of her race's
achievement, giving value to it through her own warmth, in-
cubating her species, her life's work complete and therefore
fittingly ended.

Yeats himself, though, wrote the most profound gloss on that
bird's cry in his 1922 revision of 'The Sorrow of Love'. In the
middle of that poem there arises another girl, who, like Mary
Hynes and Helen of Troy, symbolizes the sorrow of beauty in
its journey through the world; and when she arises the noise of
the brawling sparrows that opens the poem is wholly changed;
if my argument that the key to 'The Tower' is the act of aesthetic
composition has any validity at all, it should explain the last line
of 'The Sorrow of Love':

> Arose, and on the instant clamorous eaves,
> A climbing moon upon an empty sky,
> And all that lamentation of the leaves,
> Could but compose man's image and his cry.[80]

'The Tower' is a transitional poem, showing Yeats's searching for the proper function of poetry, his groping after various relationships between art and life, his grudging admission of his limitations and his joyous exercise of poetic power; yet I believe that it is Yeats's finest poetic achievement. Yeats wrote poems of greater lyric beauty, of greater structural complexity, of more rigorous intellectual development, of more incantatory intensity, but to my mind he never wrote a poem which included a greater range of human experience, both of reality and of fantasy. If 'The Tower' seems almost tentative in its affirmation, I think it is because the poem is not complex in the abstract way that poems are complex, but in the insoluble way that human experience is complex.

2

The Earthly Paradise

'The Wanderings of Oisin'

IN 'The Tower', Yeats achieves a vision of selfhood, of completed humanity; he casts himself in the role of Watcher, but he watches nothing impersonal or remote, only his body, his memories, his immediate environment—his interior landscape. As he stares from Thoor Ballylee he covers the sky with the clouds of his suffering, he conjures from the ground the swansong of his death, he animates the neighbourhood with the characters of his fantasy; the whole vista becomes swallowed in Yeats's personality, just as the walled garden in the *Roman de la Rose* contains nothing but the huge polyp-colony of one woman's mind. 'The Tower' is not an escapist voyage to Byzantium; the poet in this poem attains no mechanical clairvoyance, no abstract historical vision, only a tough-minded study of a complexity so concrete that our sensual world seems abstract in comparison.* Of course, the neighbourhood of 'The Tower' is as much a world of artifice and poetic creation as the city of 'Sailing to Byzantium', the poem with which it has so many curious analogues; but 'The Tower' is not inhuman or supernatural and cannot be found unsatisfactory on those grounds.

One of the great themes in all poetry written since Keats is the construction of an art-world designed to satisfy the human desire for perpetual joy—and the subsequent discovery that a paradise will turn cold and sterile unless it contains human pain and death as well. Keats ended his vision with the acceptance of death in 'To Autumn' and the denial of vision in 'The Fall of Hyperion'; the post-romantic poet is not expelled from Eden, he renounces it:

* I think that Yeats constructs in 'The Tower' an objectified version of himself, the autobiographical equivalent of what he meant in *The King of the Great Clock Tower* by the line, 'Mortal men our abstracts are'.

> Is there no change of death in paradise?
> Does ripe fruit never fall? Or do the boughs
> Hang always heavy in that perfect sky,
> Unchanging, yet so like our perishing earth,
> With rivers like our own that seek for seas
> They never find, the same receding shores
> That never touch with inarticulate pang?[1]

Wallace Stevens began his career with that declaration of heaven's inadequacy; Yeats, who lived with one foot always in the nineteenth century, yet always yearning toward modernity,[2] was content to repeat that process of construction and renunciation again and again, and found in that act of mythic dismantling the central structural myth of his later poems and plays. Even the city of Byzantium, which is projected with such miraculous solidity and affirmation in 'Sailing to Byzantium', has a certain degree of insubstantiality, although it is not evident in the poem itself, written in 1926, just over the threshold of the last phase of Yeats's poetic development. This poem ends, of course, with a famous denial of organic life, and a great transformation of tattered flesh into formal gold:

> Once out of nature I shall never take
> My bodily form from any natural thing,
> But such a form as Grecian goldsmiths make
> Of hammered gold and gold enamelling
> To keep a drowsy Emperor awake;
> Or set upon a golden bough to sing
> To lords and ladies of Byzantium
> Of what is past, or passing, or to come.[3]

That seems clear enough: the poet wishes to abandon his scare-crow body (instead of retaining and objectifying his body, as he does in 'The Tower') and become an artificing artifice, a dynamic equilibrium of creative energy into which shaping force has flowed and from which shaping force flows out.

Yet this clockwork ideality tends to decay on either side of the poem. In the 1904 play *The King's Threshold* Yeats conceived the only other docile apotheosized bird to appear in his work:

Seanchan.
> Has that wild God of yours, that was so wild
> When you'd but lately taken the King's pay,
> Grown any tamer? He gave you all much trouble.

> *Monk.* Let go my habit!
> *Seanchan.*   Have you persuaded him
>   To chirp between two dishes when the King
>   Sits down to table?
> *Monk.*   Let go my habit, sir!
> *Seanchan.* And maybe he has learned to sing quite softly
>   Because loud singing would disturb the King,
>   Who is sitting drowsily among his friends
>   After the table has been cleared.[4]

The poet Seanchan parodies the monk's God as a trained bird;
and here, the King is so drowsy that the bird must remain almost
inaudible lest he give offence. The golden bird in 'Sailing to
Byzantium' is even more rigid, servile, an objective puppet; and
if it contains any sort of divinity that divinity can also change
effortlessly into triviality.

There is much commentary in *A Vision* on Byzantium and
early Christianity:

A.D. 1 to A.D. 1050

God is now conceived of as something outside man and man's handiwork, and it follows that it must be idolatry to worship that which
Phidias and Scopas made, and seeing that He is a Father in Heaven,
that Heaven will be found presently in the Thebaid, where the world
is changed into a featureless dust and can be run through the fingers;
and these things are testified to from books that are outside human
genius, being miraculous, and by a miraculous Church, and this Church,
as the gyre sweeps wider, will make man also featureless as clay or dust.[5]

All human life loses its value as the Church's asceticism reduces
fertile land to desert, destroys human individuality;* and, most
ironically of all, the great art works of Phidias and Scopas are
destroyed in the iconoclasm of an earth-hating God; the world
of sheer artifice can become so empty that art can be annihilated.
This is the train of thought which tends to make Byzantium, for
all its anonymous beauty, a somewhat sinister ideal.

However, the golden bird of 'Sailing to Byzantium' is perched
in the natural world; is not entirely 'outside man and man's
handiwork'; and this fact elicited some strange criticism from
Sturge Moore:

* Similarly the golden bird of 'Sailing to Byzantium' freed Yeats of his individuality. There is an important strain in romantic thought which holds that all
individuation is deformity; this slogan is the secret motto of Keats's vale of soul-
making.

Have you read Santayana's *Platonism and the Spiritual Life*? He thinks
the Indian philosophers the most spiritual, but his arguments leave me
sceptical as to whether mere liberation from existence has any value
or probability as a consummation. I prefer with Wittgenstein, whom I
don't understand, to think that nothing at all can be said about ulti-
mates, or reality in an ultimate sense. Anyway I can say nothing that
approaches giving me satisfaction, nor am I satisfied by what others
say. Your *Sailing to Byzantium*, magnificent as the first three stanzas
are, lets me down in the fourth, as such a goldsmith's bird is as much
nature as a man's body, especially if it only sings like Homer and
Shakespeare of what is past or passing or to come to Lords and Ladies.[6]

One may agree with Moore that the deepest truth is imageless
without denying Yeats his attempt to approach ultimate reality
through images; and it is difficult to see how Moore could have
imagined Homer or Shakespeare as anything like Yeats's
passionless vatic bird. But more amazing still is the fact that
Yeats seemed to acknowledge that there was some justice in
Moore's evaluation:

Yes, I have decided to call the book *Byzantium*. I enclose the poem,
from which the name is taken, hoping that it may suggest symbolism
for the cover. The poem originates from a criticism of yours. You ob-
jected to the last verse of *Sailing to Byzantium* because a bird made by
a goldsmith was just as natural as anything else. That showed me that
the idea needed exposition. Gongs were used in the Byzantine church.[7]

It is as if Yeats were perplexed by his inability to get outside
natural life, by the hopeless embedding of his images in experiential reality. If Yeats accepted Moore's reading, he must have
felt that his imagination kept shoving him back into the world
even as he was trying hardest to escape—the old half-impotence
of 'To the Rose upon the Rood of Time'. His reply to Moore's
criticism was 'Byzantium', and if Moore was at all responsible
for the writing of that poem one can only wish that Moore had
criticized Yeats's work more often and more loudly; yet the
city of 'Byzantium', despite Yeats's 'exposition', seems even
more vulnerable to the natural world than the city of 'Sailing to
Byzantium'. The structure of 'Byzantium' is close to the structure
of the self-destructive myth:

> Marbles of the dancing floor
> Break bitter furies of complexity,

> Those images that yet
> Fresh images beget,
> That dolphin-torn, that gong-tormented sea.[8]

As Helen Vendler points out,[9] the last stanza is poised on an astonishing ambiguity, as the flood of the phenomenal world almost overwhelms the aesthetic power of the marbles, as the syntactic force of the verb 'break' slowly dissipates in the violent waves. The sea's rhythm is governed by the opposing stresses of God and sexuality, the sudden syzygy of Yeats's moon; and Yeats in old age turned increasingly away from Byzantium and towards the sea itself as its own Eden, or as something even more primitive than Eden, all tortured flux, maternal matrix:

I am deeply grateful for a mask with the silver glitter of a fish, for a dance with an eddy like that of water, for music that suggested, not the vagueness, but the rhythm of the sea. A Dublin journalist showed his scorn for 'the new paganism' by writing: 'Mr. Yeats' play is not really original, for something of the kind doubtless existed in Ancient Babylon', but a German psychoanalyst has traced the 'mother complex' back to our mother the sea—after all, Babylon was a modern inland city—to the loneliness of the first crab or crayfish that climbed ashore and turned lizard; while Gemistus Plethon not only substituted the sea for Adam and Eve, but, according to a friend learned in the Renaissance, made it symbolise the garden's ground or first original, 'that concrete universal which all philosophy is seeking'.[10]

Evolution then is a kind of perpetual fall, an alienating retreat from the well-spring of life; and similarly the soul's evolution in death, for all its metaphysical heroism, is another retreat from the sea, the 'concrete universal'. Yeats knew the Neoplatonic myths of life as the soul's voyage through the sea towards its final state;[11] and he tended to imagine death as exactly the sort of evolutionary sea-change that the crab felt when it turned into a lizard:

. . . one of my sisters said, 'I think Mr. Synge will recover, for last night I dreamed of an ancient galley labouring in a storm and he was in the galley, and suddenly I saw it run into bright sunlight and smooth sea, and I heard the keel grate upon the sand.' The misfortune was for the living certainly, that must work on, perhaps in vain, to magnify the minds and hearts of our young men, and not for the dead that, having cast off the ailing body, is now, as I believe, all passionate and fiery, an heroical thing.[12]

Synge, as it turned out, reached the same destination that cost Oisin so much pain:

. . . my sister Lolly said at breakfast, 'I think it will be all right with Synge, for last night I saw a galley struggling with a storm and then it shot into calm and bright sunlight and I heard the keel grate on the shore.' One remembers the voyages to Tir-nan-oge, certainly the voyages of souls after death to their place of peace.[13]

Yeats thought that his sister had unwittingly prophesied Synge's death, his final disembarkation. But the point of vantage of many of the last poems is not from the passionate and fiery world of the shucked souls, but from the storm of flux, underwater; and this may explain the curious refractions which twist the images of the static afterlife, the paradisal state, principally in 'News for the Delphic Oracle'.

'News for the Delphic Oracle' belongs to a genre which is almost uniquely Yeatsian, a genre which I will call the summing-up poem: it revives the *dramatis personae*, the situations and themes of the poet's previous works, as the poet continually tries to redefine, clarify, and reinterpret his own mythology, tries to subsume his myths into more inclusive mythic frameworks. 'The Tower' is the first of these summing-up poems, in that its characters are derived from ' "Dust hath closed Helen's Eye" ', *Stories of Red Hanrahan*, 'The Fisherman', and so on; but it is not until the last volumes that the genre becomes well-developed. The 'Alternative Song for the Severed Head in *The King of the Great Clock Tower*', 'News for the Delphic Oracle', and 'The Circus Animals' Desertion' are the best examples; but many other works are almost as retrospective and reinterpretative, such as 'Crazy Jane on the Mountain', 'Cuchulain Comforted', the commentary poems on 'The Three Bushes', the opening lyric of *The King of the Great Clock Tower*, and *The Herne's Egg*. Perhaps the most similar phenomenon in modern art occurs in Part V of Richard Strauss' long tone poem *Ein Heldenleben*, called 'The Hero's Works of Peace', which consists of a pot-pourri of themes from all of Strauss' previous tone poems, followed by Part VI, 'The Hero's Release from the World'— as if Strauss, still a rather young hero at thirty-five, were trying to arrange his work in one clear view before he sank at last into the night; but Strauss' ability to inflate and sentimentalize himself was legendary.

The best way to approach a summing-up poem is through its referents, and, since the paradise of 'News for the Delphic Oracle' is an ironic version of Oisin's never-discovered Tir nà nOg, it is necessary to examine first 'The Wanderings of Oisin'. If Yeats remained particularly fascinated with one early work of his, it was surely 'The Wanderings of Oisin', the longest, the most complicated, and almost the first poem that he ever published; his early letters are full of the anguish of its composition[14] and his later works show him thinking about it, reevaluating it, explaining it, disclosing new details of its composition;[15] indeed, the 'Introduction to *The Resurrection*', written about forty-five years after 'The Wanderings of Oisin', begins with one of the most remarkable commentaries he ever wrote:

For years I have been preoccupied with a certain myth that was itself a reply to a myth. I do not mean a fiction, but one of those statements our nature is compelled to make and employ as a truth though there cannot be sufficient evidence. When I was a boy everybody talked about progress, and rebellion against my elders took the form of aversion to that myth. I took satisfaction in certain public disasters, felt a sort of ecstacy at the contemplation of ruin, and then I came upon the story of Oisin in Tir nà nOg and reshaped it into my *Wanderings of Oisin*. He rides across the sea with a spirit, he passes phantoms, a boy following a girl, a hound chasing a hare, emblematical of eternal pursuit, he comes to an island of choral dancing, leaves that after many years, passes the phantoms once again, comes to an island of endless Battle for an object never achieved, leaves that after many years, passes the phantoms once again, comes to an island of sleep, leaves that and comes to Ireland, to Saint Patrick and old age. I did not pick these images because of any theory, but because I found them impressive, yet all the while abstractions haunted me. I remember rejecting, because it spoilt the simplicity, an elaborate metaphor of a breaking wave intended to prove that all life rose and fell as in my poem. How hard it was to refrain from pointing out that Oisin after old age, its illumination half accepted, half rejected, would pass in death over another sea to another island. Presently Oisin and his islands faded and the sort of images that come into 'Rose Alchemica' and 'The Adoration of the Magi' took their place.[16]

The idea of myth is used here in a rather precise but somewhat unusual sense; according to our ordinary definition, a myth is simply a re-usable story which may be, on some level, archetypal; but Yeats meant by the word a generalized embodiment of some abstract principle. He speaks of progress as a myth, and of 'The Wanderings of Oisin' as a cyclic myth designed to refute it, but the idea of progress and the idea of circularity are only structural principles; if man can embody truth but not know it, then the myth lies in the embodiment and not in the knowledge. This is clearer in the 'Introduction to *The Cat and the Moon*':

These plays, which substitute speech and music for painted scenery, should suit Cellars and Garrets, though I do not recommend *The Resurrection* to the more pious Communist or Republican Cellars; it may not be as orthodox as I think; I recommend *The Cat and the Moon*, for no audience could discover its dark, mythical secrets. Myth is not, as Vico perhaps thought, a rudimentary form superseded by reflection. Belief is the spring of all action; we assent to the conclusions of reflection but believe what myth presents; belief is love, and the concrete alone is loved; nor is it true that myth has no purpose but to bring round some discovery of a principle or a fact.[17]

The myth is warm, lovable, concrete, and not didactic, but there is always some truth behind the myth; *The Resurrection* is sufficiently tendentious that it may offend the 'pious Communist or Republican Cellars', and *The Cat and the Moon*, although it is full of unfathomable 'dark, mythical secrets', is also the embodiment of an abstract idea:

. . . I kept in mind, while only putting the vaguest suggestion of it into the play, that the blind man was the body, the lame man was the soul. . . . Doubtless, too, when the lame man takes the saint upon his back, the normal man has become one with that opposite, but I had to bear in mind that I was among dreams and proverbs, that though I might discover what had been and might be again an abstract idea, no abstract idea must be present. The spectator should come away thinking the meaning as much his own manufacture as that of the blind man and the lame man had seemed mine.[18]

First the abstract idea is reified, made vital and impressive, by the myth, and then the spectators manufacture for themselves the abstract idea, in the reverse process, through their experience with the myth. Even the scientist rebuilds his conceptions of reality out of some fundamental myth:

Science is the criticism of Myth. There would be no Darwin had there been no Book of Genesis, no electron but for the Greek atomic myth; and when the criticism is finished there is not even a drift of ashes on the pyre. Sexual desire dies because every touch consumes the Myth, and yet a Myth that cannot be so consumed becomes a spectre.[19]

If the scientist's model is correct, if it forms a proper paradigm of things, it is because the ideas flower out of a racial myth 'as if they were fruit and leaves in a preordained order.'[20] Indeed the scientist exhausts the myth by changing it from gut-wisdom into dry conceptual truth; the concrete myth and its abstract referent have the Heraclitean relationship of the gyre-form. But a myth, for all its concreteness, is wholly non-specific; the touch of any beloved woman could consume the sexual myth, and the proton and the neutron proceed out of Greek atomic myth as much as the electron.

Similarly, any work which is derived from the governing principle of circularity is employing the same myth as 'The Wanderings of Oisin'; this explains the strange *ex post facto* fusion between 'The Wanderings of Oisin' and Vico's historical writings. For instance, in *A Vision* Yeats says, in language similar to the passage cited above from the 'Introduction to *The Resurrection*', that Vico's cycles are a 'counter-myth' to the newspaper's myth of progress;[21] and finally, in the 'Introduction to *The Cat and the Moon*', Yeats distorts Vico's circle into the structure of 'The Wanderings of Oisin': 'The choral song, a life lived in common, a futile battle, then thought for its own sake, the last island, Vico's circle and mine, and then the circle joined.'[22]

There is no mention of 'The Wandering of Oisin' anywhere in the 'Introduction to *The Cat and the Moon*'—it is all ostensibly a commentary on Vico and historical process. But any reader of Vico knows that Vico's first age is stark and gigantic, with no hint of easy, song-filled communal living; and in Vico's heroic age battle was valorous, just, noble, anything but futile; clearly Yeats's late restructuring of 'The Wanderings of Oisin'—'Vain gaiety, vain battle, vain repose'—is infiltrating into his memories of Vico. However, the last element of the triad, 'thought for its own sake', seems to owe more to Vico than to 'The Wanderings of Oisin', whose last island is full of dreams, without any of that sterile conceptual thought which Yeats called 'a spider smothered in its own web';[23] if 'The Wanderings of Oisin' can distort Vico, then Vico can just as easily reinterpret

'The Wanderings of Oisin'; the two works are squeezed into the same myth with as much devil-may-care re-categorization as one can find in the criticism of Northrop Frye. Because any given myth can embrace a large number of specific works, it is fair to say that all the poems which are directly based on *A Vision*, whether in theme (e.g., 'The Phases of the Moon') or in structure (e.g., 'A Dialogue of Self and Soul'), partake of the same myth, the myth of interconsumption, something living something else's death. And I am using Yeats's concept of generalized myth when I claim that the central myth of Yeats's last poems is a myth against Yeats's own previous myths, a myth which attempts to frame transcendent myths, to show their causes, their limitations, their break-downs, to work those myths into a pattern which is simultaneously a pattern of disintegration and inclusion.

As we have seen, Yeats in old age viewed 'The Wanderings of Oisin' as a cyclic myth, but one must be careful in deciding which features of that poem are genuinely cyclical and which features are made cyclical in retrospect. I believe Yeats when he says that he rejected 'an elaborate metaphor of a breaking wave intended to prove that all life rose and fell', because fossils of that metaphor abound in the poem; but I doubt that Yeats, not then twenty-five, found it difficult to refrain from pointing out that Oisin after death 'would pass over another sea to another island'—that suggests Neoplatonic legend, the sea-mythology quoted earlier in this chapter, rather than the Celtic legends which occupied Yeats in his youth. Yeats wanted to turn 'The Wanderings of Oisin' into a perpetual cycle, like Vico's historical cycles or *A Vision's* gyres, but in fact the early poem is cyclic only in that Oisin works his way around one turn of one circle and ends more or less where he began, on Irish soil; there are just enough hints at the poem's end of one final renewal of the cycle—a last turn—to allow the older Yeats the privilege of fitting it into his later schemata. Yeats in 1934 meant that the pattern of withdrawal and re-entry, escape and nostalgia, would not be ended by Oisin's death, whereas the poem's end suggests that some termination will be achieved, in a highly modified Christian Hell; but he was thinking evidently of the amended version of the Oisin story which appears in his later works.

Yet even in the original 'Wanderings of Oisin' the germs of

much of the later mythology can be discovered; it is one of those vast semi-adolescent poems, like Keats's 'Endymion', in which a young genius lavished his power of invention and through that prodigality managed to touch on many themes not to be treated fully until later in his career. Few critics of Yeats have greatly admired this early mini-epic, but Richard Ellmann, while trying to prove the inconsistency of the poem, has hit upon the paradox which seems to me to be the core of the poem's strength: 'But the three islands, instead of being a refuge from life, are a symbolic representation of it.'[24] Thomas R. Whitaker agrees with him: 'Oisin's islands . . . are ambiguously a refuge from life and a mirror of it . . .'[25] The point is that the islands are enactments of life which have no living substance to them; when Oisin rides across the sea he enters no genuine mode of existence but only a picture,* a static image of life caught at some moment of seeming fulfillment. In an early glossary Yeats wrote that Oisin was 'The poet of the Fenian cycle of legend',[26] and Oisin is, in a sense, the artist who has cast himself as the hero of his own poem, traded his life on earth for a life in fantasy.

Oisin is not the only one of Yeats's artists who prefers pictorial to real existence; in the play *Diarmuid and Grania*, which Yeats and George Moore wrote at the turn of the century, Grania wishes that she could take refuge with Diarmuid in a tapestry instead of facing the inexorable death which awaits Diarmuid on the hunt:

> *Grania:* I stand by the door of this house, seeing the hours wane, waiting for Diarmuid to come home from his hunting. Nothing has happened until to-day, and now Diarmuid and Finn are walking up the valley together, reconciled at last. I had come to think I should never look on a stirring day again, and I had thought to send all the thread you would spin to be woven into a grass green web on which to embroider my wanderings with Diarmuid among the woods. I should have been many years embroidering it, but when it was done and hung round this room, I should have seen birds, beasts, and leaves which ever way I turned, and Diarmuid and myself wandering among them.
>
> *Laban:* But now you have thrown the doors wide open and the days are streaming in upon you again.[27]

---

* Yeats himself wrote that the poem was 'all picture, all emotion, all association, all mythology'. (*Autobiographies* [*Ireland after Parnell*, v], p. 212.)

The imaginary tapestry turns pale in the fated daylight, and events will not stop for all of Grania's control over her embroideries. But Diarmuid's friend Oisin could accomplish that transformation into art; Oisin is like one of those cartoon characters who drives a motorcycle into a billboard and is seen driving down a painted road into a painted landscape. Oona in the earliest version of *The Countess Cathleen* saw Oisin himself in a tapestry, and even foretold the fate of those who seek refuge in a picture:

> See you where Oisin and young Niam ride
> Wrapped in each other's arms, and where
>   the Finians
> Follow their hounds along the fields of
>   tapestry,
> How merry they lived once, yet men died
>   then.[28]

Each of Oisin's islands is a surrogate for some human need, but is ultimately incapable of satisfying that need; where coitus yields no depression, where battle yields no weariness of human muscle, where sleep yields no regeneration, there is only the emptiness of sterile enchantment. The islands are as tripartite as the Sphinx's riddle, yet they do not add up to 'man'; Oisin spends his youth, his middle age, and his old age living a life which seems to answer a warrior's every desire, yet wakes up at the preposterous age of three hundred years to discover that he has failed to live at all. Not only do the islands fail to constitute a human life, they fail to constitute Tir nà nOg either:

> And then lost Niamh murmured, 'Love, we go
> To the Island of Forgetfulness, for lo!
> The Islands of Dancing and of Victories
> Are empty of all power.'
>
>   'And which of these
> Is the Island of Content?
>
>   'None know', she said;
> And on my bosom laid her weeping head.[29]

In the 1889 version (in *The Wanderings of Oisin and Other Poems*) Oisin asked which is the 'Isle of Youth'; the revised version makes it clearer that, while Oisin could find Youth, he could not find final satisfaction. In Yeats's principal source, Comyn's 'The Lay of Oisin on the Land of Youth',[30] Oisin travels to two islands, the second of which is the Celtic paradise, Tir nà nOg, the Land of Youth; and there he marries Niamh and has three children. The first of Yeats's islands then is and is not Tir nà nOg: there is perpetual dancing, and all the stage-props of human joy, but there is neither marriage nor giving in marriage, no animal fertility; human life is excluded from the 'Isle of the Living' (as Yeats called it in 1889), for it is indeed (as Yeats called it in 1895) the 'Island of Dancing', full of stylized sexual activity, ritual expression without honest passion.

As Yeats noted in old age, 'The Wanderings of Oisin' is a cyclical poem, and the circular metaphors are nowhere handled with more subtlety than in Book I. The artificial metaphor of the breaking wave which Yeats rejected lingers in the tidal imagery, which in turn generates other kinds of pulsing metaphors. When Oisin asks Niamh who she is, at her Venus-like miraculous appearance, she replies,

> 'My father and my mother are
> Aengus and Edain, my own name
> Niamh, and my county far
> Beyond the tumbling of this tide.'

> 'What dream came with you that you came
> Through bitter tide on foam-wet feet? . . .'

The tide of human shores is bitter, churning, fluctuant; and Oisin's first glance at Niamh suggests the marine danger of a Celtic Helen of Troy:

> A pearl-pale, high-born lady, who rode
> On a horse with bridle of findrinny;
> And like a sunset were her lips,
> A stormy sunset on doomed ships . . .

Of course all the images of the opening scene suggest the rough heroic life, where death is the highest of all rituals; near the edge of the sea are 'the Firbolgs' burial-mounds'; and Finn's first words to Niamh declare that heroes are quiet because they are thinking of the warriors 'lying slain/ On Gabhra's raven-covered plain'. The human tide is inextricably involved in muta-bility and death; but, as Oisin goes 'Beyond the tumbling of this tide', leaving behind the ordinary cycle of human life, he enters a land governed by a counter-tide, a tide which carries no dissolution, which is as metrical and vacuous as the songs of the dancing-girls:

> 'O Oisin, mount by me and ride
> To shores by the wash of the tremulous tide,
> Where men have heaped no burial-mounds,
> And the days pass by like a wayward tune,
> Where broken faith has never been known,
> And the blushes of first love never have
>   flown . . .'

That last line suggest Keats as strongly as any line in Yeats; clearly Oscar's pencilled burial-urn has been exchanged for Keats's Grecian Urn, where the lovers never, never can kiss, though winning near the goal. The tide on the first island is tremulous, delicate, ethereal; the days pass by like a wayward tune, and life, to adapt Pater's phrase, has approached the condition of music. In the 1889 version Niamh says at this point 'the voice of change is the voice of a tune'; this line probably had to be revised, because Aengus says later that 'here there is nor Change nor Death'; but the earlier line shows very clearly the difference between the human world, where change is represented by the burial-mounds, and the Island of Dancing, where everything is aesthetic, aimless, dim, and there is no change except for the recurring modulations of the same consonant harmonies. The tide represents no threat to the island; indeed Niamh herself is possessed by a sort of internal tide, a steady languid watery motion which gently raises the seashell which binds her hair:

> And it was bound with a pearl-pale shell
> That wavered like the summer streams,
> As her soft bosom rose and fell.

The transition from the perilous human tide to the composed tide of the first island is best shown in the fine passage which describes Oisin's approach to the island:

> But now a wandering land breeze came
> And a far sound of feathery quires;
> It seemed to blow from the dying flame,
> They seemed to sing in the smouldering fires.
> The horse towards the music raced,
> Neighing along the lifeless waste;

Like sooty fingers, many a tree
Rose ever out of the warm sea;
And they were trembling ceaselessly,
As though they all were beating time,
Upon the centre of the sun,
To that low laughing woodland rhyme.

The island's music has resolved into the sound of birds, and these quite artificial birds are described in the passage immediately following. At first the siren-song draws the horse over the 'lifeless waste'—the shipwrecking ocean that the heroes know; but in only two lines the 'lifeless waste' turns into the 'warm sea', full of finger-shaped trees—the comfortable pictorial world of the first island. And the trees are ticking in that tide like so many giant metronomes, as the whole landscape turns diatonic. (The sooty-fingered trees, the mingled sunlight and moonlight, the exultant swans all reappear in a different context in 'The Tower'.) The birds also control and participate in this eternal rhythmic tapping:

And, as they sang, the painted birds
Kept time with their bright wings and feet . . .

Meanwhile, the identification between the residents of the first island and their tide is growing stronger: if Niamh's sea-shell rises and falls on her tide-like bosom, her fellow dancers are 'Unchainable as the dim tide'; and in the song which concludes Book I, the dancers imagine that the waves deplore old age as much as they do:

And the gentle waves of the summer seas,
That raise their heads and wander singing,
Must murmer at last, 'Unjust, unjust' . . .

The island's tide is part of the perpetual ticking which lies underneath the perpetual song; and that iambic movement can speak nothing except a confutation of human time and tide: ' "Unjust, unjust" '.

If there are two kinds of tide, there are also two kinds of roses:

We danced to where in the winding thicket
The damask roses, bloom on bloom,
Like crimson meteors hang in the gloom,
And bending over them softly said,

> Bending over them in the dance,
> With a swift and friendly glance
> From dewy eyes: 'Upon the dead
> Fall the leaves of other roses,
> On the dead dim earth encloses:
> But never, never on our graves,
> Heaped beside the glimmering waves,
> Shall fall the leaves of damask roses. . . .'

There are two kinds of birds as well: on the one hand, the grey
wandering osprey Sorrow, which is denied so often that it seems
to become an obsessive threat to the dancers, whose joy is so
fragile and pure that, when Oisin sings of human joy, they become
depressed enough to feel compelled to throw away his harp; and
the mortal ravens that eat the mortal heroes; on the other hand,
the song-birds which envelop the island:

> And, now our wandering hours were done,
> We cantered to the shore, and knew
> The reason of the trembling trees:
> Round every branch the song-birds flew,
> Or clung thereon like swarming bees;
> While round the shore a million stood
> Like drops of frozen rainbow light,
> And pondered in a soft vain mood
> Upon their shadows in the tide,
> And told the purple deeps their pride,
> And murmured snatches of delight;
> And on the shores were many boats
> With bending sterns and bending bows,
> And carven figures on their prows
> Of bitterns, and fish-eating stoats,
> And swans with their exultant throats . . .

The birds sing the primal music whose rhythm informs the
whole island, but they are incorporeal, without individuality or
even genus, 'frozen rainbow light'; and in their disembodied
purity they seem to scorn 'Common bird or petal' (if it is fair
to cite 'Byzantium'), can only stare at their shadows in the
inviolate involution of so many miniature Hérodiades:

> So rare a crystal is my dreaming heart,
> And all about me lives but in mine own
> Image, the idolatrous mirror of my pride,
> Mirroring this Herodiade diamond-eyed.[31]

All the creatures on the island are like the birds,* wound into
their own vain joy, their own barren pride, and have therefore
lost all substance, retreated into mere forms, 'shadows in the
tide';† the tide of the first island is so important because that
whole island seems to consist of nothing except flat images which
subtly move on the surface of the water to the beat of the tidal
pulsation. The birds are presented directly, as we have seen, as
extensions of the tide; they have surrendered everything to
their images, in contrast to the famous parrot in 'The Indian to
his Love' that rages 'at his own image in the enamelled sea',
and struggles against any collapse into impersonal enamel, the
painted seascape. Interestingly, after the description of the song-
birds, Yeats shifts without transition to the carved birds which
decorate the dancers' boats; there is a direct progression from
the carrion-eaters of the human world to the aesthetic song-birds
of the first island to the purely pictorial bitterns, stoats, and
swans carved in the wood; yet the first island is itself so pictorial
that the carved birds have at least as much vitality as the song-
birds themselves—the carved stoat can eat fish, and indeed the
carved swan is the only exultant creature on the entire island.

If life approaches the condition of music, men approach the
condition of birds; not only do the dancers sing the birds' tunes
with the birds' self-indulgent lyric inconsequence, but Niamh has
performed an act of imagination which seems to shatter Oisin
himself into a flock of birds:

> 'I loved no man, though kings besought,
> Until the Danaan poets brought
> Rhyme that rhymed upon Oisin's name,
> And now I am dizzy with the thought
> Of all that wisdom and the fame
> Of battles broken by his hands,
> Of stories builded by his words

---

* The 'trumpet-twisted shell' that dreams 'of her own melting hues' is another
example of this pervasive narcissism, and is correlative to the dancers. A twisted
shell also appears in the early poem, 'The Song of the Happy Shepherd', where its
echoes help the Shepherd to remain wrapped in his self-communion.

† In an early draft of the first stanza of 'Sailing to Byzantium', the trees are 'Clad
in such foliage that it seems a song', which suggests the rhythmic trees of 'The
Wanderings of Oisin'; and one line would have read, 'The shadow of the birds upon
the seas', again linking the Isle of Youth to the country that is not for old men.
The draft can be found in Jon Stallworthy, *Between the Lines*, p. 105.

> That are like coloured Asian birds
> At evening in their rainless lands.'

The Danaan poets, like the marbles in 'Byzantium', break the
bitter furies of Oisin's battles, his wisdom and his stories, into
something gaudy and formal, wholly artificial, coloured Asian
birds. Those Asian birds appear again at the end of Book I to
join in the chorus of the waves deprecating human time:

> A storm of birds in the Asian trees
> Like tulips in the air a-winging,
> And the gentle waves of the summer seas,
> That raise their heads and wander singing,
> Must murmur at last, 'Unjust, unjust' . . .

The end of Book I is a prophecy of destruction, however, and
the Asian birds have changed from their former poetic stasis,
decayed into animals, stormy, chaotic, as evanescent as tulip-
petals; to reverse Yeats's line, the voice of their tune is the
voice of change, and even the gentle summer waves have a
vague sense of concern in their murmuring of injustice. The
nature of birds in Book I is as complex as the nature of the tide;
and the birds, like the tide, like everything in 'The Wanderings
of Oisin', move in a circle, rise and fall, escape into frozen light
and melt back into flesh and bone. The tide, which seems so
innocent and metrical, 'tremulous', is finally a kind of threat, as
it certainly is in the 1887 *Dhoya*:

He was very happy secluded in that deep forest. Hearing the faint
murmurs of the western sea, they seemed to have outlived change.
But Change is everywhere, with the tides and the stars fastened to her
wheel. Every blood-drop in their lips, every cloud in the sky, every
leaf in the world changed a little, while they brushed back their hair
and kissed. All things change save only the fear of change. . . .

And so Dhoya grew tranquil and gentle, and Change seemed still to
have forgotten them, having so much on her hands. The stars rose and
set watching them smiling together, and the tides ebbed and flowed,
bringing mutability to all save them.[32]

Two kinds of birds, two kinds of tide, two kinds of men:

> And Niamh blew three merry notes
> Out of a little silver trump;
> And then an answering whispering flew
> Over the bare and woody land,
> A whisper of impetuous feet,

And ever nearer, nearer grew;
And from the woods rushed out a band
Of men and ladies, hand in hand,
And singing, singing all together;
Their brows were white as fragrant milk,
Their cloaks made out of yellow silk,
And trimmed with many a crimson feather;
And when they saw the cloak I wore
Was dim with mire of a mortal shore,
They fingered it and gazed on me
And laughed like murmurs of the sea . . .

The dancers are dressed in bright colours, as stylish and immaculate as stage costumes; the crimson feathers, the whispering flight of impetuous feet, show the beginning of the transition from man to bird, the transition to be continued in Book III and in a few of the lyrics written in Yeats's old age. The mire of human veins (one cannot avoid 'Byzantium') which stains Oisin's cloak is so foreign to their nature that it can produce only astonished laughter, a supremely naïve or decadent reaction; and tidal noises, 'murmurs of the sea', can be heard in the dancers' laughter, for the dancers are as much creatures of water reflection as the birds described above; Niamh herself is pearl-pale, and Oisin becomes liquid, passive, and depersonalized, as the harp which articulates his human pain is taken away and he is absorbed into the perpetual round of singing and dancing. The songs themselves are deceptively simple, for a little analysis will show that they are full of self-contradictions.

Aengus' song, the first of the series, tells us that joy is the motive force of the universe, and we may assume that Aengus, the Irish Apollo who rules the island, can be fairly definitive on this point:

'Joy drowns the twilight in the dew,
And fills with stars night's purple cup,
And wakes the sluggard seeds of corn,
And stirs the young kid's budding horn,
And makes the infant ferns unwrap,
And for the peewit paints his cap,
And rolls along the unwieldy sun,
And makes the little planets run:
And if joy were not on the earth,
There were an end of change and birth,

> And Earth and Heaven and Hell would die,
> And in some gloomy barrow lie
> Folded like a frozen fly;
> Then mock at Death and Time with glances
> And wavering arms and wandering dances. . . .'

Aengus claims, as he says in the second stanza, that 'joy is God and God is joy'; joy is the universal creator, a peculiarly hedonistic, self-centred variant of Boethius' hymn on love. Yet Aengus says in the first stanza that joy causes 'change and birth' (and enumerates some changes and births—the corn's fertility, the fern's unfolding), while he says in the second stanza that 'here there is nor Change nor Death'; the island's dancers seem to take pride in the fact that they subvert the decrees of their own God, joy. And it is not possible to argue that there is one joy-God who has two sets of standards, one for earth and one for the first island: the later songs assert that God is joy only on the first island, not for the universe in general:

> 'You stars,
> Across your wandering ruby cars
> Shake the loose reins: you slaves of God,
> He rules you with an iron rod,
> He holds you with an iron bond,
> Each one woven to the other,
> Each one woven to his brother
> Like bubbles in a frozen pond;
> But we in a lonely land abide
> Unchainable as the dim tide,
> With hearts that know nor law nor rule,
> And hands that hold no wearisome tool,
> Folded in love that fears no morrow,
> Nor the grey wandering osprey Sorrow.'

Who is the Urizenic God who subjugates the stars? Surely not joy, but instead Saint Patrick's Jehovah, who infiltrates even into the first island, who has already taken command over all except this one small refuge.

The second stanza of Aengus' song presents a myth of the fall of man which parallels this fall of God:

> 'Men's hearts of old were drops of flame
> That from the saffron morning came,
> Or drops of silver joy that fell

Out of the moon's pale twisted shell;
But now hearts cry that hearts are slaves,
And toss and turn in narrow caves;
But here there is nor law nor rule,
Nor have hands held a weary tool;
And here there is nor Change nor Death,
But only kind and merry breath,
For joy is God and God is joy.'

In the beginning, joy was a beneficent, infecundating creator, and men's hearts were 'drops of silver joy', dispersed globules partaking of God's nature; but God turned Augustinian and authoritarian, and men turned slaves, except on the first island. Yet the first island itself seems pallid and sterile compared to the great burst of natural vitality which Aengus describes in his first stanza, the one convincing passage in all the songs. If the island is deathless it must also be birthless, the 'lonely land' where hands hold 'no wearisome tool' and therefore neither consume their energy nor accomplish anything productive. The contrast between the joy-God and the iron ruler is a parody of the contrast between Fenian animism and Patrick's jealous God: the Fenians do not live for athletic titillation, and Patrick does not demand slavery, only asceticism ('The things that most of all' Oisin hates, 'Fasting and prayers'). There is imagistic pressure which tends to destroy Aengus' false dialectic, to reveal the island in its true nature: for instance, Aengus says that if joy did not exist there would be no change or birth, and 'Earth and Heaven and Hell would die . . . Folded like a frozen fly'; in a later song the word 'frozen' appears again, as the 'slaves of God' are caught in rigid Cartesian space 'Like bubbles in a frozen pond'. Clearly 'frozen' denotes something sinister, the deathlike stasis which would result from the downfall of joy and the establishment of a malevolent deity; but the dancers' island is equally lifeless and static, and the omnipresent birds look like 'drops of frozen rainbow light'.

The dancers oppose God's imaginary authoritarianism with an equally imaginary freedom:

But we in a lonely land abide
Unchainable as the dim tide,
With hearts that know nor law nor rule,
And hands that hold no wearisome tool . . .

The dancers think themselves free, while they are actually as circumscribed, patterned, and unchangeable as any slaves of God.* Insofar as joy is a human emotion, real love and not pale indulgence, it is beyond them, and Book I is an allegory of the death of Heaven, one of the deaths projected in Aengus' song; it is indeed 'Folded like some frozen fly'. Aengus himself cannot even participate in the mock joy of the dancers, but sits in a perpetual 'Druid dream of the end of days/ When the stars are to wane and the world be done'; and, finally, the dancers can only watch their island with the same expectant, almost joyless, eschatological eyes:

> 'But we are apart in the grassy places,
> Where care cannot trouble the least of our days,
> Or the softness of youth be gone from our faces,
> Or love's first tenderness die in our gaze.
> The hare grows old as she plays in the sun†
> And gazes around her with eyes of brightness;
> Before the swift things that she dreamed of were done
> She limps along in an aged whiteness; . . .
> And 'My speed is a weariness', falters the mouse,
> And the kingfisher turns to a ball of dust,
> And the roof falls in of his tunnelled house.
> But the love-dew dims our eyes till the day
> When God shall come from the sea with a sigh
> And bid the stars drop down from the sky,
> And the moon like a pale rose wither away.'

The secret of the first island is the hidden motto of most earthly paradises: *Et in Arcadia ego.* But death is so remote there that it seems meaningless on human terms; the dancers cultivate the

---

* In the 1889 version, the dancers say,

> The ever-winding wakeful sea,
> That hides us from all human spying,
> Is not so free, so free, so free.

The sea isolates the dancers and protects them, but if the sea is not absolutely free—if it too can be bound with God's iron rod—then slavery is encroaching nearer to the island than one would otherwise suspect.

† The hare appears here as an example of the terrestrial condition, where motion, speed can be achieved, but only through the expenditure of vital energy. In the early poem 'Ephemera', which records the break-up of a love affair, there is another correlative rabbit: 'A rabbit old and lame limped down the path.' Both cases foreshadow the doctrine of interconsumption and the gyre-forms of *A Vision;* and one line in 'Ephemera', ' "Passion has often worn our wandering hearts" ', anticipates 'Love's pleasure drives his love away' from 'Two Songs from a Play'.

same vapid beauty in their song of death ('the moon like a pale
rose wither away') that they do in their songs of life, so the
whole round of their existence is exposed, pure, exquisite,
impoverished.

At the core of the dancers' vision of terrestrial mortality there
is an old man 'Grown desolate', whose 'heart still dreams of
battle and love'—a picture of Oisin himself returned to earth, a
momentary glimpse of reality, a hole in the tapestry. And at last
the two tides, human and inhuman, come together, and Oisin
becomes aware that he is starving on the first island, has taken
a mess of shadows for his meat:

> When one day by the tide I stood,
> I found in that forgetfulness
> Of dreamy foam a staff of wood
> From some dead warrior's broken lance:
> I turned it in my hands; the stains
> Of war were on it, and I wept,
> Remembering how the Fenians stept
> Along the blood-bedabbled plains,
> Equal to good or grievous chance . . .

The Fenians live in a non-deterministic world, full of 'good or
grievous chance,' the danger and the transitoriness that give
meaning to human life; and Oisin craves that fullness of experience. When Oisin speaks of the 'forgetfulness/ Of dreamy foam',
he seems to realize in retrospect that the island's tide is like the
Lethe of the Greek underworld, where non-life is made tolerable
only through oblivion; but the signs of death can still inspire a
human response—tears—and he can thereby break out of his
useless dream. The most prominent feature of the dancers is that
they are desultory wanderers, made of the stuff that dreams are
made on:

> Under the golden evening light,
> The Immortals moved among the fountains
> By rivers and the woods' old night;
> Some danced like shadows on the mountains,
> Some wandered ever hand in hand;
> Or sat in dreams on the pale strand,
> Each forehead like an obscure star
> Bent down above each hookèd knee . . .

The dancers are shadowy, almost unreal; their foreheads are like obscure stars because they are too abstract, thought-enveloped, changeless, and dim to be human. Oisin of course is torn between his desire to be human and his desire to be star-like; if he is 'The poet of the Fenian cycle', we would have to say that he is a romantic poet. Therefore Oisin, for all his disenchantment, is still 'wrapped in dreams' as he leaves the first island; and he does not seem to head back towards human lands, but instead resumes the quest for the Island of Content.

As Oisin and Niamh ride over the sea towards the second island, they come upon two sets of phantoms, emblems which are gradually gaining intelligibility:

> *Oisin.* We galloped over the glossy sea:
>   I know not if days passed or hours,
>   And Niamh sang continually
>   Danaan songs, and their dewy showers
>   Of pensive laughter, unhuman sound,
>   Lulled weariness, and softly round
>   My human sorrow her white arms wound.
>   We galloped; now a hornless deer
>   Passed by us, chased by a phantom hound
>   All pearly white, save one red ear;
>   And now a lady rode like the wind
>   With an apple of gold in her tossing hand;
>   And a beautiful young man followed behind
>   With quenchless gaze and fluttering hair.

I have quoted from their first appearance, during Oisin's sea-ride in Book I; these same apparitions, even this same warning to Oisin, are recapitulated in Book II, and will reappear for a few lines at the beginning of Book III. In the 1889 version the sense of *déjà vu* is still stronger; for instance, Niamh says in Book I, 'Fret not with speech the phantoms dread', and in Book II, 'Vex not with speech the phantoms dread'. The phantoms have no dramatic interaction in any of the episodes of the poem; they remain distant, tantalizing, even more abstract and pictorial than the characters on the islands proper. Why is Niamh so insistent that Oisin should not talk to them, not look at them, utterly ignore them? Why does she call these innocuous symbols 'dread'? The first island is an image of life, a perspective drawing which can represent but not constitute a human environ-

ment; and the phantoms correspond to the islands somewhat as
the islands correspond to Finn's world, for the phantoms enact
in a generalized way the vain pursuit, whether of gaiety, battle,
or repose, which is the principle of life on the three islands.

If the Yeatsian myth is the concrete embodiment of an
abstract principle, then the phantoms constitute one of the in-
forming myths of 'The Wanderings of Oisin', the myth of the
pursuit of heroic life repeated in a finer tone. Yeats said in the
'Introduction to *The Resurrection*' that the phantoms were
'emblematical of eternal pursuit',[33] and Oisin, by Book II, is
learning that the pursuit is indeed eternal: the hound does not
catch the deer and the youth does not catch the lady. This permanent unfulfillment exposes the true human famishing which is
Oisin's lot on the islands, and this is why the phantoms are
dreadful to Niamh; if Oisin learns their significance he will understand the futility of his pursuit of the Island of Content, and the
fragile union of Oisin and Niamh will be destroyed. The phantom
of the youth chasing the phantom of the lady with the golden
apple is more than slightly suggestive of Oisin chasing Niamh
and her tantalizing island; but the Keatsian equilibrium of the
youth and lady—never drawing apart, never coming together—
also suggests the hopelessness of the poet's dream for a sublimed
version of heroic love. In Book III Oisin and Niamh sigh at the
sight of 'The immortal desire of Immortals', and Yeats offered
some commentary on this line in the notes to *The Wind among
the Reeds*:

This hound and this deer seem plain images of the desire of the man
'which is for the woman,' and 'the desire of the woman which is for the
desire of the man,' and of all desires that are as these. I have read them
in this way in *The Wanderings of Oisin*, and have made my lover sigh
because he has seen in their faces 'the immortal desire of Immortals.'[34]

It is significant that the man desires the woman, while the
woman desires the desire of the man;* women, especially
abstract immortal women, crave the pursuit more than the

* Yeats, deprecating his search for lifeless beauty, put himself in the same position as Comyn's phantoms in *Discoveries* (*Essays and Introductions*, p. 271):

Then one day I understood quite suddenly, as the way is, that I was seeking
something unchanging and unmixed and always outside myself, a Stone or an
Elixir that was always out of reach, and that I myself was the fleeting thing that

embrace, the man's love more than the man himself. This is another of the upward analogical movements which culminate in the phantoms: the phantoms not only are on the highest plane of myth in the poem, but their desire is even more rarefied and fleshless than that of the dancers in Book I, who at least hold hands; like the ghosts in 'All Souls' Night', the phantoms seem to derive their ecstasy from the most tenuous stimulus imaginable, the mere act of impalpable pursuit. The phantoms also complete the upward movement by being grouped in pairs of immortals; Oisin and Niamh, like the lovers whom Niamh sings about on the second sea-ride, are an imperfect pair in that one of them is human. It is clear that Yeats thought of the phantoms' pursuit as something perfect, universal, astronomical—symbolic of the engendering contraries which underlie temporal existence, the tensions which pull back and forth the night and the day:

A solar mythologist would perhaps say that the girl with the golden apple was once the winter, or night, carrying the sun away, and the deer without horns, like the boar without bristles, darkness flying the light. He could certainly, I think, say that when Cuchulain, whom Professor Rhys calls a solar hero, hunted the enchanted deer of Slieve Fuadh, because the battle fury was still on him, he was the sun pursuing clouds, or cold, or darkness. I have understood them in this sense in 'Hanrahan laments because of his wandering,' and made Hanrahan long for the day when they, fragments of ancestral darkness, will overthrow the world. The desire of the woman, the flying darkness, it is all one! The image—a cross, a man preaching in the wilderness, a dancing Salome, a lily in a girl's hand, a flame leaping, a globe with wings, a pale sunset over still waters—is an eternal act; but our understandings are temporal and understand but a little at a time.[35]

Yeats seems to be groping towards an archetypal realm where the world can be reduced to a few primal images, the emblems of the controlling forces; and as he approaches his apple-lady, his cross, his Salome, his winged globe, he seems to be close to

---

held out its hand. The more I tried to make my art deliberately beautiful, the more did I follow the opposite of myself, for deliberate beauty is like a woman always desiring man's desire.

The lady with the apple is the 'deliberate beauty' that the romantic poet pursues, always out of reach, always creating the desire that she cannot satisfy.

the level where Oisin and Cuchulain and Hanrahan move on the
same quest, begin to fall into one great myth.*

The reader of the *Stories of Red Hanrahan* would not instantly
associate Hanrahan with Oisin, but Hanrahan was another poet
who was loved by an immortal and sacrificed much because of that
love; and in *The Only Jealousy of Emer* (*Collected Plays*, p. 281)
Cuchulain too is bedevilled by a sea-goddess, Fand, who 'hurried
from the Country-under-Wave' to 'fish for men with dreams
upon the hook'. It is important that Niamh sings about the
coupling of mortals and immortals immediately after they see
the phantoms at the beginning of Book II:

> Now, man of croziers, shadows called our names
> And then away, away, like whirling flames;
> And now fled by, mist-covered, without sound,
> The youth and lady and the deer and hound;
> 'Gaze no more on the phantoms,' Niamh said,
> And kissed my eyes, and, swaying her bright head
> And her bright body, sang of faery and man
> Before God was or my old line began;
> Wars shadowy, vast, exultant; faeries of old
> Who wedded men with rings of Druid gold;
> And how those lovers never turn their eyes
> Upon the life that fades and flickers and dies,
> Yet love and kiss on dim shores far away
> Rolled round with music of the sighing spray:
> Yet sang no more as when, like a brown bee
> That has drunk full, she crossed the misty sea
> With me in her white arms a hundred years
> Before this day; for now the fall of tears
> Troubled her song.

The phantoms are terrifying because they have become the
reductio ad absurdum of Oisin's quest, for they show the sterile
consequences of trying to imitate the Immortals; so Niamh must
try to comfort Oisin by retreating from strict immortality into
a half-human, more possible love-affair—although she can sing

---

* Sir John Rhys tells in *Lectures on the Origin and Growth of Religion as illustrated by Celtic Heathendom* the story of Cuchulain being led across a plain by a mysterious apple; Rhys explains the story by saying, 'we have traces here of a primitive and forgotten myth which represented the sun as an apple or ball' (*Lectures*, p.
453). Cuchulain is a solar hero, and the phantom of the youth chasing the woman
with the solar apple subsumes Cuchulain himself.

of nothing that Oisin has not already rejected on the first island, and she therefore despairs. The phantoms of the youth and the lady are, then, the ironic vision of the ultimate fulfilment of Oisin's desires—ironic, because the fulfilment, the immortalized version of human love, is only an eternal insatiation, as impersonal and abstract as the laws of gravitation.*

The hound and the deer are part of the same myth, but suggest heroic battle more than heroic love, the second island more than the first; the parallels between the hunt of Oisin and the Fenians which begins the poem and the red-eared hound's hunting of the hornless deer are handled skilfully in the poem. Oisin remembers the mortal hounds Bran, Sceolan, and Lomair at several places in the poem; they focus all of his nostalgia for the rough vigorous life of the Fenians. The action of the poem begins when Niamh interrupts the hunters and their baying hounds in pursuit of a deer;† and Oisin starts his ride across the sea with the deer still uncaught, effectively stopping his participation in human affairs, keeping that scene in suspended animation in his memory. For Oisin, trapped outside clock time, the hounds of the Fenians never catch their quarry or abandon the chase, just as he expects, in the middle of Book III, that the Fenians will be alive to greet him when he returns from the third island. The red-eared hound and the hornless deer are magnified re-enactments of Oisin's memory of the real hunt which he has left behind, and of his false vision of a happy hunting ground where the joys of the hunt are prolonged forever, as immortal hounds run after an immortal deer through all time, their excitement never decaying into monotony, their keen expectation of fulfilment never losing its edge. As such, the phantoms of the hound and deer supplement the fantasy of perpetual battle which Oisin enters in Book II; and it is not by accident that Oisin, disillusioned with the second island, thinks of Bran, Sceolan, and Lomair at the beginning of Book III:

* Yeats relates the girl with the golden apple to 'night, carrying the sun away' in the notes to 'He Mourns for the Change' (*Variorum Poems*, p. 807). Some of this symbolism is carried out at the end of the 1889 version of Book I, where the dancers predict the quenching of the sun, while they themselves remain unaffected by that apocalypse. Similarly, Yeats writes in the same passage that the sun 'scares with his bustle the delicate night', suggesting the 'darkness flying the light' that the hornless deer represents.

† According to the 1889 version, the Fenians were hunting a *hornless* deer in this episode.

> Fled foam underneath us, and round us, a wandering
>   and milky smoke,
> High as the saddle-girth, covering away from our
>   glances the tide;
> The deer and the hound, and the lady and youth,
>   from the distance broke;
> The immortal desire of Immortals we saw in their
>   faces, and sighed.
>
> I mused on the chase with the Fenians, and Bran,
>   Sceolan, Lomair . . .[36]

This is directly parallel to the beginning of Book II, where Niamh sings about Immortals taking mortal lovers after the second appearance of the phantoms. In Book II, Oisin knows that he is left famished by an Immortal's love, so Niamh's song dissolves into tears; in Book III, Oisin knows that he is also left famished by a heroic feat which accomplishes nothing, so his thoughts turn to the honest joy associated with the Fenian hounds and genuine achievement.

The paired images of Comyn's phantoms were remarkably stable and powerful in Yeats's imagination, and they appear both early and late in his poetry without significant tinkering; in every case but one the emblems appear self-contained and tangential, correlative to the action rather than part of the action. The exception is 'He Mourns for the Change that Has Come upon Him and His Beloved, and Longs for the End of the World':

> Do you not hear me calling, white deer with no horns?
> I have been changed to a hound with one red ear;
> I have been in the Path of Stones and the Wood of Thorns,
> For somebody hid hatred and hope and desire and fear
> Under my feet that they follow you night and day.
> A man with a hazel wand came without sound;
> He changed me suddenly; I was looking another way;
> And now my calling is but the calling of a hound;
> And Time and Birth and Change are hurrying by.
> I would that the Boar without bristles had come from the West
> And had rooted the sun and moon and stars out of the sky
> And lay in the darkness, grunting, and turning to his rest.[37]

The speaker of this poem is either a somewhat impersonal 'lover', one of Yeats's half-dozen lyric masks, or the more fictive

Mongan, who is assigned the poem in an early printing; Mongan is a vague 'wizard and king who remembers his passed lives'[38] and has drunk ale in the Country of the Young.[39] The lover is not at all dramatic, only a disembodied mask that exists to speak a few poems, almost as impersonal as the voice of the wind among the reeds; and in this poem he is projected into a miniature analogue of 'The Wanderings of Oisin', in which the poet (or wizard) is transformed by magic into Oisin's red-eared hound. As with Oisin himself, the lover is acted upon almost passively, seems bewildered by his sudden metamorphosis; Oisin found himself inside an environment which was a projection of his wishes, a dream come true; similarly, the lover is changed by Aengus,[40] the god of love, into an emblem of perfect desire, immortal love, running on a road composed of human emotions, 'hatred and hope and desire and fear', turned hard and objective. And the lover, like Oisin, can find no joy in this dehumanized state, although he humanizes the hound as much as he can, filling it with his lamentation. He sees the hopelessness of this attenuated, purely symbolic mode of love, and is troubled that 'Time and Birth and Change are hurrying by', just as Oisin discovered that the Fenians lived and died while he was caught up in fantasy. Oisin never went so far as to change his shape, but he did try to become whatever he saw, dancing with the dancers, fighting when he was expected to fight, sleeping on the island where no living thing was awake; and Niamh twice urged him not to look at the phantoms, as if he would inevitably have galloped toward the deer and the lady if he had kept on gazing, become a fifth phantom. It is interesting that 'He Mourns for the Change' ends with exactly the same sort of apocalyptic vision as Book I of 'The Wanderings of Oisin': in the latter poem the dancers wait for the stars to drop down from the sky and the moon to wither like a pale rose, and in the former poem the Boar without bristles—akin to the 'bristless' (*sic*) boar of *Diarmuid and Grania*, which brings an end to Grania's tapestry-vision—uproots the sun and moon and stars. If Oisin had ignored the flotsam of human mortality, had become permanently assimilated into the company of the dancers, he might have felt the lover's dim frustration and desired the end of time, the consummation when the planets drop in the sun.

These themes persist far after *The Wind among the Reeds*.

The boar appears for the last time in 'Her Vision in the Wood',* the most neglected of all Yeats's masterpieces; in that poem, the woman (of 'A Woman Young and Old', suddenly turned old) finds herself absorbed into a painting:

> All stately women moving to a song
> With loosened hair or foreheads grief-distraught,
> It seemed a Quattrocento painter's throng,
> A thoughtless image of Mantegna's thought—
> Why should they think that are for ever young?
> Till suddenly in grief's contagion caught,
> I stared upon his blood-bedabbled breast
> And sang my malediction with the rest.
>
> That thing all blood and mire, that beast-torn wreck,
> Half turned and fixed a glazing eye on mine,
> And, though love's bitter-sweet had all come back,
> Those bodies from a picture or a coin
> Nor saw my body fall nor heard it shriek,
> Nor knew, drunken with singing as with wine,
> That they had brought no fabulous symbol there
> But my heart's victim and its torturer.[41]

This is the demonic inverse of the situation of *Diarmuid and Grania*: Grania wanted to retreat into the safety of a tapestry with Diarmuid; but here the woman is caught in a picture of Bacchantes, who are yet not violent or hysterical, only grieving in the stylized theatrical manner of Mantegna; the mourners are 'stately women', actresses, moving to the formal rhythm of the 'deafening music'. The woman at first sings her malediction with the rest, but this seems to be a dishonest, Latinate response to the spectacle of her gored lover; she is trying to cultivate an artificial sorrow in order to free herself from pain (just as she tried to assuage the pain of her old age in the first stanza with the 'lesser pang' of torn flesh),† not unlike Oisin's cultivation of an artificial joy on the first island. The tension of 'Her Vision in the Wood' depends on the contrast between the organic life of the woman and her lover and the painted forms of the mourners:

* The animal here is not specified, but the strong attraction to the Diarmuid and Grania legend (as well as to Venus and Adonis, a more likely subject for a Quattrocento painter) makes the animal's identification as a boar all but certain.

† The blood that flows down her fingers seems to invoke the images of the mourners; as Yeats wrote, a blood-pool is 'an ancient substitute for the medium' (*Explorations*, p. 366).

the lovers are bloody or ageing, while the mourners are 'for
ever young'; the woman shrieks, while the mourners sing; the
lover is 'no fabulous symbol', while the mourners are 'bodies
from a picture or a coin'. The lover in 'He Mourns for the Change'
had been transformed into one of Yeats's most fabulous symbols,
the red-eared hound, and found himself unhappy, trapped; but
here, as in 'The Wanderings of Oisin', the protagonists manage
to break out of stage-conventions, to face existential anguish
without the smooth mask of symbol and song.

Yeats's last interpretation of the myth of the hound and the
deer and the youth and the lady occurs at the beginning of *The
King of the Great Clock Tower*:

> *Second Attendant.* They dance all day that dance
>   in Tir-nan-oge.
> *First Attendant.* There every lover is a happy rogue;
>   And should he speak, it is the speech of birds.
>   No thought has he, and therefore has no words,
>   No thought because no clock, no clock because
>   If I consider deeply, lad and lass,
>   Nerve touching nerve upon that happy ground,
>   Are bobbins where all time is bound and wound.
> *Second Attendant.* O never may that dismal thread run loose;
> *First Attendant.* For there the hound that Oisin saw pursues
>   The hornless deer that runs in such a fright;
>   And there the woman clasps an apple tight
>   For all the clamour of a famished man.
>   They run in foam, and there in foam they ran,
>   Nor can they stop to take a breath that still
>   Hear in the foam the beating of a bell.[42]

The theme of *The King of the Great Clock Tower* is the plasticity
of the poet's beloved when caught in the poet's imagination, the
interrelation between the real woman and the transcendental
image against which the poet must judge her;* this play and a
few other short plays, for all their ritual beheadings, derive as
much from Keats's 'Eve of St. Agnes' as from the Japanese Noh
plays.

---

* I disagree with F. A. C. Wilson, who believes that the Stroller's love is
wholly exalted and that the Queen is the feminine principle of God (*W. B. Yeats and
Tradition*, p. 75), and with Helen Vendler, who would identify the Queen strictly
with the Muse (*Yeats's* VISION *and the Later Plays*, p. 145).

The Stroller first demonstrated his poetic power when he anserified his wife:

> *The Stroller.* I had a wife. The image in my head
> Made her appear fat, slow, thick of the limbs,
> In all her movements like a Michaelmas goose.[43]

And if the Queen is 'Dumb as an image made of wood or metal,/ A screen between the living and the dead', it is because she is trying to fulfil the Stroller's conception of a phase-fifteen dancer, suspended between the living and the dead, possessing the best features of both worlds. Yet although both the Stroller and the Queen herself want her to attain this ultimate status, she cannot quite do it; she is still too human:

> *The Stroller.* Neither so red, nor white, nor full in the breast
> As I had thought. What matter for all that
> So long as I proclaim her everywhere
> Most beautiful![44]

The Stroller can celebrate but not fully transform; the poet's shaping power cannot fit her flesh into the exact image of his conception. At this point in the play the story becomes remarkable. Somehow the Stroller, his ideal beloved, and the real Queen must all come together; but instead of meeting on an idealized level, remote from human experience, they meet in a most bloody manner, enacting sexual intercourse:

> He longs to kill
> My body, until
> That sudden shudder
> And limbs lie still.
>
> O, what may come
> Into my womb,
> What caterpillar
> My beauty consume?[45]

They attain the consummation for which sexual intercourse is a metaphor:

> Clip and lip and long for more,
> Mortal men our abstracts are;
> *What of the hands on the Great Clock face?*
> All those living wretches crave

> Prerogatives of the dead that have
> Sprung heroic from the grave.
> *A moment more and it tolls midnight.*[46]

At the conjunction of death and life, the Severed Head and the dancing Queen, the lovers turn mythic, become the supernaturally concrete paradigms of all human lovers; and we see that the Queen's original conception of perfect beauty (Yeats's own conception as late as Book I of *A Vision*), which entailed contempt of human life, remoteness from human affairs, was a false conception. The Queen becomes the image of all beloved women by being the most deflowered woman alive, and the Stroller becomes the image of all desiring men by being the limpest, the most wholly exhausted, used up, sacrificed, of men.

Yeats's stage poets, from Aleel onward, have the surprising ability to humanize their symbolic women even while they elevate them;* and because *The King of the Great Clock Tower* explores the theme of the chase after immortal beauty, human life versus symbolic life, it begins with 'The Wanderings of Oisin'. The late play is a much more sophisticated work than the early narrative, but even the play's most subtle theme, the Queen's downward shift from the transcendentally inhuman to the transcendentally human, is foreshadowed in 'The Wanderings of Oisin': Niamh is a much more tearful, feminine creature in Books II and III than she is in Book I. Notice the careful antithesis between the 'unhuman sound' of Niamh's laughter and the 'human sorrow' of Oisin at the first appearance of the phantoms:

> And Niamh sang continually
> Danaan songs, and their dewy showers
> Of pensive laughter, unhuman sound,
> Lulled weariness, and softly round
> My human sorrow her white arms wound.
> We galloped; now a hornless deer
> Passed by us, chased by a phantom hound
> All pearly white, save one red ear;
> And now a lady rode like the wind
> With an apple of gold in her tossing hand;
> And a beautiful young man followed behind
> With quenchless gaze and fluttering hair.

---

* I feel that the actions of humanization and elevation constitute a double gyre.

At the beginning of Book II, they see the same phantoms, Niamh
sings more Danaan songs, but there is no laughter; indeed, 'the
fall of tears/ Troubled her song'. At the beginning of Book III,
they again see the phantoms, but 'never a song sang Niamh';
her music and her laughter, the faery qualities which made her a
fit princess for Aengus on the first island, have vanished, and
she is to all intents a mortal woman:

> 'O flaming lion of the world, O when will you turn
>   to your rest?'
> I saw from a distant saddle; from the earth she
>   made her moan:
> 'I would die like a small withered leaf in the
>   autumn, for breast unto breast
> We shall mingle no more, nor our gazes empty
>   their sweetness lone
>
> 'In the isles of the farthest seas where only the
>   spirits come. . . .'

She wishes to die like any mortal woman who has lost her lover;
and she seems to have renounced the 'isles of the farthest seas
where only the spirits come' as much as Oisin has. Yeats does
not make anything of Niamh's humanization in 'The Wanderings
of Oisin'; it is only a minor theme which required decades of
imaginative thought to find its resolution; but Niamh's next
words to Oisin, the last words she speaks in the poem, her last
temptation, are directly relevant to the opening song of *The
King of the Great Clock Tower*:

> 'Were the winds less soft than the breath of a
>   pigeon who sleeps on her nest,
> Nor lost in the star-fires and odours the sound
>   of the sea's vague drum?
> O flaming lion of the world, O when will you turn
>   to your rest?'

Niamh asks, in effect, Was not the pain of the human world lost
in the supersensual splendour of the three islands? The assumption is that Oisin is tortured by the pounding rhythm of 'the sea's
vague drum', just as the phantoms in *The King of the Great Clock
Tower* are driven by the beating of a bell:

> They run in foam, and there in foam they ran,
> Nor can they stop to take a breath that still
> Hear in the foam the beating of a bell.[47]

This is not a sound which properly belongs in Tir nà nOg, except insofar as clock time is always threatening the periphery of that delicate paradise;* the Tir nà nOg of this play is another attempt to refabricate the island which Oisin repudiated, a cleverer, more substantial refabrication, yet an attempt which is still only partially successful. This last Tir nà nOg is by far the most completed version, having worked its way through 'The Wanderings of Oisin', 'Shepherd and Goatherd', 'His Bargain', and 'Byzantium'; the dancers, who were just beginning to grow feathers on Oisin's first island, now speak with the speech of birds; and they seem to have taken their form from no natural thing, to exist only as intermeshed webs of nerves, one neutral thing that both sexes fit to:

> *Second Attendant.* They dance all day that dance in
>   Tir-nan-oge.
> *First Attendant.* There every lover is a happy rogue;
>   And should he speak, it is the speech of birds.
>   No thought has he, and therefore has no words,
>   No thought because no clock, no clock because
>   If I consider deeply, lad and lass,
>   Nerve touching nerve upon that happy ground,
>   Are bobbins where all time is bound and wound.

Like the Christian God, the lovers in Tir nà nOg are known by what they are not: they are thoughtless, wordless, clockless, the utterly concrete things that mortal men are abstracts of. The lovers in death are wound filmstrips of their previous lives; but even in this dormant state there are strong suggestions of sexuality, a perfected sexuality in which lovers' nerves touch at every point instead of at just one, the mutual conflagration of 'Ribh at the Tomb of Baile and Aillinn', the double skein of 'Crazy Jane and Jack the Journeyman':

---

* The inexorable rhythm of the sea represented to Yeats the most naked sort of flux; in 'A Prayer for my Daughter', Yeats imagines

> That the future years had come,
> Dancing to a frenzied drum,
> Out of the murderous innocence of the sea.

And, of course, the sea that surrounds Byzantium is 'gong-tormented', and the spawn of images swimming there are, like the phantoms, agonized by their feverish temporality and maddened by the noise of midnight, their death. The last line of 'Byzantium' was originally very close to the last line of this opening song; according to Jon Stallworthy (*Between the Lines*, p. 126), it read 'That gong tormented current breaks in spray in foam'.

But were I left to lie alone
In an empty bed,
The skein so bound us ghost to ghost
When he turned his head
Passing on the road that night,
Mine must walk when dead.[48]

After the vision of the happy rogues dancing on the happy ground, the Second Attendant says rather sanctimoniously, 'O never may that dismal thread run loose'. Now Yeats's choruses are not necessarily any more reliable than Sophocles'; and the Second Attendant is especially suspect, because he plays the 'wicked, crooked hawthorn tree' of the last song, definitely an antagonistic character. The 'dismal thread' is of course the filmstrip of the mortal lives of the lovers, dismal because it is full of the intrigues and disappointments that beset the course of human love; the Second Attendant wants it to remain wrapped up on its cosy spool, and Yeats also found this phase-fifteen transfiguration appealing, at times:

Does not every civilisation as it approaches or recedes from its full moon seem as it were to shiver into the premonition of some perfection born out of itself, perhaps even of some return to its first Source? Does not one discover in the faces of Madonnas and holy women painted by Raphael or da Vinci, if never before or since, a condition of soul where all is still and finished, all experience wound up upon a bobbin? Does one not hear those lips murmur that, despite whatever illusion we cherish, we came from no immaturity, but out of our own perfection like ships that 'all their swelling canvas wear'?[49]

But Oisin, while contemplating the perfection of his third false Tir nà nOg, also thought of himself as a ship:

'Like me were some galley forsaken far off in
Meridian isle,
Remembering its long-oared companions, sails
turning to threadbare rags;
No more to crawl on the seas with long oars
mile after mile,
But to be amid shooting of flies and flowering
of rushes and flags.'

When one has just passed the moment of perfection, when one's dismal thread has begun to unwind, one is like a ship with swelling canvases, driven by purposiveness; but the state of perfection, if it is artificially prolonged, and does not keep shifting in and out of experiential reality, clock time, tends to tatter one's sails. The image of the ship run aground is a superb description of Oisin's vehicular form, for it shows how the islands have crippled him, loaded him with so many flowers that he cannot move, cannot float, is unfit for human activity; Niamh's lips were indeed 'A stormy sunset on doomed ships'. The Stroller, on the other hand, is more successful in his realization of transcendental love; but I believe that the parallels between Oisin and the Stroller are sufficiently strong to be used as evidence against the permanent self-sufficient paradise presented in the first stanza of the first song; indeed Yeats once described Oisin in paradise as no less thoughtless and love-wound than the happy rogues:

But when Oisin or some kingly forerunner—Bran, son of Febal, or the like—rides or sails in an enchanted ship to some divine country, he but looks for a more delighted companionship, or to be in love with faces that will never fade. No thought of any life greater than that of love, and the companionship of those that have drawn their swords upon the darkness of the world, ever troubles their delight in one another as it troubles Iseult amid her love, or Arthur amid his battles. It is an ailment of our speculation that thought, when it is not the planning of something, or the doing of something, or some memory of a plain circumstance, separates us from one another because it makes us always more unlike. . . .[50]

This is a very early, very approving statement of Oisin in the divine country; but when Yeats presses that imaginative vision hard enough, as he does in 'The Wanderings of Oisin', he discovers the unsatisfactoriness of paradise. The Tir nà nOg of *The King of the Great Clock Tower* is largely based on *A Vision's* phase fifteen,[51] yet phase fifteen is no paradise; it has enormous built-in instability, for at the moment of the interchange of the gyres the antithetical pressure reaches its maximum. The film-strip of the lovers' lives winds itself onto the reel and then starts unwinding in the opposite direction; *A Vision* offers no hope of release except the thirteenth cone, and, since that has nothing to do with phase fifteen, I see no indication that Yeats meant that in this play.* It is a mistake to emphasize the deathliness of the

---

* It is clear from 'The Hero, the Girl, and the Fool' that ultimate transcendence is beyond the wound spool as well as beyond the course of life. (*Variorum Poems*, p. 447).

consummation in *The King of the Great Clock Tower*; the consummation is finely balanced on the moment between life and death, orgasm and post-coital depression, the living Queen and the Severed Head; it seems to me that when the Second Attendant wishes for the dismal thread to remain wound, he is trying to alter the balance in favour of death.* As soon as he says it the First Attendant immediately presents two images of the dismal thread running loose:

> *Second Attendant.* O never may that dismal thread run loose;
> *First Attendant.* For there the hound that Oisin saw pursues
> The hornless deer that runs in such a fright;
> And there the woman clasps an apple tight
> For all the clamour of a famished man.
> They run in foam, and there in foam they ran,
> Nor can they stop to take a breath that still
> Hear in the foam the beating of a bell.

Here the phantoms represent the condition of mortal life, almost exactly reversed from their symbolism in 'The Wanderings of Oisin'; there they were lyric emblems of effortless, eternal pursuit, myths based on the stasis of the islands, where the joy of pursuit was seemingly prolonged forever without earning its goal; here the phantoms are sweaty, straining, trying to catch the objects of their desire before the midnight deadline. In 'He Mourns for the Change' Yeats put his lover into a phantom's body; here he puts his phantoms into mortal bodies, assigns to them mortal emotions, makes them emblems of temporal love. Indeed 'Time/ Comes from the torture of our flesh';[52] time and the condition of pursuit are identical, for the flesh is tortured by what it lacks.

It is obvious at a glance that the new phantoms are quite different from the old: Oisin's hornless deer passed by carelessly, beautifully, while the Stroller's deer runs away in a fright; Oisin's lady tossed an apple in her hand while riding like the wind, with an inhuman grace and co-ordination, while the Stroller's lady clasps the apple tightly, in desperation of letting it fall; Oisin's youth is a beautiful young man 'With quenchless

---

* As the hawthorn tree in the final lyric, the Second Attendant again frustrates the natural course of things, this time in favour of life, a Struldbruggian immortality.

gaze and fluttering hair', the romantic stupefaction and sinuous hair of a pre-Raphaelite hero, while the Stroller's youth runs noisily, hungrily, with 'all the clamour of a famished man'. Like the whole play, the first song is itself neatly balanced between the completion and death of the first stanza and the hunger and life of the second; the major theme is not love in death but love in mortality, the gyring condition which whirls from life to death and back to life; I think that this is what Yeats meant in an early draft of this song when he wrote, 'All love is shackled to mortality'.[53] F. A. C. Wilson has written that 'The physical body is a mere shell, insensitive as armour or as stone. The lover "shackled to mortality" thinks always of the far side of death, for love cannot be fully realised in the flesh.'[54] But surely Yeats did not say this in the early draft:

> I call to mind the iron of the bell
> And get from that my harsher imagery,
> All love is shackled to mortality,
> Love's image is a man-at-arms in steel;
> Love's image is a woman made of stone;
> It dreams of the unborn; all else is nought;
> To-morrow and to-morrow fills its thought;
> All tenderness reserves for that alone.[55]

The woman made of stone is not the insensitive shell of the physical body, but an image, 'Love's image', the Stroller's image of love, something transcendentalized,* and the lover 'shackled to mortality' thinks of the far side of death—but on the far side of death are 'the unborn' and the return to life. By placing the two stanzas in the order he did, with the dismal thread unwinding back into life out of Tir nà nOg, Yeats suggests the fullness of experience, the transience of fulfilment; and if Yeats had not deleted the reference to the unborn, the children conceived by the caterpillar that consumes the Queen's beauty, it would have had a force similar to the strength of the conceived Achilles, who draws his mother out of paradise in 'News for the Delphic

---

* I think this issue is settled unequivocally by the following lines (*Explorations*, p. 367):

> Let images of basalt, black, immovable,
> Chiselled in Egypt, or ovoids of bright steel
> Hammered and polished by Brancusi's hand,
> Represent spirits.

Oracle'. The man dreams of the cold hard image, phase fifteen, and the image can dream only of unborn children, clock time, 'To-morrow and to-morrow'.

Comyn's phantoms are only the first of a bewildering array of correlatives that accost Oisin at the beginning of Book II. Yeats knew from adolescence on how to manipulate images which embody a situation or a state of mind; for instance, in the short novel, *John Sherman*, written about the same time as 'The Wanderings of Oisin', there is a passage about a dog chasing a rabbit which functions in the novel in the same way that the red-eared hound functions in the poem:

Towards evening he went out. The pale sunshine of winter flickered on his path. The wind blew the straws about. He grew more and more melancholy. A dog of his acquaintance was chasing rabbits in a field. He had never been known to catch one, and since his youth had never seen one, for he was almost wholly blind. They were his form of the eternal chimera. The dog left the field and followed with a friendly sniff. . . .
    A child of four or five with a swelling on its face was sitting under a wall opposite the school door, waiting to make faces at the Protestant children as they came out. Catching sight of the dog she seemed to debate in her mind whether to throw a stone at it or call it to her. She threw the stone and made it run. In after times he remembered all these things as though they were of importance.[56]

The blind dog's pursuit of the 'eternal chimera' clearly symbolizes John's pursuit of money, a rich widow, in London; John is an inchoate poet whose love of money is as fantastic and innocuous as any of his other whims, who indeed wants money only so that he can 'remain a lounger',[57] but who is nevertheless almost corrupted by London, its deceit and its materialism. Similarly, the naughty girl who debates whether to throw a stone at the dog or call it to her, and decides in favour of cruelty, anticipates the thoughtless toying that John receives at Margaret Leland's hands later in the story. Yeats rather awkwardly tries to command the reader's attention to these symbols by writing, 'In after times he remembered all these things as though they were of importance'; but this tag-line, despite its lack of narrative sophistication, also gives the impression of John's artistic consciousness at work, slowly creating the ominousness of these omens; like Oisin's phantoms, the dog and girl are emblems which gain intelligibility only through experience.

When the phantoms vanish, Oisin and Niamh ride onto the shore on the Isle of Many Fears—a surrogate for aggression, just as the Island of Dancing was a surrogate for sexuality. Oisin left the first island because he saw the signs of human warfare floating to him over the tide; but he tries to satisfy that desire for combat, not in the world of men, but in another projection of his fantasy. Significantly, his entrance onto the second island is marked by more signs of warfare:

> A foaming tide
> Whitened afar with surge, fan-formed and wide,
> Burst from a great door marred by many a blow
> From mace and sword and pole-axe, long ago
> When gods and giants warred.

Unlike the broken lance on the tide in Book I, the signs of this combat are superhuman, titanic, almost prehistoric,* and Oisin has abandoned his godlike sexuality only to join in an equally godlike combat.

Oisin then meets some correlative statues:

> left and right
> Dark statues glimmered over the pale tide
> Upon dark thrones. Between the lids of one
> The imaged meteors had flashed and run
> And had disported in the stilly jet,
> And the fixed stars had dawned and shone and set,
> Since God made Time and Death and Sleep: the other
> Stretched his long arm to where, a misty smother,
> The stream churned, churned, and churned—his lips apart,
> As though he told his never-slumbering heart
> Of every foamdrop on its misty way.

These statues project Oisin's twin desires: on one hand, his desire to become fixed and astral, like the nocturnal dancers with star-like foreheads in Book I, or like Comyn's phantoms symbolizing 'night, carrying the sun away'; on the other hand, his desire to be submerged in human mortality, human flux, the churning tide of Finn's realm. The opposition of the two statues

---

* These remnants of warfare may have developed from the battle of the Firbolgs and the Fomoroh, alluded to at the beginning of Book I; see *Variorum Poems*, p. 795.

continues to the end of Yeats's poetry: the Soul in 'A Dialogue
of Self and Soul' sets its mind on the 'breathless starlit air',
while the Self studies the water in a blind man's ditch—and in
'Among School Children', nature is still represented by the
minute flux of foamdrops, 'a spume that plays/ Upon a ghostly
paradigm of things'. The first statue is motionless, more fixed
than the fixed stars, a student of images ('imaged meteors') like
the dancers of the first island; indeed, according to the 1889 version, he seems to be 'the watcher for a sign', just as the dancers
watch the stars and the moon and await the apocalyptic signs of
the end of time. The other statue is as vigorous as a statue (or
an emblem) can be, straining its arms towards the stream of time,
its lips apart as if it were recording in its wakeful brain every
last detail of temporal activity. Because Oisin has just entered the
second island he seems to be poised between the two statues, between permanence and process; and Book II is the story of Oisin's
discovery that the perpetual activity of mock battle is only an
illusion, that at best he can only stretch his arms towards flux,
like the second statue, without participating in it, that the demon
itself can only stare at the heavens with the same expectant eyes
as the first statue:

> 'I hear my soul drop down into decay,
> And Manannan's dark tower, stone after stone,
> Gather sea-slime and fall the seaward way,
> And the moon goad the waters night and day,
> That all be overthrown. . . .'

Oisin during his stay on the islands maintains the romantic
hope that he can balance on the knife-edge between mortal joy
and immortal stability; but just as Book I ends with a prophecy
of the withering of the moon, Book II ends with the decay of the
tower and the lunar chaos of the tide. The attempt to construct
an earthly paradise must collapse under the weight of its residual
earthiness; on an astronomical level, at least, the islands are still
part of the human world. Although the tidal imagery is not as
significant here as it is in Book I, the demon's song provides the
resolution of the problem of the two tides: the gross pressure of
the familiar lunar tide tears apart the fragile world of the islands.
There is a faint counter-tide, a watery lullaby, on the second
island as well as the first:

                                    these mild words
Fanned the delighted air like wings of birds:
'My brothers spring out of their beds at morn,
A-murmur like young partridge: with loud horn
They chase the noontide deer;
And when the dew-drowned stars hang in the air
Look to long fishing-lines, or point and pare
An ashen hunting spear.
O sigh, O fluttering sigh, be kind to me;
Flutter along the froth lips of the sea,
And shores the froth lips wet:
And stay a little while, and bid them weep:
Ah, touch their blue-veined eyelids if they sleep,
And shake their coverlet.
When you have told how I weep endlessly,
Flutter along the froth lips of the sea
And home to me again,
And in the shadow of my hair lie hid,
And tell me that you found a man unbid,
The saddest of all men.'

The lady's cyclical sigh, the refrain of her life as well as the refrain of her song, takes the place of the tremulous tide of the
first island; and the lady hopes that her sigh will bring back evidence to her of life in the land of mortals, as the first island's tide
brought a lance back to Oisin.

Indeed the parallels between the lady and Oisin himself are
remarkable in other ways as well: she imagines her kinsmen
chasing a deer, just as Oisin left Finn's world with the image of a
deer hunt imprinted in his memory; she is also homesick for (as
the 1889 version says) Eri, Oisin's home as well. Of course her
sweetheart is no immortal lover leading her over the waters,
but a man in the land of her family; but all we are told of him
is that he is 'The saddest of all men', and if there is one emotion
which is continually ascribed to Oisin from the beginning of the
poem ('My human sorrow') to the end ('the fluttering sadness
of earth'), it is sadness. Oisin must not be identified directly
with the lady's lover, but the whole island is a projection of
Oisin's fantasy: he has written for himself the role of hero
in an archetypal drama, and he has created his heroine in his own
image. The mechanism behind this allegory can perhaps be

detected in the first stanza of 'Michael Robartes and the Dancer',
where all is made explicit, even over-explicit:

> *He.* Opinion is not worth a rush;
> In this altar-piece the knight,
> Who grips his long spear so to push
> That dragon through the fading light,
> Loved the lady; and it's plain
> The half-dead dragon was her thought,
> That every morning rose again
> And dug its claws and shrieked and fought.
> Could the impossible come to pass
> She would have time to turn her eyes,
> Her lover thought, upon the glass
> And on the instant would grow wise.
> *She.* You mean they argued.[58]

This is not the solution to Book II of 'The Wanderings of Oisin',
but it shows how a beast can be protected from a human brain
and do allegorical battle. I suggest that the lady of Book II is
herself a projection of Oisin's desire for an ideal beloved, the
second island's heroic equivalent of Niamh; and that the eagles
and the demon are projections of his intellect and his naked
aggression, respectively; and that the whole drama is a legendary hero's creation of a still more superhuman legend, a still
more inhuman heroism. If it is permissible to mix Jung and
Freud for a moment, one could call the lady a version of Oisin's
Jungian *anima*, the eagles his superego (his pride, his memory
of heroic conduct), and the demon his id; or one could label them
by the more ancient terms of affection, cognition, and conation.
Yet these identifications cannot be made strictly; I only mean
that the individual elements serve a specific function in Oisin's
psychomachia, in addition to their function as attractive enigmas
in a St. George romance that is stuck like a phonograph needle
in a broken groove. In a poem written in the same year as
'Michael Robartes and the Dancer'—1918—Yeats objectifies
his hatred, projects it as a crafty demon:

> For certain minutes at the least
> That crafty demon and that loud beast
> That plague me day and night
> Ran out of my sight;

> Though I had long perned in the gyre,
> Between my hatred and desire,
> I saw my freedom won
> And all laugh in the sun.[59]

In 'Demon and Beast' Yeats does not quite do battle with his imaged hatred, but he does succeed in driving it away; he takes no credit for the victory, for 'mere growing old' has chilled his blood, routed both hatred and love. Oisin on the other hand does not grow old, and remains plagued by his demon.

What does it mean that Oisin fights continually with an image reflected from his own mind? For one thing, Oisin must fill the obliging void of the island with an obstacle sufficiently strong to demonstrate his own strength; in a little poem called 'The Realists' Yeats suggests that our modern world may be deficient in heroism because all the dragons have disappeared:

> Hope that you may understand!
> What can books of men that wive
> In a dragon-guarded land,
> Paintings of the dolphin-drawn
> Sea-nymphs in their pearly wagons
> Do, but awake a hope to live
> That had gone
> With the dragons?[60]

But this yearning for a proper obstacle, a monster as mighty, as vulnerable, and as resilient as one could wish, is not the only explanation of the demon's existence; Oisin is on another level fighting with himself, his daimon as well as his demon.* Oisin is, by glossary definition, a poet, and a poet's anti-self is powerful, active, all that is not gregarious,[61] timid, or sedentary; Yeats's autobiographical writings record everywhere his struggle with that image of unachievable heroism, passionate coldness, even from his earliest youth:

I remember vaguely that I liked Hans Andersen better than Grimm because he was less homely, but even he never gave me the knights and dragons and beautiful ladies that I longed for. I have remembered nothing that I read, but only those things that I heard or saw. When I was ten or twelve my father took me to see Irving play Hamlet, and

---

* There is an emblem of this struggle in the last Michael Robartes story, showing 'a man whipping his shadow' (*A Vision*, p. 38).

did not understand why I preferred Irving to Ellen Terry, who was, I can now see, the idol of himself and his friends. I could not think of her, as I could of Irving's Hamlet, as but myself, and I was not old enough to care for feminine charm and beauty. For many years Hamlet was an image of heroic self-possession for the poses of youth and childhood to copy, a combatant of the battle within myself.[62]

The demon is not exactly heroic, but he is an image from the heroic landscape, cold, passionate* (a revelling 'Bacchant'), and surely self-possessed. Oisin is, to be sure, already a hero, but Yeats tempts us to search for hidden personal meanings in Book II of 'The Wanderings of Oisin' (although he does not give us permission to):

In the second part of "Oisin" under disguise of symbolism I have said several things to which I only have the key. The romance is for my readers. They must not even know there is a symbol anywhere. They will not find out. If they did, it would spoil the art. Yet the whole poem is full of symbols—if it be full of aught but clouds.[63]

That reference to clouds is interesting, for Yeats, in the preface to Lady Gregory's 1904 *God and Fighting Men,* compares Oisin himself to a cloud:

. . . Oisin, his son, is made king over a divine country. The birds and beasts that cross his path in the woods have been fighting men or great enchanters or fair women, and in a moment can take some beautiful or terrible shape. We think of him and of his people as great-bodied men with large movements, that seem, as it were, flowing out of some deep below the narrow stream of personal impulse, men that have broad brows and quiet eyes full of confidence in a good luck that proves every day afresh that they are a portion of the strength of things. They are hardly so much individual men as portions of universal nature, like the clouds that shape themselves and reshape themselves momentarily, or like a bird between two boughs, or like the gods that have given the apples and the nuts; and yet this but brings them the nearer to us, for we can remake them in our image when we will, and the woods are the more beautiful for the thought.[64]

The imaginative malleability of Oisin and his companions here is astonishing. The creatures that cross Oisin's path move with a dream-like instability, 'a portion of the strength of things', 'portions of universal nature', pictures that form and re-form in the deep flux of nature, full of the insubstantial beauty

---

* In fact the lady, in the 1889 version, speaks of 'his passions cold'.

that is found through all of Yeats's three islands. The slightest pressure of desire shapes these beings, just as Oisin found forms on the islands to answer to his every dream; but Yeats in this passage does not exempt Oisin himself from this plasticity: he can be remade 'in our image when he will', remade 'the more beautiful for the thought'. This gives us, in all, an extraordinary license to construct from Oisin's voyages, especially on the second island, an allegory of Yeats's own internal struggles. The Proteus-like metamorphoses of the demon recall the above-mentioned malleability of Oisin's companions:

> And when he knew the sword of Manannan
> Amid the shades of night, he changed and ran
> Through many shapes; I lunged at the smooth throat
> Of a great eel; it changed, and I but smote
> A fir-tree roaring in its leafless top;
> And thereupon I drew the livid chop
> Of a drowned dripping body to my breast;
> Horror from horror grew; but when the west
> Had surged up in a plumy fire, I drave
> Through heart and spine; and cast him in the wave
> Lest Niamh shudder.

This passage is extremely similar to the end of 'Fergus and the Druid':

> *Fergus.* I see my life go drifting like a river
>   From change to change; I have been many things—
>   A green drop in the surge, a gleam of light
>   Upon a sword, a fir-tree on a hill,
>   An old slave grinding at a heavy quern,
>   A king sitting upon a chair of gold—
>   And all these things were wonderful and great;
>   But now I have grown nothing, knowing all. [65]

Fergus was 'the poet of the Red Branch cycle as Oisin was of the Fenian';[66] so the similarity is not by chance. Fergus knew that he had been, in his past lives, all that Oisin fought against;* and that despairing internalization (or re-internalization) of Oisin's demon suggests that Oisin is fighting something projected from himself, a dream image as labile as his imagination or his memory.

---

* The passage anticipates Yeats's own prayer in 'Mohini Chatterjee' (Collected Poems, p. 279).

I have said that the demon is a projection of aggressive feelings, and if that is true then Oisin's struggle in Book II is peculiarly involuted and fruitless; the demon's last words are 'Light is man's love, and lighter is man's rage;/ His purpose drifts and dies', and this stated vacillation of purpose—seemingly unfair, since Oisin has persisted a century—may refer to Oisin's inability to achieve control over the 'rage' that the demon's death can never satiate, since Oisin's faery sword penetrates no flesh or bone, only a fabrication of air. Yeats may be getting at another pyschological insight too, the insight that Eden destroys, that men change to a more primitive, animalistic condition, not a more angelic one, when they reach a level of maximum fulfillment. This is the theory behind the maxim that power corrupts; and it is the theme of a remarkable precursor to 'The Wanderings of Oisin', Tennyson's 'The Voyage of Maeldune'. In this poem Maeldune visits many magical islands, several of which resemble Oisin's first island,* and one of which slightly resembles his second:

> And we came in an evil time to the Isle of the
>   Double Towers,
> One was of smooth-cut stone, one carved all over
>   with flowers,
> But an earthquake always moved in the hollows
>   under the dells,
> And they shock'd on each other and butted each
>   other with clashing of bells,
> And the daws flew out of the Towers and jangled
>   and wrangled in vain,
> And the clash and boom of the bells rang into the
>   heart and the brain,
> Till the passion of battle was on us, and all took
>   sides with the Towers,
> There were some for the clean-cut stone, there were
>   more for the carven flowers,
> And the wrathful thunder of God peal'd over us all
>   the day,
> For the one half slew the other, and after we sail'd
>   away.

---

* Maeldune also visits an 'undersea isle', a calenture fantasy, reminiscent of the 'underwater land' which is part of the tripartite Tir nà nOg described in *Irish Fairy & Folk Tales*, p. 200.

On almost every island Maeldune's men exhaust their appetites
on fruit or manna or 'the poisonous pleasure of wine', and then,
thoroughly glutted, start to play games with each other, at last
start to kill each other. This surfacing of brutal passion is sublimated in 'The Wanderings of Oisin', made heroic, almost
glamorous; but it is certainly no more productive.

There is some evidence that the aggression dealt with in
Book II is specifically a result of sexual frustration, although here
the argument turns subtle and conjectural indeed. We have already seen that Oisin bears some personal resemblance to the
lady's lover, as well as to the lady herself; and behind his repeated act of battle with the demon is the necessity of liberating
the lady imprisoned in the tower. Therefore the combat is not
gratuitous, and may be described as sexually motivated. If it is
fair to discuss Oisin's demon simultaneously with the demon of
'Demon and Beast'—and I think it is—we may note that there is
a definite undercurrent of sexuality, sexual desiccation, in the
later poem:

> Yet I am certain as can be
> That every natural victory
> Belongs to beast or demon,
> That never yet had freeman
> Right mastery of natural things,
> And that mere growing old, that brings
> Chilled blood, this sweetness brought;
> Yet have no dearer thought
> Than that I may find our a way
> To make it linger half a day.
>
> O what a sweetness strayed
> Through barren Thebaid,
> Or by the Mareotic sea
> When that exultant Anthony
> And twice a thousand more
> Starved upon the shore
> And withered to a bag of bones!
> What had the Caesars but their thrones?[67]

Now it so happens that certain of Yeats's poems are associated inextricably but uncannily with some of Yeats's acquaintan-
ces; the best known example is the fat body of William Morris,
which broods over the third stanza of 'The Statues'.[68] 'Demon

and Beast', especially in its last stanza, is similarly associated
with Lionel Johnson:

'Yeats,' he said to me, 'you need ten years in a library, but I have need
of ten years in the wilderness.' When he said 'wilderness' I am certain,
however, that he thought of some historical, some bookish desert, the
Thebaid, or the lands about the Mareotic Sea. . . .

The typical men of the classical age (I think of Commodus, with his
half-animal beauty, his cruelty and his caprice), lived public lives,
pursuing curiosities of appetite, and so found in Christianity, with its
Thebaid and its Mareotic Sea, the needed curb. But what can the
Christian confessor say to those who more and more must make all out
of the privacy of their thought, calling up perpetual images of desire,
for he cannot say, 'Cease to be artist, cease to be poet', where the whole
life is art and poetry, nor can he bid men leave the world, who suffer
from the terrors that pass before shut eyes. Coleridge, and Rossetti,
though his dull brother did once persuade him that he was an agnostic,
were devout Christians, and Stenbock and Beardsley were so towards
their lives' end, and Dowson and Johnson always, and yet I think it
but deepened despair and multiplied temptation.[69]

Johnson was the Catholic artist torn between his drive to become an ascetic saint in a 'bookish desert' and the 'curiosities of
appetite', his alcoholism, his art, his inability to 'cease to be
poet', It is easy to see how this relates to 'Demon and Beast':
Johnson, like Yeats in this poem, tried to rid himself of hatred
and love, attachment to the natural world, the 'Dark Angel' of
his curious appetites:

> Dark Angel, with thine aching lust!
> Of two defeats, of two despairs:
> Less dread, a change to drifting dust.
> Than thine eternity of cares.
>
> Do what thou wilt, thou shalt not so,
> Dark Angel! triumph over me:
> *Lonely, unto the Lone I go;*
> *Divine, to the Divinity.*[70]

The lust that decays to 'drifting dust' must surely run into
the sands of the Thebaid; and both the passages quoted from
The Tragic Generation influence the great description of the
Christian desert in Book IV of *A Vision*.[71] But I have not yet mentioned the most salient fact about Lionel Johnson: he was a man
who never reached sexual maturity:

He [Dowson] was drinking, but, unlike Johnson, who, at the autopsy after his death, was discovered never to have grown, except in the brain, after his fifteenth year, he was full of sexual desire.[72]

Johnson could partially free himself of demon and beast, attain 'the austerity, the melancholy of his thoughts, that spiritual ecstasy which he touched at times',[73] because of his physiological sexlessness. For the young, the potent, 'every natural victory/ Belongs to beast or demon'—so Oisin fails to subdue the demon permanently because his sexual desire cannot find genuine satiation in a mere allegory. If it is possible to speculate further, the allegory of Book II may be based on the human insatiation of a very young, celibate poet,[74] for the interval of four days between each struggle may suggest the nocturnal sexual rhythm of late adolescence; and Yeats was indeed coy and secretive about the symbolism of Book II.

The train of Yeats's sexual associations has led me from 'The Wanderings of Oisin' to 'Demon and Beast' to *The Tragic Generation*; and there is an arrow in the middle of the Lionel Johnson section of *The Tragic Generation* which points straight back to 'The Wanderings of Oisin':

In those [Phaedria's and Acrasia's] islands certain qualities of beauty, certain forms of sensuous loveliness were separated from all the general purposes of life, as they had not been hitherto in European literature— and would not be again, for even the historical process has its ebb and flow, till Keats wrote his *Endymion*. I think that the movement of our thought has more and more so separated certain images and regions of the mind, and that these images grow in beauty as they grow in sterility.[75]

'The Wanderings of Oisin' is an allegory of art divorced from reality, for Oisin's islands are as sterile as they are beautiful;* and in the context of the passage they become as dry and bookish as Lionel Johnson's wilderness; and Oisin empties the vigour of

---

* This passage suggests that Oisin's first island may be partially based on Acra- sia's Bower of Bliss (as the Enchantress' island in 'The Island of Statues' cer- tainly is; Yeats calls attention to Spenser's influence in *Autobiographies* (*Reveries*, xxvi), p. 92). I think that Yeats's knowledge of Book II of *The Faery Queene* may have helped him with the second island as well, for in the House of Temperance in Canto IX the parts of the human mind are objectified and allegorized in a some- what similar manner; the resemblance between Maleger and the demon, who is also yielding and unsubduable, is especially noteworthy.

his youthful sexuality on a lush vision which is as bleak in its
way as the Thebaid.

　　Oisin's demon or beast (either term could be appropriate, if
the sexual interpretation is not invalid) is so much an extension
of Oisin himself that his development parallels Oisin's own: he
begins his song with 'I hear my soul drop down into decay',
which is reminiscent of Oisin's interjection to St. Patrick a few
pages before: 'There was no mightier soul of Heber's line;/
Now it is old and mouse-like'.* All through 'The Wanderings of
Oisin' one can find this entropy, this pressure which drives the
flat images, enactments, and projections into a semblance of
human mortality; as the earthly paradise strives toward imaginative completeness, it becomes subject to decay, the condition
of the created world and its plenitude. Therefore the demon of
Oisin's conation prophesies its own defeat, to be brought about
by the old age which is both enacted and undergone in the next
book; but Oisin had already stared at two other emblems of his
own destruction, near the beginning of Book II :

> A lady with soft eyes like funeral tapers,
> And face that seemed wrought out of moonlit vapours,
> And a sad mouth, that fear made tremulous
> As any ruddy moth, looked down on us;
> And she with a wave-rusted chain was tied
> To two old eagles, full of ancient pride,
> That with dim eyeballs stood on either side.
> Few feathers were on their dishevelled wings,
> For their dim minds were with the ancient things.

Wisdom is a gloomy bird of prey, not the 'ruddy moth' of the
lady's mouth; the eagles are abstract, cut off from the sensual
world, 'earless, nerveless, blind'; they have attenuated until
they are nothing except their own memories, their 'ancient
things', and as such they represent the soul, specifically Oisin's
soul:

> 'Flee from him,' pearl-pale Niamh weeping cried,
> 'For all men flee the demons'; but moved not
> My angry king-remembering soul one jot.
> There was no mightier soul of Heber's line;
> Now it is old and mouse-like. For a sign

　　* The image of Oisin as a mouse persists in Book III, when Niamh says 'if only
your shoe/ Brush lightly as haymouse earth's pebbles, you will come no more to my
side'.

> I burst the chain: still earless, nerveless, blind,
> Wrapped in the things of the unhuman mind,
> In some dim memory or ancient mood,
> Still earless, nerveless, blind, the eagles stood.

That quick juxtaposition of Oisin's old, mouse-like soul with the 'unhuman mind' of the eagles is hardly accidental; Oisin, the old man, telling his story to St. Patrick, seems to be almost aware that the eagles embodied his own 'king-remembering soul', foretold the involution into memory, the loss of all other faculties, that accompanies old age. Patrick addressed Oisin in the first line of the poem as 'You who are bent, and bald, and blind', and Oisin's first line in reply is 'Sad to remember, sick with years'; Oisin's existence has become as minimal as the eagles', as he has been beaten down to mere soul 'On the anvil of the world'. The eagles are chained to the lady because their memory is full of creatures like her, fit goals for a romantic quest or knightly love; and the brooding of the mnemonic eagles is another measure of the lady's oppression, for she is made restless, discontent, by her personal memories of her former life. Oisin's severing of the chain is an attempt to liberate her, just as his semi-weekly slaughter of the demon is an attempt to liberate her; but it is a curious feature of Oisin's three islands that, although the external drama is only a projection of the internal, nothing that happens on the outside can solve the internal problems. Therefore action tends to be meaningless: the slaughter of the demon is accomplished so often that it is never accomplished at all, and the bold sword-stroke that cuts the lady's chain is an empty gesture, for the eagles and the lady maintain the same changeless tableau that they did before: 'Still earless, nerveless, blind, the eagles stood'.

On the third island all the chains which have bound Oisin to Fenian reality seem to be at last cut, and he retreats into his dream, a dream within a dream. After leaving the 'Childe Roland' landscape of the second island, the slime, the bubbling river, the withered sedge, Oisin and Niamh find themselves among the sleeping giants in a gigantic land:

> But the trees grew taller and closer, immense
>   in their wrinkling bark;

> Dropping; a murmurous dropping; old silence and
>   that one sound;
> For no live creatures lived there, no weasels
>   moved in the dark:
> Long sighs arose in our spirits, beneath us
>   bubbled the ground.
>
> And the ears of the horse went sinking away in
>   the hollow night,
> For, as drift from a sailor slow drowning the
>   gleams of the world and the sun,
> Ceased on our hands and our faces, on hazel and
>   oak leaf, the light,
> And the stars were blotted above us, and the whole
>   of the world was one.

The trees expand, grow enormous and dim, diffuse into darkness; the whole island attains a nocturnal homogeneity, as Oisin has crossed from the pre-Raphaelite art of the first island to the minimal art of the last, the black canvas, the 'un-imaged night'.[76] It is true that 'no live creatures lived there', for the third island is so abstracted and catatonic that it is for all purposes lifeless; the other islands are, in their way, equally lifeless, but all the trends which have been building through the poem culminate on the third island. Even the blackness has been developing through the first two books: the first island is approached as the moon rises 'like a white rose' and abandoned in the 'wood's old night', with a prophecy that the moon will wither away 'like a pale rose'; and the second island is first seen by moonlight and last perceived through a 'lone/ And drifting greyness'. The 'monstrous slumbering folk' that inhabit the island, naked, beautiful, golden, with beautiful and golden armour, seem to be vague creatures from some forgotten legend that has long ago been drained of all vitality:

> And my gaze was thronged with the sleepers;
>   no, not since the world began,
> In realms where the handsome were many,
>   nor in glamours by demons flung,
> Have faces alive with such beauty been known
>   to the salt eye of man,
> Yet weary with passions that faded when the
>   sevenfold seas were young.

> And I gazed on the bell-branch, sleep's forebear,
>   far sung by the Sennachies.
> I saw how those slumberers, grown weary, there
>   camping in grasses deep,
> Of wars with the wide world and pacing the shores
>   of the wandering seas,
> Laid hands on the bell-branch and swayed it, and
>   fed of unhuman sleep.

The dancers of Book I opposed their inhuman joy to Oisin's human sorrow; and some of the old contrast remains in the building tension between the sleepers' beauty and the human 'salt eye', or the sleepers' 'unhuman sleep' and Oisin's restless curiosity. The sleepers are bird-like, with feathered ears and golden claws, even more bird-like and soulful than the dancers of Book I; and these least human of Oisin's companions can blend easily into the magnified forest, for their beards are full of owls' nests:

> The wood was so spacious above them, that He
>   who has stars for His flocks
> Could fondle the leaves with His fingers, nor
>   go from His dew-cumbered skies;
> So long were they sleeping, the owls had builded
>   their nests in their locks,
> Filling the fibrous dimness with long generations
>   of eyes.

Even God, the iron ruler of the stars in Book I, has become a sleepy, pastoral, tenderized deity, resting in his dew-cumbered skies as if He found Himself in a sentimental painting. Book III is much more self-consciously beautiful and picturesque than the preceding books; Yeats himself said that it 'has most art',[77] and he clearly intended that the third island should be the most lyrical, hypnotic, and sterile of all. The lulling effect of the metre is remarkable, for the clear pulse of the quick, irregularly-rhymed tetrametre of Book I and of the heroic couplets of Book II vanishes at the first line: 'Fled foam underneath us, and round us, awandering and milky smoke'. The milky smoke of those long lines blots out all form as surely as the trees blot out the starlight; the metre gutters out into a shadowy intricacy of rhythm, as Oisin spends his last hundred years on the most subtle, the most aesthetic island of all. He joins the mythic sleepers

and tries to lose himself in their company, to simulate a young
man's dream of a soothing, spent old age; and for the first time
his years seem to fall on him:

> Wrapt in the wave of that music, with weariness
>   more than of earth,
> The moil of my centuries filled me; and gone like
>   a sea-covered stone
> Were the memories of the whole of my sorrow and
>   the memories of the whole of my mirth,
> And a softness came from the starlight and filled
>   me full to the bone.

This is a false, imaginary version of what happens when he returns to Ireland and rejoins human toil:

> And there at the foot of the mountain, two carried a
>   sack full of sand,
> They bore it with staggering and sweating, but fell
>   with their burden at length.
> Leaning down from the gem-studded saddle, I flung it
>   five yards with my hand,
> With a sob for men waxing so weakly, a sob for the
>   Fenians' old strength.
>
> The rest you have heard of, O croziered man; how,
>   when divided the girth,
> I fell on the path, and the horse went away like a
>   summer fly;
> And my years three hundred fell on me, and I rose,
>   and walked on the earth,
> A creeping old man, full of sleep, with the spittle
>   on his beard never dry.

Oisin might have learned from his experience with the 'forget-
fulness/ Of dreamy foam' in Book I that Lethe was essentially
vapid, unfulfilling; but he must exhaust his pictures of an ideal
old age, just as he exhausted his pictures of youth and middle
age. He falls under the spell of the bell-branch,[78] and sleeps, and
forgets; but he dreams, and in those dreams he creates, impara-
dises, a vision of the heroic past:

> But in dreams, mild man of the croziers, driving
>   the dust with their throngs,
> Moved round me, of seamen or landsmen, all who
>   are winter tales;

> Came by me the kings of the Red Branch, with roaring
>   of laughter and songs,
> Or moved as they moved once, love-making or piercing
>   the tempest with sails.

The Red Branch kings were not Oisin's companions, for the Red Branch warriors 'preceded the Fenian circle by about two hundred years',[79] but they are part of Oisin's past mythology, 'winter tales' come alive, full of their old laughter, their old love. This stanza is climactic, for it represents the deepest penetration into vision that Oisin achieves in the poem: he has filled the most ethereal of the islands with human heroism, all the exhilaration and joy of human experience. But the dream represents mortal life so perfectly that it is pregnant with mortality:

> Came Blanaid, MacNessa, tall Fergus who feastward
>   of old time slunk,
> Cook Barach, the traitor; and warward, the spittle
>   on his beard never dry,
> Dark Balor, as old as a forest, car-borne, his
>   mighty head sunk
> Helpless, men lifting the lids of his weary and
>   death-making eye.
> And by me, in soft red raiment, the Fenians moved
>   in loud streams,
> And Grania, walking and smiling, sewed with her
>   needle of bone.
> So lived I and lived not, so wrought I and wrought
>   not, with creatures of dreams,
> In a long iron sleep, as a fish in the water goes
>   dumb as a stone.

The vision of the earthly paradise tends always towards plenitude, over-inclusion; it is a self-contaminating vision, for the traitors file past once the procession of heroes has run its course; Balor, 'the leader of the hosts of darkness'[80] follows Conchubar MacNessa, the king of the Red Branch kings, and Barach follows Fergus, the poet-king whom he betrayed. Finally, Oisin imagines the Fenians, his own friends, closer still to his experiential Ireland, and last of all Grania, sewing with her needle of bone, sewing the tapestry which offered her no shelter from mortality. Thus his dream reaches completeness, as he lives and lives not, suspended between the dumb coldness of the third island and the full resplendent life of his dream.

But at last the sleep runs out its century and he awakes with
'the ancient sadness of men', knowing that all dreams are unsatisfactory when compared to life itself, even the dream that
approximates most closely the richness of life. Oisin's disengage-
ment from oblivion is handled very beautifully, for whole
stanzas reappear almost verbatim from the beginning of the
book, only in reverse, as if Oisin's horse is stepping backward,
in slow motion, from mid-forest to seashore; after the coda ends
with the 'Fled foam underneath us' line, Oisin's memory is fully
restored, painfully sharp; 'the fluttering sadness of earth', the
tears that fall with the terrestrial fecundity of berries, have destroyed the spell of the bell-branch. He sees the degenerate primary populace that has grown in Ireland since the coming of
Patrick's Catholicism, and he learns that 'The Fenians a long
time are dead'; indeed, he might have observed the first sign of
decay before he left, for Gabhra was 'The great battle in which
the power of the Fenians was broken'.[81] The Fenians withered
and died 'in old age', the gods 'a long time are dead', and Oisin's
years fall on him; but although he is wracked by old age and the
death of his friends, he retains all of his old heroic will, and has
learned to deal with reality instead of dreams:

> If I were as I once was, the strong hoofs crushing
> the sand and the shells,
> Coming out of the sea as the dawn comes, a chaunt
> of love on my lips,
> Not coughing, my head on my knees, and praying, and
> wroth with the bells,
> I would leave no saint's head on his body from
> Rachlin to Bera of ships.

This anger, this savage indignation, contrasts strongly with his
flaccid existence in the first part of the book as a male sleeping
beauty who wastes a century waiting to be nudged by his horse.
But he cannot regain the strength that he dissipated* in his three
hundred years of dreaming, and he realizes that he is fit for little
more than Patrick's subservient Catholicism; indeed he per-
ceives a certain resemblance between Patrick and himself:

---

* Yeats believed, as Matthew Arnold did in 'The Scholar-Gypsy', that the life
of the imagination, cut off from reality, dissipated one's energies very slowly indeed, if at all; see the essay 'Magic', especially pages 38 to 41, in *Essays and Introductions*.

> What place have Caoilte and Conan, and Bran,
>   Sceolan, Lomair?
> Speak, you too are old with your memories,
>   an old man surrounded with dreams.
> *St. Patrick.* Where the flesh of the footsole clingeth on
>   the burning stones is their place;
> Where the demons whip them with wires on the
>   burning stones of wide Hell,
> Watching the blessèd ones move far off, and
>   the smile on God's face,
> Between them a gateway of brass, and the howl
>   of the angels who fell.
> *Oisin.* Put the staff in my hands; for I go to the
>   Fenians, O cleric, to chaunt
> The war-songs that roused them of old; they
>   will rise, making clouds with their breath,
> Innumerable, singing, exultant; the clay underneath
>   them shall pant,
> And demons be broken in pieces, and trampled
>   beneath them in death.

Oisin, amazingly enough, has still another poetic vision left in him; and he wants to find the Island of Content, Tir nà nOg, in Hell itself. This great transfiguration of Hell from a Christian torture-chamber to a hero's Valhalla is Oisin's last attempt to impose the Ought on the Is, and it is Oisin's most magnificent attempt of all. The key word is 'exultant', as it is in a passage in Book II where the Irish sea-god Manannan cries out to a 'mightier race':

> That sea-god's name, who in a deep content
> Sprang dripping, and, with captive demons sent
> Out of the sevenfold seas, built the dark hall
> Rooted in foam and clouds, and cried to all
> The mightier masters of a mightier race;
> And at his cry there came no milk-pale face
> Under a crown of thorns and dark with blood,
> But only exultant faces.

Christ is Nietzsche's passive, pitiful God, and his pallor contrasts with the ruddy, exultant faces of the heroes. But medieval Christianity, if it had a rather unimpassioned vision of heaven, had a powerful vision of hell, and the apparatus of demons and whips seems to stir Oisin's combative nature.

Yeats's last word on 'The Wanderings of Oisin' appears in
'The Introduction to *The Resurrection*', and there he says that
Oisin 'half accepted, half rejected' the illumination of his old age;
and perhaps we can see what he means from the description of
the Fenians' victory over the demons:

> We will tear out the flaming stones, and batter
> 　　the gateway of brass
> And enter, and none sayeth 'No' when there enters
> 　　the strongly armed guest;
> Make clean as a broom cleans, and march on as oxen
> 　　move over young grass;
> Then feast, making converse of wars, and of old
> 　　wounds, and turn to our rest.

Oisin has accepted the illumination of his old age in that he
craves nothing except what he could have had in terrestrial life,
the Fenian round of warfare, wounds, feasting, and resting; but
he has rejected its illumination in that he is still looking for an
enactment of life, an invincible, purified, perpetual heroism, not
life itself. When he wants to break the demons in pieces, one
may suspect that the lesson of the second island has not been
fully understood; and when he wants to make 'converse of wars,
and of old wounds, and turn to our rest', it seems the vision of
the third island is still alluring. But Patrick denies Oisin's con-
quest, tells him to pray for his soul, 'kneel and wear out the
flags';* Patrick suggests that Oisin has lost his soul partially
because of 'the demon love of its youth', and that is on some
level true, for Oisin on the islands chose poetry against life, in
the earliest version of 'The Choice', and therefore stands to
lose 'A heavenly mansion, raging in the dark'.[82] Oisin is moved
by Patrick's arguments, for he feels acutely the emptiness of old
age; and he renounces both the blessèd and the isles of the
blessèd, his own perfected Fenian war-hall:

> *Oisin.* Ah me! to be shaken with coughing and broken
> 　　with old age and pain,
> Without laughter, a show unto children, alone
> 　　with remembrance and fear;

---

* In the 1889 version, there is a scene in Book II where a chorus of monks fall on
the flags in terror of God's thunder; in both cases, there is an earthly prefiguration
of the devils who whip 'with wires on the burning stones of wide Hell'.

> All emptied of purple hours as a beggar's
>   cloak in the rain,
> As a hay-cock out on the flood, or a wolf
>   sucked under a weir.
>
> It were sad to gaze on the blessèd and no
>   man I loved of old there;
> I throw down the chain of small stones! when
>   life in my body has ceased,
> I will go to Caoilte, and Conan, and Bran,
>   Sceolan, Lomair,
> And dwell in the house of the Fenians, be
>   they in flames or at feast.

Oisin, although he casts down the rosary,* must accept something of Patrick's despoiling of his vision, for he is an antithetical man who has lingered on into a primary era, and he is therefore deformed, like Judas in *Calvary*. He cannot be certain that his friends (and his dogs) are not in flames instead of at feast, and the mention of Conan, who was noteworthy for his 'slanderous tongue' earlier in Book III, suggests that he may find some unsavoury characters in Hell; for all he knows he may be confronted with the same Hell that the visionary Aleel saw in *The Countess Cathleen*:

> *Aleel.* The brazen door stands wide, and Balor comes
>   Borne in his heavy car, and demons have lifted
>   The age-weary eyelids from the eyes that of old
>   Turned gods to stone; Barach, the traitor, comes
>   And the lascivious race, Cailitin,
>   That cast a Druid weakness and decay
>   Over Sualtim's and old Dectora's child;
>   And that great king Hell first took hold upon
>   When he killed Naoise and broke Deirdre's heart. . . .[83]

This cast of characters is identical in three out of four instances with the list in Oisin's dream earlier in Book III; but Oisin is willing to cast his lot with his old companions, and accept whatever else he may find in Hell. This is his point of maximum wisdom in the poem, for he has pared away everthing unessential,

---

* Oisin's wearing of the rosary suggests that he has already half accepted St. Patrick's wisdom; indeed, in some of the early versions of the dialogues of Oisin and St. Patrick, Oisin surrendered to Patrick's arguments and agreed to baptism (see Russell K. Alspach, *Irish Poetry*, p. 64).

the exultation of war, the images and the pomp of victory, and wishes to keep only those things which he loved on earth:

> What thou lov'st well shall not be reft from thee
> What thou lov'st well is thy true heritage
> Whose world, or mine or theirs or it is of none?
> First came the seen, then thus the palpable
>   Elysium, though it were in the halls of hell,
> What thou lovest well is thy true heritage. . . .[84]

Pound wrote that, in Canto LXXXI, but it seems very close to the thoughts of Oisin's long-delayed maturity; and perhaps Pound knew all that Yeats himself ever hoped to find in heaven when he wrote, in Canto CXIV,

> Sea, blue under cliffs, or
> William murmuring: 'Sligo in heaven' when the mist came
>   to Tigullio. And that the truth is in kindness.[85]

3

The Poverty of Heaven

'News for the Delphic Oracle'

YEATS used Oisin in 'The Wanderings of Oisin' to criticize the myth of the poet's search for the immortal: Oisin is magical hero as well as poet, can consummate that which Yeats can only wish for, and so Oisin manifests the flaws inherent in the pursuit of supernatural beauty. Oisin in 1889 tended to vitiate the Rose by following her to her actual lair; and over forty years later Yeats hunts out Oisin in a new dwelling place for the purpose of making *A Vision* less visionary. Yeats finds Oisin, macerated by much ocean voyaging, on a fourth island, where he seems to have followed the advice of the first part of 'The Tower', and chosen Plato and Plotinus for his friends:

> There all the golden codgers lay,
> There the silver dew,
> And the great water sighed for love,
> And the wind sighed too.
> Man-picker Niamh leant and sighed
> By Oisin on the grass;
> There sighed amid his choir of love
> Tall Pythagoras.
> Plotinus came and looked about,
> The salt-flakes on his breast,
> And having stretched and yawned awhile
> Lay sighing like the rest.[1]

This is 'News for the Delphic Oracle', Yeats's funniest, most beautiful vision of paradise; the study and analysis of Yeats's previous poems can only increase the shock of finding these heroes and philosophers, fifteen nights or 180° out of phase, yawning together on the same island. Yeats's heaven, according to *A Vision*, is the place where all antinomies are resolved, the gyres turned into a sphere; and Yeats, whose mind turned increasingly ironic and sceptical in the 1930s, decided at last to resolve his antinomies by making their representatives lie on the same beach with the same smiling and indifferent faces. It is true that the act of stretching and yawning is Yeats's usual periphrasis for post-coital depression, for instance, in 'Three Things', one of Yeats's own favourite lyrics;[2] but it is also true that stretching and yawning can be a sort of pre-coital depression, as in *A Full Moon in March*, where the Queen stretches and yawns three times in unconscious anticipation of the drop of blood which will enter her womb and beget a child. Yeats was always keenly conscious of the post-coital state of mind; indeed I believe that the last stanza of 'Lullaby' is designed to supplement from a feminine point of view the aftermath of the rape presented in 'Leda and the Swan'. In 'News for the Delphic Oracle' the golden codgers do not seems to be engaging in sexual activity; Oisin is 300 years old, as much a codger as 'golden-thighed Pythagoras', and it is unthinkable that the old ascetic Plotinus would take a lover, even in a poem that is loaded with surprises; but their stretching and yawning can nevertheless anticipate the frantic sexuality of the last stanza, as Yeats neatly splits the copulation and the depression between two sets of characters. It is important to make this argument clear, because it ruins the balance of the stanzas if we assume that the golden codgers have just stopped making love when the poem begins; the codgers are in a state of post-coital depression associated with no act of coitus, a perpetually fulfilled condition which is the ironic reversal of the Keatsian condition where the lovers never, never kiss, though winning near the goal. It is possible to associate this paradise with Oisin's third island, because of the sleepiness, the advanced age—one could even relate the golden codgers to the sleepers with their golden nails—but it is probably more accurate to say that the paradise is Oisin's first island turned inside-out, a prolonged satiation instead of a prolonged coitus which never satiates; and Yeats was demonstrably interested in making the myth of Oisin's wanderings even more cyclical than it already was, so the circularity of a voyage from the third island to Ireland and back to an analogue of the first island would have appealed to him. Yeats had proven on the first island that Keats's Grecian Urn was the wrong place for an artist to look for paradise; and now in 'News for the Delphic Oracle' Yeats proves that it is equally useless for lovers to try to stop the clock several heavy breaths later.

'News for the Delphic Oracle' is one of Yeats's subtlest poems, so incongruous in its parts yet so masterfully constructed that it has the poised ricketiness of one of Tinguely's self-destroying machines. F. A. C. Wilson has drawn many parallels between the details of this island and the Neoplatonic caves from Porphyry to the Witch of Atlas,[3] with varying success; I will not repeat his findings, and will limit myself to other sources, principally 'The Wanderings of Oisin' itself. The first four lines of the poem suggest the animism of heaven's landscape, the perfect inter-animation between the golden codgers and the waters and the wind; in paradise the landscape mirrors immediately the state of mind of its residents. The correlative landscape is a standard fixture of 'The Wanderings of Oisin', as we have seen, and a few passages foreshadow the sighing of the great water and the wind; perhaps the most striking example occurs in Niamh's song about mortal and immortal lovers at the beginning of Book II:

> those lovers never turn their eyes
> Upon the life that fades and flickers and dies,
> Yet love and kiss on dim shores far away
> Rolled round with music of the sighing spray . . .

The spray sighs while the lovers kiss by some distant shore; and in Niamh's first song the ecstatic waters seem to embody her faery laughter:

> And Niamh sang continually
> Danaan songs, and their dewy showers
> Of pensive laughter, unhuman sound . . .

The 'dewy showers' also remind us of the silver dew which the poet points to in the second line of the poem; dew is a prominent feature of Oisin's first island as well, where the falling of the dew, interestingly enough, seems to exert a calming effect on the revellers:

And in a wild and sudden dance
We mocked at Time and Fate and Chance
And swept out of the wattled hall
And came to where the dewdrops fall
Among the foamdrops of the sea,
And there we hushed the revelry. . . .

On the third island the dew drops sleep over the Immortals and Oisin; there is a clear antithesis between Oisin's restless sadness and the Immortals' nepenthic dew:

I awoke: the strange horse without summons out
of the distance ran,
Thrusting his nose to my shoulder; he knew in
his bosom deep
That once more moved in my bosom the ancient
sadness of man,
And that I would leave the Immortals, their dimness,
their dews dropping sleep.

Surely the silver dew in 'News for the Delphic Oracle' is the soothing soporific dew of 'The Wanderings of Oisin', not the flaming dew of 'The Secret Rose', on which the passionate Cuchulain lost the world and Emer for a kiss. Dew seems to be a standard ingredient of the Homeric paradise as well, for in Book XIV of the *Iliad* Zeus and Hera make love on Olympus as a shower of dew falls around them:

So speaking, the son of Kronos caught his wife
in his arms. There
underneath them the divine earth broke into young,
fresh
grass, and into dewy clover, crocus and hyacinth
so thick and soft it held the hard ground deep
away from them.
There they lay down together and drew about them a
golden
wonderful cloud, and from it the glimmering dew
descended.[4]

It is interesting that just before this passage Homer mentions Ocean, Minos, and Rhadamanthus—and just after this passage Zeus falls into a deep sleep, perhaps suggesting that the passage was on Yeats's mind when he wrote the poem. The line 'And the wind sighed too' (which, incidentally, is one of Yeats's most amazing achievements as a metrist, a trimetre line with all three stresses in succession) is perhaps anticipated when Niamh asks Oisin in Book III, 'Were the winds less soft than the breath of a pigeon who sleeps on her nest', hoping that the thought of the seductive winds of the islands will lure Oisin away from mortal lands.

There are a few other slight resemblances between 'The Wanderings of Oisin' and 'News for the Delphic Oracle': Thetis' limbs are 'delicate as an eyelid', and the lady in the tower hopes that her sigh will touch her brothers' 'blue-veined eyelids', very delicate eyelids indeed; and the beauty of the sleepers in Book III is contrasted to the 'salt eye of man', just as the beauty of Plato, Minos, and Pythagoras contrasts to the 'Salt blood' that blocks the eyes of the swimming Plotinus in 'The Delphic Oracle upon Plotinus'. At the beginning of Book III, Oisin and Niamh, meeting the phantoms for the last time, saw the immortal desire of Immortals in the faces, and sighed; but the water and the winds in 'News for the Delphic Oracle' sigh for a love that is exactly opposite to the love of the fleeing, insatiable phantoms, a love grown fat, sleepy, and satisfied. Oisin in particular seems quite out of place in the almost Christian stasis of this paradise, so monotonous, so utterly consonant and fulfilled, like a C major chord prolonged through eternity—nearly as much out of place as the hippo performing on a harp of gold in Eliot's 'The Hippopotamus';* and if this paradise is designed only to fall apart, it is not really cemented together in the first place.

Richard Ellmann has Yeats's copy of Milton's poems, a gift he received from Mrs. Yeats, and in the back of that book Yeats wrote the first few lines of 'News for the Delphic Oracle'. This suggests that Milton has something to do with the poem, and there is a definite (though difficult to define) Miltonic feeling about the beginning of the poem, probably due to its comfortable, diffuse love, the combination of Christian and classical references, the great unison of its landscape. One need not read far in Milton to discover where the first four lines of 'News for the Delphic Oracle' came from:

> But peaceful was the night
> Wherein the Prince of light
> His reign of peace upon the earth began:

* A poem that Yeats anthologized in *The Oxford Book of Modern Verse*, p. 280.

> The Winds, with wonder whist,
> Smoothly the waters kiss't,
>   Whispering new joys to the mild Ocean,
> Who now hath quite forgot to rave,
> While Birds of Calm sit brooding on the charmed wave.

This is 'On the Morning of Christ's Nativity', stanza five. This poem also solves the joke implicit in the title, for Milton is the man who has the news for the Delphic Oracle:

> The Oracles are dumb,
> No voice or hideous hum
>   Runs through the arched roof in words deceiving.
> *Apollo* from his shrine
> Can no more divine,
>   With hollow shriek the steep of *Delphos* leaving.
> No nightly trance, or breathed spell,
> Inspires the pale-ey'd Priest from the prophetic cell.

And as the hideous hum of the oracle fades into inaudibility, as Apollo runs away shrieking, another Pan arrives on the scene:

> The Shepherds on the Lawn,
> Or ere the point of dawn,
>   Sat simply chatting in a rustic row;
> Full little thought they then,
> That the mighty *Pan*
>   Was kindly come to live with them below;
> Perhaps their loves, or else their sheep,
> Was all that did their silly thoughts so busy keep.
>
> When such music sweet
> Their hearts and ears did greet,
>   As never was by mortal finger struck,
> Divinely-warbled voice
> Answering the stringed noise,
>   As all their souls in blissful rapture took:
> The Air such pleasure loath to lose,
> With thousand echoes still prolongs each heav'nly close.

Yeats's great joke is to substitute the lecherous earthly Pan for Milton's heavenly Pan, the Virgilian Christ, with his superbly tolerable music; and in place of the 'smiling Infancy' of the baby Christ Yeats has put the foetal Achilles. The oracle's vision of the blessèd isles, as explained in 'The Delphic Oracle upon

Plotinus' and its source in Porphyry, is driven out by the sexuality of Pan's nymphs and satyrs; I believe that 'News for the Delphic Oracle' is a triumphant renunciation of the blessèd isles in favour of generative life. Yeats may have noted with some amusement the relevance of one stanza of the Nativity Ode to 'The Wanderings of Oisin':

> For if such holy Song
> Enwrap our fancy long,
>   Time will run back, and fetch the age of gold,
> And speckl'd vanity
> Will sicken soon and die,
>   And leprous sin will melt from earthly mold,
> And Hell itself will pass away,
> And leave her dolorous mansions to the peering day.

It is possible that the 'age of gold' that Time has fetched is related to the golden codgers and their classical Elysium; and it is possible that Yeats in old age noted the resemblance between 'And Hell itself will pass away' to a line in 'The Wanderings of Oisin', 'And Earth and Heaven and Hell would die'.

Thetis also appears in Milton as a minor character, for instance, in 'In Quintum Novembris' and 'Comus', but Yeats probably derived more of his third stanza from the stanza of the Nativity Ode immediately following the stanza on the oracle:

> The lonely mountains o'er,
> And the resounding shore,
>   A voice of weeping heard, and loud lament;
> From haunted spring and dale
> Edg'd with poplar pale,
>   The parting Genius is with sighing sent;
> With flow'r-inwov'n tresses torn
> The Nymphs in twilight shade of tangled thickets mourn.

Yeats, reversing everything, lets the nymph Thetis destroy the mighty harmony of the waters and the wind which Milton identifies with Christ's reign of peace; Homer was Yeats's example, and his unchristened heart. The 'choir of love' also appears in the Nativity Ode, in the introduction, as the 'Angel Choir' into which the Magi join their voices, and later on as the 'glittering ranks' of cherubim and seraphim 'Harping in loud and solemn choir,/ With unexpressive notes to Heav'n's new-born Heir'. Milton, by the word 'unexpressive', meant 'inex-pressible'; Yeats, if he read the poem with 'News for the Delphic Oracle' in mind, must have seen the possibilities of filling a heaven with a genuinely unexpressive choir.

As for Yeats's deliberate confusion of Pan and Christ, it must be remembered that Yeats had been quite familiar with the prophetic interpretation of Virgil's fourth eclogue for at least four decades; he used echoes from Virgil (via Shelley's *Hellas*) in his own prophecies of a Second Coming in 'Two Songs from a Play', and there is a passage in his 1897 short story. 'The Adoration of the Magi', which blends Virgil's fourth eclogue (although it is mis-numbered) with the pagan vision of Tir nà nOg:

Years passed, and one day, when the oldest of the old men, who had travelled in his youth and thought sometimes of other lands, looked out on the grey waters, on which the people see the dim outline of the Islands of the Young—the Happy Islands where the Gaelic heroes live the lives of Homer's Phaeacians—a voice came out of the air over the waters and told him of the death of Michael Robartes. While they were still mourning, the next oldest of the old men fell asleep whilst he was reading out the Fifth Eclogue of Virgil, and a strange voice spoke through him, and bid them set out for Paris, where a dying woman would give them secret names and thereby so transform the world that another Leda would open her knees to the swan, another Achilles beleaguer Troy.*

One hears the themes, even the verbal rhythms, of the second stanza of 'Two Songs from a Play'; and 'the oldest of the old men, who had travelled in his youth' may foreshadow the golden codgers, in the context of the 'Happy Islands where the Gaelic heroes live the lives of Homer's Phaeacians'.

To trace this pattern of association further, we must turn to the essay on 'Blake's Illustrations to Dante':

. . . and to us one-half of the philosophy of Dante is less living than his poetry, while the truth Blake preached and sang and painted is the root of the cultivated life, of the fragile perfect blossom of the world born

---

* *Mythologies*, pp. 309–10. Yeats added the reference to Leda and the swan in a 1925 revision (as Giorgio Melchiori has observed in *The Whole Mystery of Art*, p. 83), but the references to the Islands of the Young, Homer's Phaeacians, and the 'Fifth Eclogue' were present from the beginning; however, in the original version the Virgilian prophecy '. . . another Argo shall carry heroes over sea, and another Achilles beleaguer another Troy' was located a few pages after this paragraph.

in ages of leisure and peace, and never yet to last more than a little season; the life those Phaeacians, who told Odysseus that they had set their hearts in nothing but in 'the dance and changes of raiment, and love and sleep,' lived before Poseidon heaped a mountain above them; the lives of all who, having eaten of the Tree of Life, love, more than did the barbarous ages when none had time to live, 'the minute particulars of life,' the little fragments of space and time, which are wholly flooded by beautiful emotion because they are so little they are hardly of time and space at all.[5]

So the Phaeacians are kin to the dancers of Book I of 'The Wanderings of Oisin', happy Blakean fellows who think only of 'the dance . . . and love and sleep'; indeed, they are 'hardly of time and space at all', like the first island's dancers, who are also outside ordinary time and space; this chain has led us from the first stanza of 'News for the Delphic Oracle' straight to the first island of 'The Wanderings of Oisin', without the need of any reference to Oisin himself.

The *Odyssey*-like quality of Oisin's voyages, if we may hunt further on the track of the Phaeacians, can hardly be exaggerated; for instance, in Yeats's 1898 essay 'The Autumn of the Body', he writes, referring to Mallarmé's preference for intense, symbolic, apocalyptic poetry,

I think there will be much poetry of this kind, because of an ever more arduous search for an almost disembodied ecstasy, but I think we will not cease to write long poems, but rather that we will write them more and more as our new belief makes the world plastic under our hands again. I think that we will learn again how to describe at great length an old man wandering among enchanted islands. . . .[6]

So far any student of Yeats who did not know this essay would think that Yeats was talking about his own attempt to write a long poem in 'The Wanderings of Oisin'. But let me complete the sentence:

. . . his return home at last, his slow-gathering vengeance, a flitting shape of a goddess, and a flight of arrows, and yet to make all of these so different things 'take light from mutual reflection, like an actual trail of fire over precious stones,' and become 'an entire word,' the signature or symbol of a mood of the divine imagination as imponderable as 'the horror of the forest or the silent thunder in the leaves.'[7]

Yeats means that the symbolist movement will be able to retell

the *Odyssey*; but he leaves the impression that he has already
tried to retell something like the *Odyssey*. Indeed Oisin's three
islands bear a certain resemblance to some of the episodes in the
Odyssey: Circe suggests Niamh and the futility of sexual enchantment, Polyphemus the demon of the second island, and the
Lotus-Eaters the narcotized dreamers of the third island.

Pythagoras and Plotinus, the primary philosophers who
balance the antithetical Oisin and Niamh, are also fairly well-
defined in Yeats's mythology. Pythagoras is known to history
as the discoverer of the mathematical ratios which determine the
relative frequencies of fixed strings; therefore his research, in a
sense, founded Western music, and he is a fit leader for the
heavenly 'choir of love'. He could even articulate, bring to
earth, the music of the spheres:

> World-famous golden-thighed Pythagoras
> Fingered upon a fiddle-stick or strings
> What a star sang and careless Muses heard:
> Old clothes upon old sticks to scare a bird.[8]

Yeats commented on these lines, 'Pythagoras made some measurement of the intervals between notes on a stretched string'.[9]
In paradise Pythagoras is, of course, no longer victimized by
the old age which reduced him to a scarecrow on earth; he has
graduated upward from gross flesh to pure music, perhaps by
means of the celestial digestion which Raphael described in
Paradise Lost. This upward analogical movement was a genuine
feature of Pythagoras' thought; he postulated animal spirits
which allied men to the gods:

'In the *Timaeus* of Plato,' writes Berkeley, 'there is something like a
net of fire, and rays of fire in the human body. Doth this not seem to
mean the animal spirit flowing, or rather darting, through the nerves?'
This fire is certainly that energy which in *Séraphita* is distinguished
from will, and it is doubtless through its agency that will can rise above
the human lot, or act beyond the range of the normal senses. 'If we
believe Diogenes Laertius,' writes Berkeley, 'the Pythagorean philosophers thought there was a certain pure heat or fire which had something divine in it, by the participation whereof man becomes allied to
the Gods. And according to the Platonists, Heaven is not defined so
much by its local situation as by its purity. The purest and most excel-
lent fire, that is Heaven, saith Facinus.'[10]

Pythagoras was famous on earth for founding a mathematical society which studied the occult and geometrical properties of numbers; and his research in this field led to Euclid on one hand and to various secret societies on the other, whispered down the centuries until his doctrines finally filter into Madame Blavatsky's thought:

It is recognized by modern science that all the higher laws of nature assume the form of quantitative statement. This is perhaps a fuller elaboration or more explicit affirmation of the Pythagorean doctrine. Numbers were regarded as the best representations of the laws of harmony which pervade the cosmos. We know too that in chemistry the doctrine of atoms and the laws of combination are actually and, as it were, arbitrarily defined by numbers. As Mr. W. Archer Butler has expressed it: 'The world is, then, through all its departments, a living arithmetic in its development, a realized geometry in its repose.' . . . The mystic Decad $1 + 2 + 3 + 4 = 10$ is a way of expressing this idea. The One is God, the Two, matter; the Three, combining Monad and Duad, and partaking of the nature of both, is the phenomenal world; the Tetrad, or form of perfection, expresses the emptiness of all; and the Decad, or sum of all, involves the entire cosmos. The universe is the combination of a thousand elements, and yet the expression of a single spirit—a chaos to the sense, a cosmos to the reason.[11]

This antithesis between sensual chaos and rational numerical abstraction is fundamental to Yeats's thought, even more in his old age than in his youth, and Yeats chose Pythagoras to express all that was stark, finite, impersonal—soulful, according to Yeats's definition of the word. Pythagoras is best known from 'The Statues':

> Pythagoras planned it. Why did the people stare?
> His numbers, though they moved or semeed to move
> In marble or in bronze, lacked character.
> But boys and girls, pale from the imagined love
> Of solitary beds, knew what they were,
> That passion could bring character enough,
> And pressed at midnight in some public place
> Live lips upon a plummet-measured face.
>
> No! Greater than Pythagoras, for the men
> That with a mallet or a chisel modelled these
> Calculations that look but casual flesh, put down
> All Asiatic vague immensities,

> And not the banks of oars that swam upon
> The many-headed foam at Salamis.
> Europe put off that foam when Phidias
> Gave women dreams and dreams their looking-glass.[12]

These stanzas are invariably glossed with a passage from the end of *On the Boiler*, perhaps the best gloss Yeats ever wrote on one of his poems:

There are moments when I am certain that art must once again accept those Greek proportions which carry into plastic art the Pythagorean numbers, those faces which are divine because all there is empty and measured. Europe was not born when Greek galleys defeated the Persian hordes at Salamis; but when the Doric studios sent out those broad-backed marble statues against the multiform, vague, expressive Asiatic sea, they gave to the sexual instinct of Europe its goal, its fixed type. In the warm sea of the French and Italian Riviera I can still see it. I recall a Swedish actress standing upon some boat's edge between Portofino and Rapallo, or riding the foam upon a plank towed behind a speed-boat, but one finds it wherever the lucky or the well-born uncover their sunburnt bodies. There, too, are doubtless flesh-tints that Greek painters loved as have all the greatest since; nowhere upon any beautiful body, whether of man or woman, those red patches whereby our democratic painters prove that they have really studied from the life.[13]

Phidias reified the Pythagorean numbers because the proportions of his figures were determined mathematically; I am sure that Yeats was thinking of the sculptors' rules popular among the Greeks, such as the rule that the body should be seven times as long as the head. Pythagoras' system becomes almost the Platonic form of the statue, because the statue was generated from something as abstract and numerical as a computer programme.* The sea is Asiatic because it is sprawling, vague, the mother of formlessness; but its bitter furies are broken by the Doric statues, just as the 'warm sea' of the Riviera is divided by the wake of the water skis that the Swedish actress rides on; perhaps in 'The Statues' one is supposed to imagine the wakes of the 'bank of oars' trying in vain to draw lines and partitions†

---

* The people should not stare at what Pythagoras planned (in line 1 of 'The Statues'), because his numbers are no more exotic than the fingers on their hands.
† In *Coole Park, 1929*, Yeats compares the Irish intelligentsia to swallows and speaks of the 'intellectual sweetness' of the tracks they leave in the 'dreaming air'.

on 'The many-headed foam at Salamis'. The actress is as perfectly proportioned as a statue, casual flesh that seems a calculation— she shows the metamorphosis opposite from that of Phidias' statue, as her flesh tint changes from democratic red to artificial, sun-burnt bronze, as her form reverts to the form of the sexual 'fixed type' on which her distant ancestor stared in Phidian Greece.

The eugenic teleology of art appears in Yeats's writings as early as 1904, in *The Kings' Threshold*:

> I said the poets hung
> Images of the life that was in Eden
> About the child-bed of the world, that it,
> Looking upon those images, might bear
> Triumphant children.[14]

But Pythagoras, although his number system underlies Phidias' antithetical miracles,* is only half-Western; numbers are finite, but they are not concrete. Pythagoras is assigned his position as heaven's choir-leader because of the services he performed for the arts,† but it is clear, even from *On the Boiler*, that mathematics can cause as much ontological mischief as good. There exist two visions of reality which can be generated from numbers, which may be labelled as proportional and Cartesian reality. Proportional reality is what I have been discussing, the system whereby each object in the phenomenal world is considered as unique and incommensurable, but nevertheless analyzable according to the ratios between the lengths of its parts; proportional reality consists of concrete shapes and hard Blakean lines.‡ This is the type of measure implicit in the phrase 'Measurement began our might' in 'Under Ben Bulben'. Cartesian reality, on the other hand, breaks up the world into a three-dimensional

---

* Phidias is so antithetical that he seems to be personally identified with the full moon itself in *A Vision*, p. 270.

† There is some evidence that the statues belong in heaven with him: their faces are 'divine', 'empty and measured', and Yeats wrote of Swedish statues which seem to 'come down from some Roman heaven' (*Autobiographies*, (*The Bounty of Sweden*, XIII), p. 555.)

‡ Blake anticipated this line of thought when he wrote, '"I know too well that the majority of Englishmen are fond of the indefinite . . . a line is a line in its minutest subdivisions, straight or crooked. It is itself, not intermeasurable by anything else . . . but since the French Revolution"—since the reign of reason began, that is—"Englishmen are all intermeasurable by one another. . . ."' (quoted by Yeats, *Essays and Introductions*, p. 126.)

mathematical grid on which objects can be reduced to formulae, since space has usurped the function of matter:

Space was to antiquity mind's inseparable 'other', coincident with objects, the table not the place it occupies. During the seventeenth century it was separated from mind and objects alike, and thought of as a nothing yet a reality, the place not the table, with material objects separated from taste, smell, sound, from all the mathematician could not measure, for its sole inhabitants, and this new matter and space, men were told, had preceded mind and would live after. Nature or reality as known to poets and tramps has no moment, no impression, no perception like another, everything is unique, and nothing unique is measurable.[15]

Yeats thought that Berkeley had refuted Cartesian space, and was angry that Cartesian reality still dominated the popular mind, substituting cheese-men for heroes:

No educated man to-day accepts the objective matter and space of popular science, and yet deductions made by those who believed in both dominate the world, make possible the stimulation and condonation of revolutionary massacre and the multiplication of murderous weapons by substituting for the old humanity with its unique irreplaceable individuals something that can be chopped and measured like a piece of cheese; compel denial of the immortality of the soul by hiding from the mass of the people that the grave-diggers have no place to bury us but in the human mind.[16]

The Irish think proportionally, the English in the Cartesian manner:

'Because Ireland is a backward country everybody is unique and knows that if he tumbles down somebody will pick him up. But an Englishman must be terrified, for there is a man exactly like him at every street corner.'[17]

Yeats describes this degeneration into Cartesian abstraction in a striking passage at the end of his 1909 diary *The Death of Synge*, in which 'straight lines' replace 'instinctive motion', and the idea of doing something is 'more vivid than the doing of it'; when life is over-intellectualized, all sense of weight and shape, the palpable texture of reality, vanishes into the awkward geometry of the mind:

I noticed in the train, as I came to Queenstown, a silent, fairly well-dressed man, who struck me as vulgar. It was not his face, which was quite normal, but his movements. He moved from his head only. His arm and hand, let us say, moved in direct obedience to the head, had not the instinctive motion that comes from a feeling of weight, of the shape of an object to be touched or grasped. There were too many straight lines in gesture and in pose. The result was an impression of vulgar smartness, a defiance of what is profound and old and simple. I have noticed that beginners sometimes move this way on the stage. They, if told to pick up something, show by the movement of their body that their idea of doing it is more vivid than the doing of it. One gets an impression of thinness in the nature. I am watching Miss V— to find out if her inanimate movements when on the stage come from lack of experience or if she has them in life. I watched her sinking into a chair the other day to see if her body felt the size and shape of the chair before she reached it. If her body does not so feel she will never be able to act, just as she will never have grace of movement in ordinary life.[18]

On the Boiler goes through the same gyre as 'The Double Vision of Michael Robartes', trying to escape from the puppets of phase one, all wood and fixed strings, trying to find the dancer of phase fifteen who out-dances thought, or at least a Swedish actress posing for publicity, the profanest perfection of mankind; and it is interesting that Pythagoras can take some of the credit for both the puppets and the actress. Pythagoras is such a transitional figure, caught between the singing of the stars and the old clothes of his flesh, between his Western finiteness and his Asiatic abstraction, between mathematical art and mathematical science, that he becomes in heaven a minor tutelory deity unobjectionable to any faction, even blander than the bland Rhadamanthus* of 'The Delphic Oracle upon Plotinus'.

Plotinus contributed so much to so many different aspects of Yeats's thought that it is difficult to be sure exactly what his structural function in the poem is. Because, having confronted his daimon directly, he was closer to the divine than any other man, he was the most primary, the most objective, the most world-transcending of men. Plotinus, whose vision was at the core of what Yeats called phase one, emptied the material world

---

* The epithet 'bland Rhadamanthus' may be derived subliminally from a scrambling of the words 'blandishments' and 'Rhadamanthus', which appear near to each other in MacKenna's translation of the Delphic Oracle's encomium to Plotinus (*The Enneads*, p. 16).

of meaning, even of substance; he asks his readers to make a mental picture of the universe:

Bring this vision actually before your sight, so that there shall be in your mind the gleaming representation of a sphere, a picture holding all the things of the universe moving or in repose or (as in reality) some at rest, some in motion. Keep this sphere before you, and from it imagine another, a sphere stripped of magnitude and of spatial differences; cast out your inborn sense of Matter, taking care not merely to attenuate it: call on God, maker of the sphere whose image you now hold, and pray Him to enter. And may He come bringing His own Universe with all the gods that dwell in it—He who is the one God and all the gods, where each is all, blending into a unity, distinct in powers but all one god in virtue of that one divine power of many facets.[19]

This is one pole of the gyre which dominates Yeats's thinking in old age, the gyre of self and soul; this gyre is distorted from Book I of *A Vision*, where both extremes are transcendental, and made into a double cone, rotating from transcendence back to earth, with the Plotinian One on one cone, the whole multiplicity of historical flux on the other.

Yeats's ability to regard these two extremes dispassionately, analytically, is at times remarkable:

I think that two conceptions, that of reality as a congeries of beings, that of reality as a single being, alternate in our emotion and in history, and must always remain something that human reason, because subject always to one or the other, cannot reconcile. I am always, in all I do, driven to a moment which is the realisation of myself as unique and free, or to a moment which is the surrender to God of all that I am. I think that there are historical cycles wherein one or the other predominates, and that a cycle approaches where all shall [be] as particular and concrete as human intensity permits. Again and again I have tried to sing that approach—*The Hosting of the Sidhe*, 'O sweet everlasting voices', and those lines about 'The lonely majestical multitude'—and have almost understood my intention. Again and again with remorse, a sense of defeat, I have failed when I would write of God, written coldly and conventionally. Could those two impulses, one as much a part of truth as the other, be reconciled, or if one or the other could prevail, all life would cease.[20]

Oisin is 'unique and free', a developed self, while Plotinus surrenders everything to God; and in their reconciliation in

'News for the Delphic Oracle' all life has indeed ceased, until the poem falls apart at the end of the third stanza. Yet the doctrine of the 'congeries of beings', although it suggests heroic free will, autonomous selves, everything that is not Plotinian, is associated in a strange way with Plotinus:

If reality is timeless and spaceless this is a goal, an ultimate Good. But if I believe that it is also a congeries of autonomous selves I cannot believe in one ever-victorious Providence, though I may in Providences that preside over a man, a class, a city, a nation, a world—Providences that may be defeated, the tutelary spirits of Plotinus.[21]

Yeats chooses, for the moment at least, against the One, as he also does in 'A Dialogue of Self and Soul', preferring the ugly vitality of the blind man's ditch to the dead wisdom of the tower —and he seems to find an ally in Plotinus. Plotinus first turns heroic in the note to 'The Tower' in which Yeats decides that the doctrine of 'Death and life were not/ Till man made up the whole' does not confute Plotinus, only repeat him.[22]

Later on Plotinus is conceived as Plato's humanizer, the man who replaced Plato's forms with the individual souls of men:

It was perhaps obvious, when Plotinus substituted the archetypes of individual men in all their possible incarnations for a limited number of Platonic Ideas, that a Greatest Year for whale and gudgeon alike must exhaust the multiplication table.[23]

Plotinus has become so much the champion of human flux that he even muddies the great mathematics of Plato's great year. This absorption of Plotinus' philosophy into Yeats's at last reaches the point where Plotinus is made to choose the individuated souls of men rather than ratiocination:

It is fitting that Plotinus should have been the first philosopher to meet his daimon face to face, though the boy attendant out of jealousy or in convulsive terror strangled the doves, for he was the first to establish as sole source the timeless individuality or daimon instead of the Platonic Idea, to prefer Socrates to his thought.[24]

Plotinus, of course, much preferred Socrates 'restored to the All' to Socrates the man; a human being, at least on earth, is *not* archetypal:

To me, moreover, it seems that if we ourselves were archetypes, Ideas, veritable Being, and the Idea with which we construct here were our

veritable Essence, then our creative power, too, would toillessly effect
its purpose: as man now stands, he does not produce in his work a true
image of himself: become man, he has ceased to be the All; ceasing to
be man—we read—'he soars aloft and administers the Cosmos entire';
restored to the All he is maker of the All.[25]

But Yeats's pressure towards multiplicity, the doctrine of the
'congeries of being', was strong enough to absorb even Plotinus:

We may come to think that nothing exists but a stream of souls, that
all knowledge is biography, and with Plotinus that every soul is
unique. . . .

There is perhaps no final happy state except in so far as men may
gradually grow better; escape may be for individuals alone who know
how to exhaust their possible lives, to set, as it were, the hands of the
clock racing.[26]

That preference of eugenics to heaven, the denial of the 'finaj
happy state' except for those who have transcended time, like
Plotinus, through scorn,* or, like Oisin, through the intensity
of life,† shows the intellectual background of 'News for the
Delphic Oracle', its conscious manipulation of the grand Miltonic style bent to serve a discredited goal, its chiselled magnilo-
quence‡ combined with the most facile-sounding short lines and
cant expressions to be found in Yeats's poetry. The thought of
Plotinus also led Yeats to deny the final happy state in his 1930
Diary:

Plotinus calls well-nigh the most beautiful of Enneads *The Impassivity
of the Disembodied* but, as he was compelled to at his epoch, thought of
man as re-absorbed into God's freedom as final reality. The ultimate
reality must be all movement, all thought, all perception extinguished,
two freedoms unthinkably, unimaginably absorbed in one another.
Surely if either circuit, that which carries us into man or that which

---

* Plotinus thought that time is 'sensation' (according to *A Vision*, p. 70), subjective, no proper state for the soul.

† The heroic Robert Gregory similarly set the hands of his clock running ('In
Memory of Major Robert Gregory', *Collected Poems*, p. 151):

> Some burn damp faggots, others may consume
> The entire combustible world in one small room
> As though dried straw, and if we turn about
> The bare chimney is gone black out
> Because the work had finished in that flare.

‡ Yeats wrote that Milton's 'flesh had partly been changed to stone' (*Essays and
Introductions*, p. 376).

carries us into God, were reality, the generation had long since found its term.[27]

Here Yeats is playing his old game of sifting out that part of a man's thought which is most congenial to his own while dismissing as chaff what 'he was compelled to' think because of his epoch; but in 1930 he seemed to have a more accurate picture of Plotinian philosophy than he did in the 1934 *Wheels and Butter-flies*. Yeats's association of Plotinus with the 'stream of souls' doctrine, the congeries of beings, serves no particular purpose in the poem except to allow Plotinus to retain his individuality in heaven, not to become sucked up into the One; Yeats may have preferred Plotinus to his thought—God—but Yeats could have put Plotinus into his heaven only for the sake of his abstraction, those eyes 'staring at miracle'.[28]

We have seen that Pythagoras was the patron saint of sculptors; and Plotinus was quite interested in sculpture, because the statue provided him with a model for the problem of the creator's conception versus its imposition onto matter:

Let us go to the realm of magnitudes:—suppose two blocks of stones lying side by side: one is unpatterned, quite untouched by art; the other has been minutely wrought by the craftsman's hands into some statue of god or man, a Grace or a Muse, or if a human being, not a portrait but a creation in which the sculptor's art has concentrated all loveliness.
Now it must be seen that the stone thus brought under the artist's hand to the beauty of form is beautiful not as stone—for so the crude block would be as pleasant—but in virtue of the Form or Idea introduced by the art.[29]

Phidias also is mentioned: 'Thus Pheidias wrought the Zeus upon no model among things of sense but by apprehending what form Zeus must take if he chose to become manifest to sight'.[30] Pythagoras provided sculptors with the means to move down-ward from the conception to the embodiment; but Plotinus scorns the stone, scorns the plucked strings,[31] scorns the human body, loves only the idea, the pattern, the melody, the soul; if Pythagoras was abstract, but involved with analogical movement (because he translated the melody into the strings), Plotinus' abstraction is so intense that he rejects everything material,

everything that is not God.* But Plotinus, if he is to be imagined
in any material form, is to be imagined as a self-perfecting statue:

Withdraw into yourself and look. And if you do not find yourself
beautiful yet, act as does the creator of a statue that is to be made
beautiful: he cuts away here, he smoothes there, he makes this line
lighter, this other purer, until a lovely face has grown upon his work.
So do you also: cut away all that is excessive, straighten all that is
crooked, bring light to all that is overcast, labour to make all one glow
of beauty and never cease chiselling your statue, until there shall shine
out on you from it the godlike splendour of virtue, until you shall see
the perfect goodness surely established in the stainless shrine.[32]

The golden codgers seem all to be fairly rigid beings, slightly
animated statues; the paradise of 'News for the Delphic Oracle'
is another aesthetic refuge for Oisin, who in life kept seeking
refuge inside pictures, and surely Plotinus and Pythagoras belong
in the classical heaven that Yeats imagined in *The Bounty of
Sweden*, when he saw the statues of the Swedish kings:

These myth-makers and mask-makers worked as if they belonged to
one family, and the great walls where the roughened surface of the
bricks, their carefully varied size and tint, takes away all sense of
mechanical finish; the mosaic-covered walls of the 'Golden Room'; the
paintings hung upon the walls of the committee-rooms; the fresco
paintings upon greater surfaces with their subjects from Swedish
mythology; the wrought iron and the furniture, where all suggests
history, and yet is full of invention; the statuary in marble and in
bronze, now mythological in subject, now representations of great
Swedes, modelled naked as if they had come down from some Roman
heaven. . . .[33]

In 'News for the Delphic Oracle', the frescoes of Oisin and
Niamh, subjects from Irish mythology, are found in the same
'Roman heaven' as the statues of Pythagoras and Plotinus.
Plotinus is of course a new arrival, having just completed the
journey described in 'The Delphic Oracle upon Plotinus':

> Behold that great Plotinus swim,
> Buffeted by such seas;
> Bland Rhadamanthus beckons him.
> But the Golden Race looks dim,
> Salt blood blocks his eyes.[34]

---

* Yeats's line in 'Blood and the Moon', 'Everything that is not God consumed
with intellectual fire', is derived from Plotinus, *Ennead* I, p. 62.

The journey through the water is sometimes related to the swimming described in the 'Introduction to *Fighting the Waves*':

Certain typical books—*Ulysses*, Virginia Woolf's *The Waves*, Mr. Ezra Pound's *Draft of XXX Cantos*—suggest a philosophy like that of the *Samkara* school of ancient India, mental and physical objects alike material, a deluge of experience breaking over us and within us, melting limits whether of line or tint; man no hard bright mirror dawdling by the dry sticks of a hedge, but a swimmer, or rather the waves themselves. In this new literature announced with much else by Balzac in *Le Chef-d'œuvre inconnu*, as in that which it superseded, man in himself is nothing.[35]

This passage is about the contrast between the novel of the eighteenth and nineteenth centuries and the modern novel: the older novels modelled the human consciousness as a mirror (Stendhal's mirror, which becomes the dominant metaphor of Yeats's introduction to *The Oxford Book of Modern Verse*), passively reflecting external reality instead of creating and dominating that reality in the manner of the consciousness of 'The Tower'; and in the twentieth century, as the world grows even more objective and mechanical, the mind loses even the minimal identity of a mirror, and becomes wholly indistinguishable from the deluge of perceptions which overwhelms it. When the mind cannot differentiate itself from ambient reality, the body loses all coenesthesis, and therefore the swimmer becomes so passive, so liquid, that he becomes dissolved into the waves themselves. These waves are further defined in *On the Boiler*:

Events in time come upon us head-on like waves, each wave in some main character the opposite of its predecessor. But there are other events that lie side by side in space, complements one of another. Of late I have tried to understand in its practical details the falsehood that is in all knowledge, science more false than philosophy, but that too false. Yet, unless we cling to knowledge, until we have examined its main joints, it comes at us with staring eyes.[36]

Plotinus' waves, which are not so random and fluid that their crests and troughs do not bear some sinusoidal resemblance to the gyre-form, have at last carried us back to Pythagoras and 'The Statues', where 'knowledge increases unreality', and 'Mirror on mirror mirrored is all the show'. Although Yeats's mirror metaphor springs from Stendhal and Coleridge, Plotinus himself uses it as the dominant metaphor of Yeats's favourite Ennead,[37] 'The Impassivity of the Unembodied', in which Plotinus, himself deriving much from Plato's cave, compares matter to a mirror:

> Its every utterance, therefore, is a lie; it pretends to be great and it is little, to be more and it is less; and the Existence with which it masks itself is no Existence, but a passing trick making trickery of all that seems to be present in it, phantasms within a phantasm; it is like a mirror showing things as in itself when they are really elsewhere, filled in appearance but actually empty, containing nothing, pretending everything. Into it and out of it move mimicries of the Authentic Existents, images playing upon an image devoid of Form, visible against it by its very formlessness. . . .[38]

The images in Plotinus' mirror may be compared to the abstract knowledge of positivistic science, which is mathematical and therefore a falsification of reality, but that knowledge cannot be ignored, or it will come 'at us with staring eyes'. Yeats declares elsewhere in *On the Boiler* that children must be taught 'nothing but Greek, Gaelic, mathematics',[39] and the reason he gives for mathematics is interesting: 'being certainty without reality it is the modern key to power'. [40] Our age is so unreal, so contaminated with abstraction, that ignorance of mathematics is a fatal response to its unreality; mathematics attacks us with staring, empty, Buddha-like eyes if we do not 'examine its main joints'. This passage is partly derived from a speech in *The Hour-Glass*, where the Wise Man compliments himself for 'educating' his pupil:

> And all the while
> What were they all but fools before I came?
> What are they now but mirrors that seem men
> Because of my image? Fool, hold up your head.
> What foolish stories they have told of the ghosts
> That fumbled with the clothes upon the bed,
> Or creaked and shuffled in the corridor,
> Or else, if they were pious bred,
> Of angels from the skies,
> That coming through the door,
> Or, it may be, standing there,
> Would solidly out-stare
> The steadiest eyes with their unnatural eyes,
> Aye, on a man's own floor.[41]

The staring angel in this play proves that if we examine *only* the joints of knowledge, then another antithesis will arise to destroy us; here the Wise Man is abstract, while the angel represents transcendent beauty. Pythagoras in heaven can represent mathematical knowledge, and Plotinus can represent philosophical knowledge; if Plotinus can be further identified with the swimmer who turns into the waves, then Plotinus was in danger of fuzzing out into flux, losing all concrete identity on earth, until he attained the abstract safety of paradise; and Plotinus, because of his objective surrender to God, was indeed of approximately the same phase as the wave-like Leopold Bloom.

The codgers are golden because gold is the proper substance for those who have shed the dross of the flesh and emerged as numerical or divine abstraction, as Yeats imagined in his vision in 'Rosa Alchemica' of the stars as innumerable alchemical furnaces 'turning lead into gold, weariness into ecstasy, bodies into souls, the darkness into God';[42] but the image is so profane that the codgers seem to be merely dipped in gold, seem to have attained the sentimental immortality of a bronzed baby shoe.

The second stanza of 'News for the Delphic Oracle' floods the divine old-age home with an influx of youth.

> Straddling each a dolphin's back
> And steadied by a fin,
> Those Innocents re-live their death,
> Their wounds open again.
> The ecstatic waters laugh because
> Their cries are sweet and strange,
> Through their ancestral patterns dance,
> And the brute dolphins plunge
> Until, in some cliff-sheltered bay
> Where wades the choir of love
> Proffering its sacred laurel crowns,
> They pitch their burdens off.

Just as Pythagoras and Plotinus balanced the heroic, antithetical Oisin and Niamh, so the Innocents balance the primary classical philosophers with a mindless primary Christianity. The Innocents do not have a particularly rich tradition as a subject for poetry, but it is conceivable that Yeats could have picked them up from Milton, in this case from *Paradise Regained* II:

> a Stable was our warmth,
> A Manger his; yet soon enforc't to fly
> Thence into *Egypt*, till the Murd'rous King
> Were dead, who sought his life, and missing fill'd
> With Infant blood the streets of *Bethlehem*.

I doubt, however, that Yeats would have found *Paradise Regained* an attractive work. Yeats does not use the Innocents in a significant way in any other work,* and I suspect that their most important aspect is the extreme disparity in age and intellect between them and the golden codgers. The shift from the codgers to the Innocents is the first sign in the poem of the shift from the effete paradise of the first stanza back into the generative world. The Innocents 're-live their death', are involved in the Dreaming Back process[43] which will eventually return them to the mortal world; and surely the Innocents are not among those few who reach a 'final happy state', for they have done nothing to set the hands of their clocks racing. Indeed the paradise of the first stanza is beginning to look a little like Spenser's Garden of Adonis, where Old Genius

> letteth in, he letteth out to wend,
> All that to come into the world desire;
> A thousand naked babes attend
> About him day and night, which doe require,
> That he with fleshly weedes would them attire:
> Such as him list, such as eternall fate
> Ordained hath, he clothes with sinfull mire,
> And sendeth forth to liue in mortall state,
> Till they againe returne backe by the hinder gate.
>
> After that they againe returned beene,
> They in that Gardin planted be againe;
> And grow afresh, as they had neuer seene
> Fleshly corruption, nor mortall paine.
> Some thousand yeares so doen they there remaine;
> And then of him are clad with other hew,

---

* Father Hart in *The Land of Heart's Desire* invokes 'The Holy Martyrs and the Innocents,/ The adoring Magi in their coats of mail', in a passage so unimportant that Yeats asked amateurs to omit it entirely from their performances.

> Or sent into the chaungefull world againe,
> Till thither they returne, where first they grew:
> So like a wheele around they runne from old to new.

The Garden of Adonis, somewhat like Yeats's paradise, is peculiarly poised between mutability and a condition that Spenser calls 'eterne in mutability', referring to Adonis, 'the father of all formes', who does not die but changes perpetually, a high analogue of the reincarnative cycles; as we have seen, all of Oisin's paradisal states spring from the desire to eternalize the most attractive features of mutability. Yeats was quite aware of the Garden of Adonis, as is shown by his essay on Spenser, which speaks of Spenser's pagan cult of beauty:

And in his *Hymne of Heavenly Beautie* he sets a woman little known to theology, one that he names Wisdom or Beauty, above Seraphim and Cherubim and in the very bosom of God, and in the *Faerie Queene* it is pagan Venus and her lover Adonis who create the forms of all living things and send them out into the world, calling them back again to the gardens of Adonis at their lives' end to rest there, as it seems, two thousand years between life and life. He began in English poetry, despite a temperament that delighted in sensuous beauty alone with perfect delight, that worship of Intellectual Beauty which Shelley carried to a greater subtlety and applied to the whole of life.[44]

Venus and Adonis bear a slight resemblance to Oisin and Niamh (and a strong resemblance to Diarmuid and Grania), and in 'News for the Delphic Oracle' it would seem that Oisin and Niamh have grown almost as formal and pompous as Venus and Adonis, have turned from sensuous beauty to a mock Intellectual Beauty. Yeats insists again that Spenser was basically a sensual poet before Puritanism soured him, made him moral and intellectual:

He is a poet of the delighted senses, and his song becomes most beautiful when he writes of those islands of Phaedria and Acrasia, which angered 'that rugged forehead,' as it seems, but gave to Keats his *Belle Dame sans merci* and his 'perilous seas in faery lands forlorn,' and to William Morris his 'Water of the Wondrous Isles.'[45]

It is fascinating that he should mention *The Water of the Wondrous Isles*, for in that romance there is an 'Isle of the Old and the Young', which Yeats mentions in his essay on Morris, 'The Happiest of the Poets':

The evils their [his bad women's] enchantments make are a disordered abundance like that of weedy places, and they are cruel as wild creatures are cruel and they have unbridled desires. One finds these evils in their typical shape in that isle of the Wondrous Isles, where the wicked witch has her pleasure-house and her prison, and in that 'isle of the old and the young,' where until her enchantment is broken second childhood watches over children who never grow old and who seem to the by-stander who knows their story 'like images' or like 'the rabbits on the grass.'[46]

On the 'Isle of the Old and the Young' the heroine Birdalone finds only old men and babies; the babies remain unnaturally young, never grow up, while the old men slowly die. But this is evil, because it is a frustration of the generative process, and Birdalone, when she returns the second time to the Wondrous Isles, finds all the enchantments broken: the witch-wife's own 'Isle of Increase Unsought' (the name of which suggests the satiation of desire in Oisin's first island) has turned barren, the kings and queens of the 'Isle of Kings' and the 'Isle of Queens' have lost their waxy paralysis, turned human; the 'Isle of Nothing' has changed from an empty wasteland to a bountiful farming community; and on the 'Isle of the Old and the Young' the old men have died off and been forgotten, while the babies have aged into a prosperous adolescence. These transformations from posed figurines to living people are not unlike certain features of Oisin's islands, although Morris's romance, written in 1892, could not have influenced the earlier poem; but subliminal influence on 'News for the Delphic Oracle', of course, is not precluded. The golden codgers do not die off, but they do fade away as the focus shifts to the vitality of the ocean and Pan's cavern. When Yeats writes that the babies of the 'Isle of the Old and the Young' seem ' "like images" or like "the rabbits in the grass" ', he is referring to this passage:

Birdalone stood there, and was now perplexed and downhearted; for now the look of the elder scarce liked her, and the children began to seem to her as images, or at the best not more to her than the rabbits or the goats; and she rued her word that she would abide there the night through. For she said to herself: I fear some trap or guile; is the witch behind this also? for the old man is yet stark, and though he be foolish at whiles, yet may wizardry have learned him some guile.[47]

Birdalone wonders whether the babies are human at all, whether they are only unnaturally jolly pieces of bait designed to tempt her into some wizard's den; but if they are indeed images in never-never land in Part II, they have been fully humanized by the time of Birdalone's return voyage in Part VI. Similarly, Yeats's Innocents are transitional figures, children entering the golden codgers' paradise, dead but nevertheless uncomfortably vigorous.

Morris thought, as Yeats clearly did in 'The Wanderings of Oisin', that a frozen, artificial landscape is a manifestation of enchantment, not an earthly paradise. But Morris's vision of the true Earthly Paradise was far from Yeats's own, for Morris's landscapes were not wholly satisfying to Yeats, far too placid, bucolic, almost bovine:

> When William Morris describes a house of any kind, and makes his description poetical, it is always, I think, some house that he would have liked to have lived in. . . . Indeed all he writes seems to me like the make-believe of a child who is remaking the world, not always in the same way, but always after its own heart; and so, unlike all other modern writers, he makes his poetry out of unending pictures of a happiness that is often what a child might imagine, and always a happiness that sets mind and body at ease. Now it is a picture of some great room full of merriment, now of the wine-press, now of the golden threshing-floor, now of an old mill among apple-trees. . . .
> His poetry often wearies us as the unbroken green of July wearies us, for there is something in us, some bitterness because of the Fall, it may be, that takes a little from the sweetness of Eve's apple after the first mouthful; but he who did all things gladly and easily, who never knew the curse of labour, found it always as sweet as it was in Eve's mouth. [48]

Yeats, at the beginning of 'The Happiest of the Poets', contrasts this orderly farmers' Eden with Rossetti's 'rejection of Nature', his love of intensity, his desire for 'a world of essences, of unmixed powers, of impossible purities', [49] the Morning and Evening Star; and at the end of the essay Yeats contrasts Morris's vision with that of the early Christians:

> The early Christians were of the kin of the Wilderness and of the Dry Tree, and they saw an unearthly Paradise, but he was of the kin of the Well and of the Green Tree and he saw an Earthly Paradise. [50]

The Innocents were not early Christians, but they were nevertheless honorary Christian martyrs, made ascetic by Herod's fiat; yet they are no kin of the Dry Tree, for they are thoroughly wet, sporting in the water with the dolphins. They are playful, but there is surely an unearthly intensity in the sweetness of their reopening wounds; and in that condition of suspended intensity they approach Yeats's vision of an earthly paradise, where aimless joy is sustained through no barren Thebaid but in the midst of flux itself, Plotinus's waves—the vision of the 'Self' rejoicing in the frog-spawn of a blind man's ditch. The Innocents are appointed as the representatives of Christianity on the island (although we never see them actually come to land, and they indeed belong in the water, in generation) because Yeats regarded Christianity as somewhat regressive, infantile, inculcating self-surrender, a passive suffering unworthy of an adult; this childlike quality of Christianity is indicated by the fact that Christ appears in Yeats's poetry typically as a child, and a rather squalid child at that:

> The true faith discovered was
> When painted panel, statuary,
> Glass-mosaic, window-glass,
> Amended what was told awry
> By some peasant gospeller;
> Swept the sawdust from the floor
> Of that working-carpenter.
> Miracle had its playtime where
> In damask clothed and on a seat
> Chryselephantine, cedar-boarded,
> His majestic Mother sat
> Stitching at a purple hoarded
> That He might be nobly breeched
> In starry towers of Babylon
> Noah's freshet never reached.
> King Abundance got Him on
> Innocence; and Wisdom He.
> That cognomen sounded best
> Considering what wild infancy
> Drove horror from His Mother's breast.[51]

The irony of 'Wisdom' is not the subtlest that Yeats ever exercised, but it is clear that art considerably 'improved' Christ's clothing and his Nazareth before they were acceptable for a major religion. The pictorializing of Christ is again reminiscent of 'The Wanderings of Oisin', 'Her Vision in the Wood', and all the other poems generated from the tension between aesthetic images and the natural world; in this poem, however, the disjunction between the picture and the reality is complete: Noah's puny stream never reaches the 'starry towers of Babylon', and hypostatized Wisdom is a mere cognomen for Christ's all-too-human babyhood. This poem is far from unique: in 'The Magi', the stiff, painted figures of the Magi look down with disdain at the spasmodic humanity of 'The uncontrollable mystery on the bestial floor', and in 'A Nativity' Delacroix, Landor, Irving, and Talma become the interior decorators and stage-mechanics of Christ's birth. The Innocents retain something of the infant Christ's primitive simplicity, transfigured only by the ordinary transfiguration in which all souls participate after death; the Innocents are not the pathetic little martyrs of a sentimental Catholicism[52] but dead souls charged with aesthetic joy, the memories of their one passionate moment turned cold and sweet during the Dreaming Back. In the first stanza the great waters sighed for love, but in the second stanza the ecstatic waters laugh in sympathy with the sweet, strange cries of the Innocents; the calm, depressed harmony of the golden codgers and the ocean has changed into something roiling, vibrant, intense.

This combination of ecstasy and infant torture is not a common theme in literature, but appears notably in Blake's 'Mental Traveller':

> And if the Babe is born a Boy
> He's given to a Woman Old
> Who nails him down upon a rock
> Catches his shrieks in cups of gold
>
> She binds iron thorns around his head
> She pierces both his hands & feet
> She cuts his heart out at his side
> To make it feel both cold & heat
>
> Her fingers number every Nerve
> Just as a Miser counts his gold
> She lives upon his shrieks & cries
> And she grows young as he grows old. . . .
>
> . . . he becomes a wayward Babe
> And she a weeping Woman Old
> Then many a Lover wanders here
> The Sun & Stars are nearer rolld

> The trees bring forth sweet Extacy
> To all who in the desert roam
> Till many a City there is Built
> And many a pleasant Shepherds home
>
> But when they find the frowning Babe
> Terror strikes thro the region wide
> They cry the Babe the Babe is Born
> And flee away on Every side. . . .

Here again is the gyring between youth and age, age and youth, which can be seen in the Garden of Adonis and 'News for the Delphic Oracle'; Blake's Babe delights only the woman, not the ocean, by his shrieks,* but the apocalyptic landscape, the close connection between this poem and *A Vision*, would seem to establish some resemblance between Blake's Babe and the Innocents.

In most of the analogues we have studied there is some pressure driving the children away from the state of perfection; in 'Wisdom' there is even a somewhat equivocal mockery of the painted background; and I think this helps to explain the strong counter-pressure that is developing in 'News for the Delphic Oracle', even as the Innocents ride closer and closer to the island, carrying the seeds of generative destruction. The vitality of the second stanza cannot be overestimated; and the plunging of the brute dolphins shows that these animals still retain the joyous swirling energy which Yeats associated with them from the beginning of his career:

Seagulls came out of the mist and plunged into the sunlight, and out of the sunlight and plunged into the mist. To the westward gannets were striking continually, and a porpoise showed now and then, his fin and back gleaming in the sun. Sherman was more perfectly happy than he had been for many a day, and more ardently thinking. All nature seemed full of a Divine fulfilment.[53]

The third stanza of 'News for the Delphic Oracle' begins with painted nudes, the cool classical beauty which the first stanza lightly burlesques, and ends with the nudes coming to life in the most embarrassing manner possible:

---

* The line 'She cuts his heart out at his side' is surely the source of 'And tear the heart out of his side' in 'Two Songs from a Play'.

Slim adolescence that a nymph has stripped,
Peleus on Thetis stares.
Her limbs are delicate as an eyelid,
Love has blinded him with tears;
But Thetis' belly listens.
Down the mountain walls
From where Pan's cavern is
Intolerable music falls.
Foul goat-head, brutal arm appear,
Belly, shoulder, bum,
Flash fishlike; nymphs and satyrs
Copulate in the foam.

Until the last few lines, everything in the poem suggests paint-ings; the first two lines of the first stanza sound as if details of a painting are being pointed out, and the ancestral patterns of the dancing waters in the second stanza suggest some geometrical form used to represent waves; but in the third stanza, if T. R. Henn is correct, there is an actual source painting, Poussin's 'The Marriage of Peleas and Thetis' (known before and after Yeats's time as 'Acis and Galatea'). I am not convinced that there exists a 'startlingly exact correspondence'[54] between the painting and the poem: as Richard Ellmann has said,[55] Poussin's Peleus does not stare at Thetis, except perhaps at her cheek; Peleus is not even fully stripped, and the nymphs and satyrs and the intolerable musicians are right next to the lovers, not 'Down the mountain walls'—indeed Peleus and Thetis seem to be embracing on a sort of beach-blanket. However, Poussin's nymphs and satyrs do copulate in the water, in exotic positions, with that posed lubricity to which only the French have the secret; and, as far as I know, Yeats never borrowed anything from any painting without changing some of the details. I will add a few suggestions, in any case, about other possible sources for the third stanza.

Yeats included only one of Pound's Cantos in *The Oxford Book of Modern Verse*, Canto XVII:

Chrysophrase,
And the water green clear, and blue clear;
On, to the great cliffs of amber.
Between them,
Cave of Nerea,

> she like a great shell curved,
> And the boat drawn without sound,
> Without odour of ship-work,
> Nor bird-cry, nor any noise of wave moving,
> Nor splash of porpoise, nor any noise of wave moving,
> Within her cave, Nerea,
>   she like a great shell curved
> In the suavity of the rock,
>   cliff green-gray in the far,
> In the near, the gate-cliffs of amber,
> And the wave
>   green clear, and blue clear,
> And the cave salt-white, and glare-purple,
>   cool, porphyry smooth,
>   the rock sea-worn.
> No gull-cry, no sound of porpoise,
> Sand as of malachite, and no cold there,
>   the light not of the sun.
> Zagreus, feeding his panthers,
>   the turf clear as on hills under light.
> And under the almond-trees, gods,
>   with them, *choros nympharum*.[56]

The Cave of Nerea suggests the Nereid Thetis, and this may also be the location of the 'cliff-sheltered bay'; the porpoises do not splash and make no sound, but Yeats could easily have added a little more animation to the seascape; the epithet 'salt-white' recalls the 'salt flakes' on Plotinus's breast, and the 'Salt blood' that blocked his eyes; if there is no 'choir of love', there is at least a *'choros nympharum'*; and, although as a pun it would be outrageous, there is no reason why porphyry rock cannot evoke Porphyry's cave of the nymphs. There are several hints that Pound is describing an imaginary painting: his expressions 'in the far/ In the near' sound like an artist's background and foreground, and the impression of the unnatural stillness of artifice, which is strong in the cited passage because of the soundlessness, the odourlessness, 'the light not of the sun', becomes still stronger as the poem proceeds:

> 'There, in the forest of marble,
> the stone trees—out of water—
> the arbours of stone—
> marble leaf, over leaf. . . .[57]

All this contrasts sharply with the canto's first lines, which suggest Dionysiac fertility, a somewhat sleepy variant of the last lines of 'News for the Delphic Oracle':

> So that the vines burst from my fingers
> And the bees weighted with pollen
> Move heavily in the wine-shoots:
>   chirr—chirr-chir-rikk—a purring sound,
> And the birds sleepily in the branches.
> ZAGREUS! IO ZAGREUS!⁵⁸

As for Peleus and Thetis, they may be derived from Homer as well as from Poussin; in Book XVIII, lines 79–87, of the *Iliad*, Achilles, despairing because of the loss of Peleus's armour to the Trojans, wishes that his mother had never married Peleus. And in Book XXIV of the *Odyssey* there is a curious scene in which the gibbering souls of the slain suitors gather around Achilles and Agamemnon, who are talking to each other in Hades; Agamemnon tells Achilles about the ceremonies the Achaians gave to honour the dead Achilles:

>   Your mother gave you
> a golden jar with handles. She said that it
>   was a present
> from Dionysos, and was the work of renowned
>   Hephaistos.
> In this your white bones are laid away, O
>   shining Achilleus,
> mixed with the bones of the dead Patroklos,
>   son of Menoitios,
> and apart from those of Antilochos, whom you
>   prized above all
> the rest of your companions after the death
>   of Patroklos. . . .
>
> Then your mother, asking the gods for the
>   gift of beautiful
> prizes, set them in the field for the best of
>   the Achaians.
> I in my time have attended the funerals of
>   many
> heroes, at those times when, because a king
>   has perished,

> the young men gird themselves for sport and
>   set up the prizes;
> but these your heart would have admired
>   beyond any others,
> such beautiful prizes as were set up by the
>   goddess, silver-footed
> Thetis, for your sake.[59]

If Thetis is waiting to send Achilles out into the world of flux in 'News for the Delphic Oracle', she is also willing to provide him with a proper return voyage to the afterlife.

The last lines of the poem seem to turn the painting of Peleus and Thetis into a scrim screen that suddenly disappears as the brilliant revelry is illuminated behind it, but the nymphs and satyrs are as much part of Poussin's painting as Peleus and Thetis themselves. It seems as if the nymphs and satyrs express the sexuality that Peleus and Thetis cannot on account of their heroic formality, and such correlatives are not uncommon in paintings; for instance, in Giotto's fresco 'The Lamentation' the mourners stand around Christ's body with the most controlled rigidity, while the angels above weep, contort themselves in the extremity of grief, seemingly more human than any man. Yeats uses this technique, not only in 'News for the Delphic Oracle', but in 'Lullaby' as well:

> Sleep, beloved, such a sleep
> As did that wild Tristram know
> When, the potion's work being done,
> Roe could run or doe could leap
> Under oak and beechen bough,
> Roe could leap or doe could run. . . .[60]

The frenzied roe and doe enact the wild sexuality that Iseult's aphrodisiac causes, evidently inverting themselves once before the act is consummated. Peleus's formality, his elegant weeping, is only a theatrical posture, as the existence of Achilles proves; and that attentive foetus tears the poem's delicate fictions apart, responding even *ab ovo* to the intolerable music of generative reality. 'Intolerable music' is a strangely powerful term, and perhaps some of that power derives from Plato's banishing of all musical modes not conducive to courageous or temperate emotions (*Republic* 399); certainly Yeats's 'intolerable music' has all the power to deprave which Plato ascribed to the ignoble modes. The presence of Pan, as well as the presence of Achilles, tends to give the lie to the first stanza's paradise, for the classical writers never thought that Pan had any business in an abstract Elysium, that he lived anywhere but in the fertile woodlands of earth. 'News for the Delphic Oracle' was written near the end of Yeats's life, yet it begins with 'The Wanderings of Oisin' and ends with Pan, a character mentioned in an even earlier poem, 'The Island of Statues':

> *The Sleeper.* As here I came I saw god Pan.
>   He played
> An oaten pipe unto a listening fawn,
> Whose insolent eyes unused to tears would weep.
> Doth he still dwell within the woody shade,
> And rule the shadows of the eve and dawn?[61]

The Sleeper is one of the statues who has just come back to life after the Enchantress's spell was broken; he is not revived by Pan's 'oaten pipe', but he associates that music with whatever he has known of love or human emotion. The statues are freed from the Enchantress's spell, but they remain on the Island of Statues, hidden from the course of generative life (although not from death itself), electing a picturesque king and queen to rule them; but in old age Yeats was able to humanize quite thoroughly the statue-like residents of Elysium, whip them into a sexual fury. Peleus straddles perfectly the world of the codgers and the world of the satyrs, his tears linking him on one hand to the great landscape sighing for love in the first stanza, yet on the other hand hinting at a much more human, violent response to love, just as Oisin's tears in 'The Wanderings of Oisin' serve to break him out of petrification. We have seen how the stresses in the poem tend to break down the fragile paradise of the first stanza with the steady pressure of Thetis's most benign tumour; and Yeats found that Eden was even closer to earth than the Platonic form of Coole Park described in the introductory poem to *The Shadowy Waters:*

> Is Eden far away, or do you hide
> From human thought, as hares and mice and coneys
> That run before the reaping-hook and lie
> In the last ridge of the barley? Do our woods
> And winds and ponds cover more quiet woods,
> More shining winds, more star-glimmering ponds?[62]

Earth Unparadised

'The Circus Animals' Desertion'

EARTHLY paradises are never earthly enough, or else they are indistinguishable from earth. We have examined Yeats's holo-thurian vision of paradise, seen how it everts, throws out its innards when it is threatened by the outer world; and in this chapter we shall trace the decay of apocalypse, the shrinking of millennium. Yeats's most famous poems are perhaps his middle-period millennial poems, such as 'Leda and the Swan' and 'The Second Coming'; but the concept of millennium, defined with such power in these poems, was originally closely allied in Yeats's mind to Tir nà nOg, the Celtic paradise. In the 1897 'Adoration of the Magi' the oldest man looks out on the waters 'on which the people see the dim outlines of the Islands of the Young—the Happy Islands where the Gaelic heroes live the lives of Homer's Phaeacians'. In the same paragraph (according to the revised 1925 version) the second oldest man falls asleep reading Virgil's prophetic eclogue, and hears a voice saying that a dying woman would 'so transform the world that another Leda would open her knees to the swan, another Achilles beleaguer Troy'.[1] All the pictures that poets have made of the heroic life raised to its uttermost intensity, the *Odyssey's* Phaeacia, the sack of Troy, become prophetic of what the next millennium will bring, just as Tir nà nOg turns into something heroic, Oisin's three islands, including Phaeacian gaiety and an Achillean combat, the frag-mented vision of various kinds of intensities. Both the millen-nium and the paradise are thus informed by Homer and Virgil, and the same acceptance of ordinariness that defeats the paradise can defeat the millennium. The renunciation of Virgil's prophecy does not come quickly; in the 1904 *Samhain* called 'First Prin-

ciples', perhaps the best-written of the series, we find that same
patient waiting for the second coming, the second Troy:

A civilisation is very like a man or a woman, for it comes in but a few
years into its beauty, and its strength, and then, while many years go
by, it gathers and makes order about it, the strength and beauty going
out of it the while, until in the end it lies there with its limbs straightened
out and a clean linen cloth folded upon it. That may well be, and yet we
need not follow among the mourners, for, it may be, before they are at
the tomb, a messenger will run out of the hills and touch the pale lips
with a red ember, and wake the limbs to the disorder and the tumult
that is life. Though he does not come, even so we will keep from among
the mourners and hold some cheerful conversation among ourselves;
for has not Virgil, a knowledgeable man and a wizard, foretold that
other Argonauts shall row between cliff and cliff, and other fair-haired
Achaeans sack another Troy?[2]

The anticipation of *A Vision*'s historical gyres is remarkable;
and one can even hear the same Virgilian rhythm of 'The Adoration of the Magi', 'other Argonauts . . . other fair-haired
Achaeans . . . another Troy'. Only in the phrase 'the disorder
and tumult that is life' is there a hint of resurrection into the imperfect, the merely vital. Yeats quotes part of the Fourth Eclogue
again at the beginning of Book IV of *A Vision*, but in his poetry
Yeats turns from Second Troy to 'No Second Troy', from the
new heroism of the millennium to the increasing chaos which
will darken the world just before the millennium. 'The Second
Coming', for all the power of its description of the 'brazen
winged beast' that Yeats associated with 'laughing, ecstatic destruction',[3] has no clue to what sort of civilization the rough
beast will create, what new authoritarianism will replace the old
anarchy. The brazen winged beast which embodies the millennium of 'The Second Coming' appeared previously in the 1902
Where There is Nothing, in which Paul Ruttledge seems to decide that he will father the rough beast singlehandedly, lead the
peasants to a peasant millennium. But he discovers that his millennial vision is self-destructive, because in practical terms a
peasants' revolt will degenerate into a structured society no
better than the society he wishes to destroy:

Paul Ruttledge. We will have one great banner that will go in
front, it will take two men to carry it, and on it we will have
Laughter, with his iron claws and his wings of brass and his
eyes like sapphires—

Aloysius. That will be the banner for the front, we will have different troops, we will have captains to organize them, to give them orders—

Paul Ruttledge. To organize? that is to bring in law and number? Organize—organize—that is how all the mischief has been done. I was forgetting, we cannot destroy the world with armies, it is inside our minds that it must be destroyed, it must be consumed in a moment inside our minds. God will accomplish his last judgment, first in one man's mind and then in another. He is always planning last judgments. And yet it takes a long time, and that is why he laments in the wind and in the reeds and in the cries of the curlews.[4]

In other words, the society which follows millennium will recapitulate the same, very Blakean, Fall of Man that Paul described earlier when he was in a monastery:

Paul Ruttledge . . . They gathered the green Earth to their breasts and their lips, as I gather these boughs to mine, in what they believed would be an eternal kiss.

Second Friar. I see a light about his head.

Third Friar. I wonder if he has seen God.

Paul Ruttledge. It was then that the temptation began. Not only the Serpent who goes upon his belly, but all the animal spirits that have loved things better than life, came out of their holes and began to whisper. The men and women listened to them, and because when they had lived according to the joyful Will of God in mother wit and natural kindness, they sometimes did one another an injury, they thought that it would be better to be safe than to be blessèd, they made the Laws. The Laws were the first sin. They were the first mouthful of the apple, the moment man had made them he began to die; we must put out the Laws as I put out this candle.[5]

Paul sees the oceanic blessedness of earth destroyed by partitions, by the rectilinear 'big houses and big towns'; and he sees the holiness that God put into everything that lives congeal into church-buildings, turn inhuman and ungodly. When Paul refuses to lead the peasants' army under the banner of the brazen winged beast, he becomes the first character in Yeats, I believe, to reject millennium in the way that Oisin rejected paradise. Paul turns his back on temporal power, in imitation of Christ, so that he may face solitary death, 'the invisible heart of flame'; but after *A Vision* Yeats found that he could consider the failure of

millennium on strictly secular terms. There are no specific pre-
dictions in *A Vision* on the exact nature of the civilization which
will emerge after A.D. 2000, although it will clearly be an antithetical society analogous to Homer's Greece, 'the *antithetical
multiform influx*'.[6] But Yeats obviously had great hope for that
influx; indeed he thought he saw in modern mathematical
thought—his letters to Sturge Moore indicate that he meant
Whitehead[7]—some exciting developments:

. . . when the moment of surrender is reached, when the new gyre
begins to stir, I am filled with excitement. I think of recent mathematical
research; even the ignorant can compare it with that of Newton—so
plainly of the 19th Phase—with its objective world intelligible to intellect; I can recognise that the limit itself has become a new dimension,
that this ever-hidden thing which makes us fold our hands has begun to
press down upon multitudes. Having bruised their hands upon that
limit, men, for the first time since the seventeenth century, see the
world as an object of contemplation, not as something to be remade,
and some few, meeting the limit in their special study, even doubt if
there is any common experience, doubt the possibility of science.[8]

If science has reached its limit, if intellect has made intelligible
all that can be made intelligible, then men will no longer watch
the world passively, communally, but will experience, enjoy, un-
fold their hands and struggle. Although Yeats rarely explains
that science and Christianity are two aspects of the same surrender to an absolute, either to Cartesian mirror-reality or to God,
he makes this clear in a passage in his 1930 Diary which is, to my
knowledge, his first realization that the year 2000 will bring no
titanic change, no civilization better able to live up to its ideal
than we can to ours:

We approach influx. What is its form? A civilisation lasts two thousand
years from nadir to nadir—Christ came at the Graeco-Roman meridian,
physical maturity, spirit in celestial body, and was the first beginning
of the One—all equal in the eyes of One. Our civilisation which began
in A.D. 1000 approaches the meridian and once there must see the
counterbirth. What social form will that birth take? It is multitudinous,
the seat of the congeries of autonomous beings each seeing all within
its own unity. I can only conceive of it as a society founded upon unequal
rights and unequal duties which if fully achieved would include all
nations in the European stream in one harmony, where each drew its
nourishment from all though each drew different nourishment. But this

ideal will be no more achieved than are the equal rights and duties before the One—God with the first Christians, Reason with Rousseau. There will be a weak unforeseen life moulding itself upon poor thought, war in all likelihood, discord till it become in its turn concord (spirit in celestial body), Olympus just as it breaks. It is founded by a Teacher not a Victim, and this Teacher is what he is because he creates and expresses the congeries, or concord of many, which must impose itself in the course of centuries.[9]

The post-millennial civilization will still be antithetical, still dedicated to individuality instead of common, submissive experience, still amorous of inequality and hierarchy instead of democracy, but men will live there as they have always lived, with a 'weak unforeseen life', discord and imposed concord, a broken euphemerized pantheon.

This recognition of human recalcitrance, human inability to fit into the geometry of the ideal millennium, is developed much further. The Teacher who is the 'Daimon' (or embodied spirit) of the new dispensation seems quite prosaic next to Leda and her indifferent swan (who incarnated the last antithetical age), prosaic next to the Victim Christ, so diffuse that he 'is not a being but a harmony of beings'.[10] The mere fact that the coming age is antithetical and not primary helps to rid it of the paraphernalia of the miraculous:

Yet I must bear in mind that an antithetical revelation will be less miraculous (in the sense of signs and wonders), more psychological, than a primary which is from beyond man and mothered by the void. It is developed out of man and is man.[11]

Yeats states in the same diary that he is no believer in millenniums:

But I am no believer in Millenniums. I but foresee another moment of plasticity and disquiet like that which was at and before the commencement of our era, re-shaped by the moral impulse preserved in the Gospels, and that other present, according to Mr. Mackail, in Virgil. At the moment it seems more important that I should try the lots in Virgil than in the Gospels. What idea of the State, what substitute for that of the toga'd race that ruled the world, will serve our immediate purpose here in Ireland?[12]

The era that laboured to give birth to the rough beast of 'The Second Coming', the blood-dimmed tide, has at last produced only a little 'moment of plasticity and disquiet'; and the Argonauts, the fair-haired Achaeans, are resurrected to sit in the Irish Senate* and cogitate on what model of the state 'will serve our immediate purpose in Ireland'. That pragmatic impulse has turned the immense switch of the gyres from primary to antithetical civilization, from the Gospels to Virgil, into something strictly secular, human, relentlessly non-apocalyptic; as Yeats says in *On the Boiler*, 'Yet we must hold to what we have that the next civilisation may be born, not from a virgin's womb, nor a tomb without a body, not from a void, but of our own rich experience.'[13] It is that richly individuated, private experience that will be the keynote of the new era; men, if they cannot be fair-haired Achaeans, can at least develop themselves into a reasonably full selfhood; therefore the new civilization will proceed out of all of us collectively, not out of some apocalyptic animal, or Mary's inhuman conception, or Christ's 'tomb without a body', or any other void. After the millennium the new antithesis will be comparatively primitive, bodily, free of the intellectual strait-jacket of Cartesian space:

Perhaps now that the abstract intellect has split the mind into categories, the body into cubes, we may be about to turn back towards the unconscious, the whole, the miraculous; according to a Chinese sage darkness begins at midday. Perhaps in my search, as in that first search with Lady Gregory among the cottages, I but showed a first effect of that slight darkening.[14]

The sense that underneath geometrical form one ought to be able to find a human body is usually strong in Yeats's imagination; and Yeats's first half-repudiation of *A Vision* was written before that book was finished, 'The Gift of Harun Al-Rashid':

> The signs and shapes;
> All those abstractions that you fancied were
> From the great Treatise of Parmenides;
> All, all those gyres and cubes and midnight things
> Are but a new expression of her body
> Drunk with the bitter sweetness of her youth.[15]

This uncovering of the body's primitive wisdom from beneath

* Yeats's seeming intention to dress the senators in togas is reminiscent of his campaign in the Senate to dress judges in 'very dignified and very simple' modern costumes (see *The Senate Speeches of W. B. Yeats*, p. 125).

the mind's 'gyres and cubes' is implicit in Yeats's late millennial imagery; the 'congeries of beings' is not only a Plotinian gathering of archetypes, but an assembly of bodies as well.

Yeats pushes his imaginative construction of the post-millennial society to its furthest in a passage in the 'Introduction to *Fighting the Waves*':

I once heard Sir William Crookes tell half a dozen people that he had seen a flower carried in broad daylight slowly across the room by what seemed an invisible hand. His chemical research led to the discovery of radiant matter, but the science that shapes opinion has ignored his other research that seems to those who study it the slow preparation for the greatest, perhaps the most dangerous, revolution in thought Europe has seen since the Renaissance, a revolution that may, perhaps, establish the scientific complement of certain philosophies that in all ancient countries sustained heroic art. We may meet again, not the old simple celebration of life tuned to the highest pitch, neither Homer nor the Greek dramatists, something more deliberate than that, more systematised, more external, more self-conscious, as must be at a second coming, Plato's Republic, not the Siege of Troy.[16]

Like much of Yeats's later prose, this passage is pregnant, elliptical, and seems simpler than it actually is. William Crookes' scientific shock at finding a phantom with a beating heart is behind 'the central situation'[17] of the play *The Resurrection*. This association links Crookes to the millennial theme, to the apparitions which announce a new dispensation. The 'radiant matter' that Crookes discovered seems curiously related to the ectoplasmic radiance of the ghost he saw; it is as if his scientific studies grew out of 'the criticism of Myth'[18] in the manner Yeats described in his most famous letter to Sturge Moore. Yet Yeats immediately separates Crookes' activities by indicating that popular science has ignored Crookes' psychic investigations in favour of his 'chemical research'; this crop of mummy wheat maturing in the dark is, however, preparing a revolution. The phantom brewing new revolution is not the Christ of *The Resurrection*, but is instead more nearly identified with an invisible hand carrying a flower, something simple and organic.

There is a passage in the 'Introduction to *The Words upon the Window-pane*' which perhaps defines more fully the phantoms awaiting resurrection:

. . . the Irish country-woman did see the ruined castle lit up, the bridge across the river dropping; those two Oxford ladies did find themselves in the garden of the Petit Trianon with Marie Antoinette and her courtiers, see that garden as those saw it; the gamekeeper did hear those footsteps the other night that sounded like the footsteps of a stag where stag has not passed these hundred years. All about us there seems to start up a precise inexplicable teeming life, and the earth becomes once more, not in rhetorical metaphor, but in reality, sacred.[19]

The earth all around us is charged with sacred 'teeming life', charged with the electric dead. The fruition then will be nothing fierce or preternatural, only the life we have always known, a little freer, a little more aristocratic, antithetical. The second coming is 'not the old celebration of life tuned to the highest pitch' simply because it is a second coming and not the first; Virgil is repudiated, for the post-millennial men will sack no second Troy, only try as best they can to live in a philosopher's schematized, law-ridden Utopia. Beyond apocalypse there is no heroism but a 'scientific complement' of heroic philosophy, an antithetical world as bedevilled by science as our old primary world. Finally neither of Crookes' discoveries can be denied; his phantoms must learn to live in harmony with his wave-form equations; Yeats has followed Hegelian dialectic to his personal limit, and must take the new subjectivity in uncomfortable synthesis with the old objectivity. The thought of Homeric life turned rigid and objective produced nothing in Yeats's mind but Plato's Republic; and it seems that Yeats, like many others, did not find Plato's Republic purely Edenic. A state governed by moralistic philosophers, where most art is banished, is clearly a compromise at best; and Yeats was at last willing to accept a distinctly debased, humanized millennium.

At the end Yeats seemed to be willing to swap all historical theory in return for a woman's body:

> How can I, that girl standing there,
> My attention fix
> On Roman or on Russian
> Or on Spanish politics?
> Yet here's a travelled man that knows
> What he talks about,
> And there's a politician

>   That has read and thought,
>   And maybe what they say is true
>   Of war and war's alarms,
>   But O that I were young again
>   And held her in my arms![20]

According to Jon Stallworthy,[21] Yeats intended this dismissal of
war, of wrangling politics, to conclude the volume now called
Last Poems; and 'Politics' was to be preceded immediately by
'The Circus Animals' Desertion'. 'The Circus Animals' Desertion' is Yeats's last word on the interface between fantasy and
fact, between poetry and reality, between the mirror-resembling
dream and Locke's excrement.* The Tir nà nOg of 'The Wanderings of Oisin' becomes the first ring of a three-ring circus,
where Oisin is an ageing show-horse trotted out for one final
round of applause:

>   What can I but enumerate old themes?
>   First that sea-rider Oisin led by the nose
>   Through three enchanted islands, allegorical dreams,
>   Vain gaiety, vain battle, vain repose,
>   Themes of the embittered heart, or so it seems,
>   That might adorn old songs or courtly shows;
>   But what cared I that set him on to ride,
>   I, starved for the bosom of his faery bride?[22]

The gaiety, the battle, and the repose were vain, soured, because Yeats the man could not attain the supernatural consummation he longed for, the consummation which he tried in vain
to project onto Oisin. That is why sea-rider Oisin is himself
horselike, 'led by the nose': Yeats was attempting to ride Oisin
to Niamh's faery bosom. The theme of the poet who desires to
make love to a supernatural woman is common in early Yeats
(for example in the *Stories of Red Hanrahan*) and later on the
supernatural woman turns into the poet's own created, visionary
woman (for example in *The King of the Great Clock Tower*); but
this stanza is, I think, the first time that Yeats *in propria persona*
read back this theme into one of his former works, posited a
strictly psychoanalytic explanation of one of his created women.
The image of the poet himself running in Niamh's direction is

---

* Yeats called the materialistic world of Locke excrementious in his 1930 Diary
(*Explorations*, p. 325).

not however, unique to 'The Circus Animals' Desertion';
Niamh beckons temptingly in 'The Hosting of the Sidhe', and
there is a sequel to 'The Lake Isle of Innisfree' called 'The Danaan Quicken Tree', published in 1893 but not included in the
Collected Poems, in which the poet rows to Innisfree and decides
to eat a faery berry which is either poisonous to mortals or 'able
to endow them with more than mortal powers':[23]

> Cast out all hope, cast out all fear,
> And taste with me the faeries' meat,
> For while I blamed them I could hear
> Dark Joan call the berries sweet,
> Where Niam heads the revelry.
> (Ah, mournful Danaan quicken tree!)[24]

Human love here is transfigured to Niamh's level; but the
implicit warning of the poison suggests that this revelry may
prove even vainer than Oisin's. The counter-theme that human
love is spoiled by the search for transcendence is as strong as the
original theme; in the 1903 'Baile and Aillinn', the narrator compares common earthly love with the heroic love of Naoise and
Deirdre:

> *And when we walk with Kate or Nan*
> *About the windy water-side,*
> *Our hearts can hear the voices chide.*
> *How could we be so soon content,*
> *Who know the way that Naoise went?*[25]

At one point in the poem he asserts that temporal love is the
only valuable thing that life can provide:

> *And our poor Kate or Nan is less*
> *Than any whose unhappiness*
> *Awoke the harp-strings long ago.*
> *Yet they that know all things but know*
> *That all this life can give us is*
> *A child's laughter, a woman's kiss.*[26]

This narrative exploration of the relative value of natural and
supernatural love is continued in the 1914 'The Two Kings', an
impressive poem despite the fact that almost no one reads it.
This poem straddles *Dhoya* and 'The Three Bushes' in the most
curious manner imaginable: King Eochaid's wife is an incarnated
faery, 'betrayed into a cradle', who must choose between the

faery love of her faery lover and the human love of King
Eochaid; her two lovers struggle, a king fighting a huge white
stag, in an enactment of the struggle within the queen's mind.
The faery tempts the queen with the same vision with which
Niamh tempted Oisin:

> "What happiness
> Can lovers have that know their happiness
> Must end at the dumb stone? But where we build
> Our sudden palaces in the still air
> Pleasure itself can bring no weariness,
> Nor can time waste the cheek, nor is there foot
> That has grown weary of the wandering dance,
> Nor an unlaughing mouth, but mine that mourns,
> Among those mouths that sing their sweethearts' praise,
> Your empty bed."[27]

The queen replies that love is given meaning by its transitoriness, that coitus could not be intense without the subsequent depression that the faery mocks:

> "How should I love," I answered,
> "Were it not that when the dawn has lit my bed
> And shown my husband sleeping there, I have sighed,
> 'Your strength and nobleness will pass away'?
> Or how should love be worth its pains were it not
> That when he has fallen asleep within my arms,
> Being wearied out, I love in man the child? . . .
>
> "Never will I believe there is any change
> Can blot out of my memory this life
> Sweetened by death, but if I could believe,
> That were a double hunger in my lips
> For what is doubly brief."[28]

This pure humanism reaches its culmination in 'The Circus
Animals' Desertion', where Oisin's islands are explicitly declared to be imagined evasions of reality, Niamh a tormenting
succuba who drew Yeats, as she drew Oisin, to desires which
admitted no gratification.

The wish-fulfilment of 'The Wanderings of Oisin' leads Yeats
to the sublimation fantasy of *The Countess Cathleen*:

> And then a counter-truth filled out its play,
> *The Countess Cathleen* was the name I gave it;

> She, pity-crazed, had given her soul away,
> But masterful Heaven had intervened to save it.
> I thought my dear must her own soul destroy,
> So did fanaticism and hate enslave it,
> And this brought forth a dream and soon enough
> This dream itself had all my thought and love.

The play is a 'counter-truth' because Yeats was then starved for
the bosom of Maud Gonne, for no faery Niamh; in one, the
dream brought forth a woman, and, in the other, the woman
brought forth a dream. *The Countess Cathleen* is a repainted,
prettified version of Maud Gonne's revolutionary activities,
where the blood and the fury settle into merciful philanthropy,
where the endless rancour finally eases into a contrived heaven.
Cathleen literally did try to destroy her soul, but only for the
sake of other Irish souls, not through the '*Hysterica passio* of its
own emptiness',[29] through its fanaticism and hate. The hate-
crazed Maud changes into the benevolent, 'pity-crazed' Cathleen,
but there are many signs in the play that Aleel regards Cathleen
with almost as much alarm as Yeats regarded Maud Gonne.
Cathleen is so overcome with the plight of the poor that she says,

> Till I have changed my house to such a refuge
> That the old and ailing, and all weak of heart,
> May escape from beak and claw; all, all, shall come
> Till the walls burst and the roof fall on us.
> From this day out I have nothing of my own.[30]

That last line surely hints at a fanaticism which is trying to
surface from life into allegory. Oona comments to Aleel after
hearing that speech, 'you and I are of no more account/ Than
flies upon a window-pane'; and Aleel certainly feels that Cathleen has traded Aleel's love for her good deeds. Later in the play
Aleel gives his soul to the Merchants for free, and the peasant
Shemus suspects that Aleel has gone mad:

> *Shemus.*
>   How can you sell your soul without a price?
>   I would not listen to his broken wits.
>   His love for Countess Cathleen has so crazed him
>   He hardly understands what he is saying.
> *Aleel.* The trouble that has come on Countess Cathleen,
>   The sorrow that is in her wasted face,

> The burden in her eyes, have broke my wits,
> And yet I know I'd have you take my soul.
> *First Merchant.* We cannot take your soul, for it is hers.[31]

Clearly all sorts of craziness are hovering around the fringes of
The Countess Cathleen; and Cathleen's possession of Aleel's soul
throws a new light on the line 'The dream itself had all my
thought and love'—Aleel's uncompromising, uncompromised
love for Cathleen has replaced the tortured, unassertive love of
Yeats for Maud Gonne. Yeats frankly admitted that he tried to
elevate his love for Maud into something mythic, eternal,
worthy of a Tristram:

> I disliked Moore's now sentimental, now promiscuous amours, the main
> matter of his talk. A romantic, when romanticism was in its final
> extravagance, I thought one woman, whether wife, mistress, or incite-
> ment to platonic love, enough for a lifetime: a Parsifal, Tristram, Don
> Quixote, without the intellectual prepossessions that gave them
> solidity.[32]

The descent from the holy Parsifal to the secular Tristram to the
foolish Don Quixote should be observed. Aleel, for all the bra-
very of his final scene, tends to turn abject and Yeats-like in certain situations, most notably at his first entrance:

> *Aleel.*   A man, they say,
>   Loved Maeve the Queen of all the invisible host,
>   And died of his love nine centuries ago.
>   And now, when the moon's riding at the full,
>   She leaves her dancers lonely and lies there
>   Upon that level place, and for three days
>   Stretches and sighs and wets her long pale cheeks.
> *Cathleen.* So she loves truly.
> *Aleel.*   No, but wets her cheeks,
>   Lady, because she has forgot his name[33]

If Yeats replaced the unsatisfactory Maud with the fictive,
pliable Cathleen, then Aleel can replace the still-intransigent
Cathleen with the still more fictive, still more pliable Maeve.
Maeve ignored the man who died for her, forgot his name (just
as Cathleen and Maud failed to pay enough attention to Aleel
and Yeats), so Aleel condemns Maeve to weep for her loss.
Maeve is an allegory within an allegory, and Aleel's song about
Maeve's dancers changes from the sorrow of an imagined loss to

the joy of an imagined sexual fulfilment, as the dancers abandon
their literary raving to lift their skirts:

> *Aleel.* . . .
>   Lift up the white knee;
>   Hear what they sing,
>   Those young dancers
>   That in a ring
>   Raved but now
>   Of the hearts that broke
>   Long, long ago
>   For their sake.
> *Oona.* New friends are sweet.
> *Aleel.* But the dance changes,
>   Lift up the gown,
>   All that sorrow
>   Is trodden down.[34]

As *The Countess Cathleen* proceeds, it increasingly becomes less
a reflection of the situation between Yeats and Maud Gonne,
more a wish-fulfilment of a poet turned hero, of a beloved whose
shattered soul is artificially repaired: 'But masterful Heaven
had intervened to save it'. The *deus ex machina* at the end of the
play is obviously the part of the play that is falsest to Yeats's
personal emotional life; Heaven may be masterful but human
life will allow no such neat, imposed pattern. The word 'masterful' suggests the phony teleology of the well-made play, and
it is significant that the word is repeated at the beginning of
Part III of the poem: 'Those masterful images because com-
plete/ Grew in pure mind'. The masterful intervention in *The
Countess Cathleen* is this sort of abstract, purely mental construct, unnaturally complete, unreal, a circus trick suspended between the miraculous and the trivial. The masterful Heaven that
grows in pure mind, grows from our hopeless need for exterior
order, is anticipated in a mocking passage in *The Hour-Glass*:

> For I am certain that there is no God
> Nor immortality, and they that said it
> Made a fantastic tale from a starved dream
> To plague our hearts.[35]

In my first chapter I described how a blind man's art could
spring from his sexual frustration; here Yeats shows how his own
art sprang from his sexual frustration, his fear for Maud's safety,

just as Keats in 'Ego Dominus Tuus', shut out from all the luxury of the world, made luxuriant song. Although Yeat's perception that the beauties of his art were the ghostly emanations of his personal stresses was not a theme for his poetry until the six-weeks' search of 'The Circus Animals' Desertion', he touched on something of that theme in his 1906 *Discoveries*:

Presently I found that I entered into myself and pictured myself and not some essence when I was not seeking beauty at all, but merely to lighten the mind of some burden of love or bitterness thrown upon it by the events of life. We are only permitted to desire life, and all the rest should be our complaints or our praise of that exacting mistress who can awake our lips into song with her kisses.[36]

It is clear from innumerable passages in *Wheels and Butter-flies* that Yeats thought his later plays continually threatened by abstraction. Even *The Countess Cathleen* flirted with naked moral precept:

In Christianity what was philosophy in Eastern Asia became life, biography and drama. A play passes through the same process in being written. At first, if it has psychological depth, there is a bundle of ideas, something that can be stated in philosophical terms; my *Countess Cathleen*, for instance, was once the moral question, may a soul sacrifice itself for a good end? but gradually philosophy is eliminated until at last the only philosophy audible, if there is even that, is the mere expression of one character or another. When it is completely life it seems to the hasty reader a mere story.[37]

'The Circus Animals' Desertion' employs the opposite theory of *The Countess Cathleen*'s creation, the theory that it was shaped into beauty from the garbage of the concrete; but the danger of abstraction in plays is a theme repeated in the next stanza, which refers to *On Baile's Strand*:

> And when the Fool and Blind Man stole the bread
> Cuchulain fought the ungovernable sea;
> Heart-mysteries there, and yet when all is said
> It was the dream itself enchanted me:
> Character isolated by a deed
> To engross the present and dominate memory.
> Players and painted stage took all my love,
> And not those things that they were emblems of.

This demands comparison with a passage in the 'Introduction to *The Resurrection*':

So did the abstract ideas persecute me that *On Baile's Strand*, founded upon a dream, was only finished when, after a struggle of two years, I had made the Fool and Blind Man, Cuchulain and Conchubar whose shadows they are, all image, and now I can no longer remember what they meant except that they meant in some sense those combatants who turn the wheel of life.[38]

The Fool and the Blind Man are the shadows of Cuchulain and Conchubar (indeed the shadows play their roles, enact the crucial oath-taking scene at the beginning of the play), and Cuchulain and Conchubar are themselves but the images of rather shadowy ideas, wheel-shaped ideas. The dialectical nature of the play is easy to follow, for Cuchulain and the Fool represent the self, all body, strength, and appetite, while Conchubar and the Blind Man represent the soul, all wisdom, morality, and restraint. They are indeed 'combatants who turn the wheel of life':

> *Cuchulain*. No wonder in that, no wonder at all in that.
>   I never have known love but as a kiss
>   In the mid-battle, and a difficult truce
>   Of oil and water, candles and dark night,
>   Hillside and hollow, the hot-footed sun
>   And the cold, sliding, slippery-footed moon—
>   A brief forgiveness between opposites
>   That have been hatreds for three times the age
>   Of this long-'stablished ground. . . .
>
> *Conchubar*.
>   You are but half a king and I but half;
>   I need your might of hand and burning heart,
>   And you my wisdom.[39]

The Fool and the Blind Man become abstracted into the poles of the major gyre:

> *First Woman*. Life drifts between a fool and a blind man
>   To the end, and nobody can know his end.[40]

When the Fool and the Blind Man come together as characters and not as truths, collaborate to steal the bread, when Cuchulain steps down from his lofty selfhood to flog the sea, Yeats could see 'Heart-mysteries'—the insoluble complexities of human behaviour—emerging from the dialectic; but Yeats knew that the play was written to display the enchanting dream, the mind-mysteries which turned into *A Vision*, rather than the profound experiential reality which lay underneath the wheel:

> Those wild hands that have embraced
> All his body can but shove
> At the burning wheel of love
> Till the side of hate comes up.[41]

Too many wheels, too little love and hate. The character isolated by a deed is a part of the enchanting dream, the emblems, and not a part of the heart-mysteries, because the isolated tragic hero is cut free of all human context, like a purged soul striving towards God. Yeats once described Hamlet as 'a soul lingering on the storm-beaten threshold of sanctity',[42] and such a tragic character is passing away from the heart-mysteries, from the ordinary trash of the human, towards something remote, impersonal. The best gloss on 'Character isolated by a deed' is perhaps in a 1904 *Samhain*:

A farce and a tragedy are alike in this, that they are a moment of intense life. An action is taken out of all other actions; it is reduced to its simplest form, or at any rate to as simple a form as it can be brought to without our losing the sense of its place in the world. The characters that are involved in it are freed from everything that is not a part of that action; and whether it is, as in the less important kinds of drama, a mere bodily activity, a hairbreadth escape or the like, or as it is in the more important kinds, an activity of the souls of the characters, it is an energy, an eddy of life purified from everything but itself.[43]

That contempt for 'mere bodily activity', as opposed to pure intense denatured life, is exactly what Yeats renounces in 'The Circus Animals' Desertion'; he prefers Cuchulain's physical struggle with the waves to the tragic ecstasy of his madness. In this poem Yeats seems contemptuous of the players and painted stage that had usurped his human love, but in a passage in *On The Boiler* Yeats clasps the 'dead art' of tragedy to his bosom, revels in the players and the painted stage, the whole tragic artifice of simplicity, and seems to scorn the gross humanity that the stage is an emblem of, the humanity that he holds at arm's length:

What does it matter that it belongs to a dead art and to a time when a man spoke out of an experience and a culture that were not of his time alone, but held his time, as it were, at arm's length, that he might be a spectator of the ages? I am haunted by certain moments: Miss O'Neill in the last act of Synge's *Deirdre*, 'Draw a little back with the squabbling of fools'; Kerrigan and Miss O'Neill playing in a private house that scene in Augusta Gregory's *Full Moon* where the young mad people in their helpless joy sing *The Boys of Queen Anne;* Frank Fay's entrance in the last act of *The Well of the Saints;* William Fay at the end of *On Baile's Strand;* Mrs. Patrick Campbell in my *Deirdre,* passionate and solitary; and in later years that great artist Ninette de Valois in *Fighting the Waves.* These things will, it may be, haunt me on my deathbed; what matter if the people prefer another art, I have had my fill.[44]

Yeats could not quite free himself from the isolated characters that 'engross the present and dominate memory'.

Yeats defeats the aesthetic transcendence, even the wisdom, of his own constructs, but he does not repudiate them; by integrating his old myths into the greater myth of his life he imbues his former works—for all their beautiful flatness, their pretension, their heavy coats of paint—with a greater poignance, a more intimate personal value. The poet comes to terms with his works, learns that he can enjoy them as objectifications, enactments, of his personal crises and desires. *The King of the Great Clock Tower,* in its first version, reached its climax with the revelry of poets with their imagined women, a great summit conference of Yeats's *dramatis personae:*

> What brought them there so far from their home,
> Cuchulain that fought night long with the foam,
> *What says the Clock in the Great Clock Tower?*
> Niam that rode on it; lad and lass
> That sat so still and played at the chess?
> What but heroic wantonness?
> *A slow low note and an iron bell.*
>
> Aleel, his Countess; Hanrahan
> That seemed but a wild wenching man;
> *What says the Clock in the Great Clock Tower?*
> And all alone comes riding there
> The King that could make his people stare,
> Because he had feathers instead of hair.
> *A slow low note and an iron bell.*[45]

The severed head of the Stroller, himself a poet in love with his imagination, speaks with a voice similar to Yeats's own, a voice which conjures up the major achievements of Yeats's career. The characters all stop suddenly at their moment of greatest intensity: Cuchulain stops flogging the tide long enough to join the meeting, Niamh gallops over from Tir nà nOg, Deirdre and Naoise rise from their chess-game—all attend the *Walpurgisnacht*, all descend from their emblematic niches, all turn their thoughts to wantonness. The tension is most note-worthy in the case of Deirdre and Naoise, whose chess-game in *Deirdre* is full of an unbearable passion held in the most rigid control; their chess-moves compose a frozen enactment of their game with Conchubar, while their game with Conchubar is it-self a pre-ordained re-enactment of another, still more mythic game that Lugaidh Redstripe played; and in *The King of the Great Clock Tower* all this sitting-still, this tension, dissolves into 'heroic wantonness'. Aleel and Countess Cathleen are there too, no longer trapped in a ritual of fanatic good-will, finally able to consummate the desire that Aleel sublimated into a vision of Maeve and that Cathleen sublimated into philanthropy. And Hanrahan, broken knees and all, finds a place among the heroes—Hanrahan, who seemed but a wild wenching man but was as much a poet as Aleel, and therefore allowed, at last, to wench with his imagination. Last to come riding in, all alone, is the pitiful king of 'The Wisdom of the King', the imaginative ruler whose beloved rejected him in favour of a tall ordinary man who did not have feathers growing on his head; the story sug-gests the dual nature of the poet, as king and as outcast (a naïve version of *The King's Threshold*), and may be read as an allegory of Yeats's early relation with Maud Gonne;[46] but on the moun-tain-side even the timid self-projection of the embryonic Yeats can find the fulfilment of his dream. In this way, through Yeats's disguises of himself—Aleel, Hanrahan, and the feather-haired king—Yeats can wanton with his own characters, become the master of ceremonies at his personal revels.

The integrative myth of 'The Circus Animals' Desertion' does not end with the players and painted stages that projected, usurped Yeats's passions, but on a lower level among the detritus of those passions, the refuse of the human heart. 'The Circus Animals' Desertion', however, at one point in its development was typed as a complete poem without the stanza that we now know as the final one; in its place was the following stanza:[47]

> O hour of triumph come and make me gay!
> If burnished chariots are put to flight
> Why brood upon old triumph, prepare to die;
> Even at the approach of the un-imaged night
> Man has the refuge of his gaity;
> A dab of black enhances every white,
> Tension is but the vigour of the mind,
> Cannon the god and father of mankind.

It seems disconcerting that the poem was ended with a statement of the joy of catastrophe, the same rejoicing at the approach of night that is found in 'The Gyres' and 'The Man and the Echo'. The night is 'un-imaged', wholly black, because Yeats partially renounced his images in Part II, put his 'burnished chariots' to flight; and white is enhanced by black because the coming of night makes the doubly-brief images of day doubly-sweet. Cannon is the god and father of mankind* because Yeats saw that the world was moving toward a black secular millennium, the war foretold, too accurately, in 'Politics' and other places:

The drilled and docile masses may submit, but a prolonged civil war seems more likely, with the victory of the skilful, riding their machines as did the feudal knights their armoured horses. During the Great War Germany had four hundred submarine commanders, and sixty per cent of the damage done was the work of twenty-four men. The danger is that there will be no war, that the skilled will attempt nothing, that the European civilisation, like those older civilisations that saw the triumph of their gangrel stocks, will accept decay.[48]

If war is bad, placid decay is worse; cannon fathers mankind by keeping it in perpetual political flux, but revolution may bring only change, not improvement:

> Hurrah for revolution and more cannon-shot!
> A beggar upon horseback lashes a beggar on foot.
> Hurrah for revolution and cannon come again!
> The beggars have changed places, but the lash goes on.[49]

This is the historical gyre of *A Vision* reduced to its bleakest minimum, a mere interchanging of beggar on horseback with

---

* Yeats's line is a paraphrase from Heraclitus: 'It was this Discord or War that Heraclitus called "God of all"' (*A Vision*, p. 67).

beggar on foot; and the poem's title, 'The Great Day', is
Yeats's most ironic name for millennium. The association of
poignant, rather transitory, artistic images with warfare which
is made in the cancelled stanza of 'The Circus Animals' Desertion' makes the poem almost a re-writing of 'Lapis Lazuli', in
which Yeats's own all-too-fragile works of art are substituted
for Callimachus's handiworks (all destroyed) and the lapis
lazuli Chinamen. The Chinamen of 'Lapis Lazuli' seem to be
able to hold history at arm's length, safe in the refuge of their
gaiety; but the same forces that undermined Callimachus's
works are undermining the Chinamen:

> Every discoloration of the stone,
> Every accidental crack or dent,
> Seems a water-course or an avalanche,
> Or lofty slope where it still snows
> Though doubtless plum or cherry-branch
> Sweetens the little half-way house
> Those Chinamen climb towards, and I
> Delight to imagine them seated there;
> There, on the mountain and the sky,
> On all the tragic scene they stare.
> One asks for mournful melodies;
> Accomplished fingers begin to play.
> Their eyes mid many wrinkles, their eyes
> Their ancient, glittering eyes, are gay.[50]

The destruction of the stone becomes absorbed into the imaginative vision—indeed the beauty of the stone is heightened by the
discoloration, cracks, and dents; the Chinamen, who seem to take
such disinterested aesthetic pleasure in the devastation and re-
building of civilizations, finally must rejoice over their own destruction.

The similarity between 'Lapis Lazuli' and the old version of
'The Circus Animals' Desertion' even extends to the tragic
heroes presented in the middle sections of both poems: in the
former, Yeats explores the ability of men to cast themselves
unintentionally as tragic heroes (as he does, with modifications,
in 'Easter 1916' and 'Parnell's Funeral'), and in the latter Yeats
explains, in the reverse manner, how the experiences of tragic
heroes are rooted in common humanity. The tendency of Yeats's
mind to move towards war can be seen, not only in King Billy's

bomb-balls and the divine cannon, but in an early draft of Part III of 'Under Ben Bulben' as well:

> Before he can accomplish fate
> He recovers all his mind
> For an instant stand at ease
> Laughs aloud as though in peace.
> Let children should an airplane
> Some neighbouring city pavement stain
> Or the deadly cannon sound
> Catch their hands & dance in a round
> That passing moment makes it sweet
> When male & female organ meet. . . .[51]

Here is the same joy in destruction; if the 'passing moment makes it sweet', the sweetness springs from the transitoriness, as in 'The Two Kings'. The sudden transition to sexual intercourse suggests that the falling bombs rid the world of all that is not purely human; the explosions are as orgasmic, fecund, as they are destructive—indeed fecundity and destruction, according to 'Lapis Lazuli', are two halves of the same act. 'Where there is nothing, there is God', yet at the end of the draft of Part III of 'Under Ben Bulben' the bombs leave dancing children, explicit sexuality; and Part IV of the poem presents, through circuitous imagery, a God closely identified with the human sexual principle. The work of poets, sculptors, and painters is to 'Bring the soul of man to God';[52] and the scene immediately shifts to the Sistine Chapel, where Michelangelo's fresco shows the fingertip connection of the soul of man to God. But this stirs no holy thoughts in the bowels of the globe-trotting Madam, only sexual desire for the naked, sleepy-eyed Adam; she, like the girls who kissed the statue's face in 'The Statues', has been connected to a eugenic ideal; human teleology is the profanest sort of perfection, working not towards any abstract deity, only towards well-filled cradles.

The structure of the original version of 'The Circus Animals' Desertion' is almost exactly like the structure of Part I of the 'Introduction to *The Resurrection*', which moves from the myth of 'The Wanderings of Oisin' to the millennium of 'The Adoration of the Magi' to the abstractions of *On Baile's Strand* to the 'laughing, ecstatic destruction' of *Where There is Nothing*. The original 'Circus Animals' Desertion' provided a similar account of the intellectual history of Yeats's art, substituting only *The Countess Cathleen* for 'The Adoration of the Magi'; it did not end with a discussion of *Where There is Nothing*, but it did end with the same ecstatic destruction. Yet Yeats felt that there was something wrong about the stanza which concluded his poem on the note of tragic gaiety. Perhaps the clue to the new direction of Yeats's thoughts is in *Where There is Nothing*, at the end of Act IV, where Paul Ruttledge takes off his monk's habit and says, 'One by one I am plucking off the rags and tatters of the world'.[53] Yeats did not want to dismiss the rags and tatters of his threadbare art and sink into the night; he wanted instead to wallow in felt reality, in those remnants of his life that still had personal value:

> Those masterful images because complete
> Grew in pure mind, but out of what began?
> A mound of refuse or the sweepings of a street,
> Old kettles, old bottles, and a broken can,
> Old iron, old bones, old rags, that raving slut
> Who keeps the till. Now that my ladder's gone,
> I must lie down where all the ladders start,
> In the foul rag-and-bone shop of the heart.

At the end Yeats did not want the God of nowhere and nothing, a vacant transcendence, but instead was content with excremental reality; when the cannon-smoke of the cancelled stanza cleared away, only a devastated landscape remained. Having spent his mythopoeic life exploring the desolation of unreality, Yeats was now ready to embrace the 'desolation of reality'.[54] The oddity of Yeats's career is that he was never so close to naked reality, the foul rag-and-bone shop of his last correlative landscape, or the rabbit's agony of 'The Man and the Echo', as he was when about to die; and it is astonishing that Yeats wanted to put at the end of his last book a poem which dedicated a new beginning to his poetry, which promised an infinity of new poetic themes, new techniques, a rebirth. He prophesied that rebirth, perhaps, in 'A General Introduction for my Work' when he compared himself to the raving slut who keeps the till:

. . . I tried to make the language of poetry coincide with that of passionate, normal speech. I wanted to write in whatever language comes most naturally when we soliloquise, as I do all day long, upon the events of our own lives or of any life where we can see ourselves for the moment. I sometimes compare myself with the mad old slum women I hear denouncing and remembering. . . .[55]

I think he could have mined his new poetics too, except for that day in January, 1939, when Yeats superseded all his myths, created his death.

'The Circus Animals' Desertion' is an attempt to reconcile an antinomy: 1) art is art because it is not life; 2) no poet has any myth except autobiography. The thesis derives from Goethe, but has the force of Wilde's aesthetics and de l'Isle Adam's *Axël* behind it; and the antithesis as well is curiously associated with Wilde, with his dictum in 'The Critic as Artist' that criticism, the highest form of art, is autobiography. The whole circus metaphor suggests that art has nothing to do with life, that art is so evasive that it is almost nugatory; but the end of the poem indicates that a radical breakdown in the wall between life and art is occurring. The most remarkable aspect of the poem is its suggestion that the breakdown has been struggling to occur since the beginning of Yeats's career, that it is a continuously recurring process which keeps art honest, prevents it from veering into clownish sterility. The breakdown, however, is not only in the wall between life and art; it is a collapse of the analogical levels of reality as well.

The artist at the beginning lived in a world which was not our world. Yeats said in 'The Moods' (1895) that the artist 'belongs to the invisible life', and the impalpable, immeasurable, incomprehensible life as well.

. . . the only restraint he can obey is the mysterious instinct that has made him an artist, and that teaches him to discover immortal moods in mortal desires, an undecaying hope in our trivial ambitions, a divine love in sexual passion.[56]

The very core of Yeats's occultism was the message on Hermes' emerald tablet, which announced that the physical world was only a low analogue of the higher world; life is not in our control, for we enact in our daily lives a drama in which higher beings indifferently make use of our bodies for their sport. These higher beings have many names: the moods; the Sidhe of *The Wind Among the Reeds*; the gods of 'Rosa Alchemica'

who take possession of Michael Robartes and his friends, who
need human bodies to consummate an ecstatic dance before
casting the bodies away like so many 'hollow masks';[57] the
Gate-keepers of *Hodos Chameliontos* who have no meat and drink
but human passion, who 'through their dramatic power' bring
our souls to crisis, rejoice indifferently at Juliet's wedding and
Cleopatra's death;[58] and the invisible hypnotist of *Estrangement*
who holds civilization together with his 'artificially created
illusions'.[59] All men are under their control but it is the artist's
business to become the most sensitive vehicle for the transmis-
sion of ultimate truth, prophecy, or those emotions which,
according to the doctrine of the moods, have an inhuman referent. This is partly responsible for Yeats's interest in the
mediumistic trance:

. . . I am full of uncertainty, not knowing when I am the finger, when
the clay. Once, twenty years ago, I seemed to awake from sleep to find
my body rigid, and to hear a strange voice speaking these words through
my lips as through lips of stone : 'We make an image of him who sleeps,
and it is not he who sleeps, and we call it Emmanuel.'[60]

By the time of *A Vision* the drama of human life has reduced
its scale to a *Commedia dell'Arte*,[61] and the stage-manager is not
a higher alien being but the Daimon, the higher version of the
human, the ultimate self which moves through each reincarnative state. This humanizing shows the increasing *rapprochement*
of the analogical levels; and in Yeats's later career the forces
which control the huge drama of history, as well as the small
drama of individual life, begin to seem more pleasant in aspect:

History seems to me a human drama, keeping the classical unities by
the clear division of its epochs, turning one way or the other because
this man hates or that man loves. Had any trade question at the opening
of the eighteenth century as great an effect on subsequent history as
Bolingbroke's impotence and Harley's slowness and secrecy ? Was the
French Revolution caused by the peasants' poverty or by that which
used it ? The peasant had been poor for centuries. Yet the drama has its
plot, and this plot ordains character and passions and exists for their
sake.[62]

The form of history at first seems determined by human provo-
cations, but that is not an adequate description: it is the plot
that is the given, and that plot 'ordains character and passions';

still, there is a certain friendliness about a plot which exists *for the sake* of those same characters and passions. At one point in the 'Introduction to *Fighting the Waves*', it seems that the controlling forces will always be wholly alien: science can only prove 'the poverty of the human intellect, that we are lost amid alien intellects, near but incomprehensible, more incomprehensible than the most distant stars'.[63] Yet, since Yeats is always anxious to show the futility of science, as opposed to other modes of cognition, I believe that the key word in that passage is 'near'; but only in one poem, 'Whence Had They Come?', do we see how near the forces can actually come to us:

Eternity is passion, girl or boy
Cry at the onset of their sexual joy
'For ever and for ever'; then awake
Ignorant what Dramatis Personae spake;
A passion-driven exultant man sings out
Sentences that he has never thought;
The Flagellant lashes those submissive loins
Ignorant what that dramatist enjoins,
What master made the lash. Whence had they come,
The hand and lash that beat down frigid Rome?
What sacred drama through her body heaved
When world-transforming Charlemagne was conceived?[64]

The forces, who seemed such alien intellects in the 'Introduction to *Fighting the Waves*', have become wholly immanent in the ordinary lovers; the strength of any incarnation can be measured by seeing how low it goes, and here the forces have reached their human nadir. Any incarnation is a collapse of analogical levels, at least momentarily, and this poem suggests that the flux of common life is perpetually incarnational, an undistorted response to the will of the forces. The persistence of the incarnation is as remarkable as its vulgarity; by contrast, the gods of 'Rosa Alchemica' descended only in holy ritual, and only for a short time. The lovers are ignorant, just as science found the forces incomprehensible; but that is because the forces are so close, so pervasive, that it is as difficult to be conscious of them as it is to be conscious of air; and the strings by which the forces manipulate us are not external but inside us, our own sexual desires. Indeed the forces of this poem correspond to the Gate-keepers, Sidhe, and moods of Yeats's earlier mythology roughly as the sexual principle of 'Under Ben Bulben' corresponds to a transcendental god. The analogical breakdown is clearest when Charlemagne's incarnation is compared to that of, say, 'Leda and the Swan'. Charlemagne has always been somewhat embarrassing to Yeats scholars: there is the recalcitrant historical fact that he was born over two hundred years before the millennium he is supposed to incarnate, according to *A Vision*; and he does not seem quite the same sort of creature as Christ or Leda's egg or the rough beast. I believe, however, that being undisputably human he is a most satisfactory incarnational figure for Yeats's secularized historical force. The 'sacred drama' of his conception obeys the classical unities but will not have any *deus ex machina* scenes; the playwright must keep himself concealed, internalized, Zeus swallowed by Leda.

The lovers in 'Whence Had They Come?' are 'Dramatis Personae', and *Dramatis Personae, 1896–1902* is the title of a long section of Yeats's *Autobiographies*. The volume called the *Autobiographies*, no matter how judiciously compiled, would be a fragmented work; the individual fragments are, however, coherent, fiercely organized. *Dramatis Personae, 1896–1902* begins with a strong tension between opposites, as Yeats starts arranging his friends into dialectical patterns: 'Moore and Martyn were indeed in certain characteristics typical peasants, the peasant sinner, the peasant saint'[65]—and they were the original persons in Yeats's drama *The Cat and the Moon*. The two peasant friends are, of course, balanced by the more noble characters of that six-year period, Yeats himself for one; when Moore and Yeats collaborate on *Diarmuid and Grania*, Yeats is the poet, Moore the 'realist'.[66] In this manner *Dramatis Personae, 1896–1902* proceeds, providing not only accounts of the mechanics of writing plays, but accounts of the dramatic form of life itself; the tendency of the fragment is so literary that Yeats records how he liked to imagine himself as a character in a book, 'a Parsifal, Tristram, Don Quixote'.[67] If in certain of Yeats's later poems the form of the poem is autobiographical, we see in Yeats's prose how the form of his autobiography is poetical; in this way life and art interpenetrate.

Yeats's later treatment of symbols and metaphors shows another aspect of analogical breakdown. For the young Yeats 'the gross is the shadow of the subtle',[68] and never more than a shadow, and as late as the 1920s Yeats had a strong sense that the symbol and what it symbolizes are quite distinct; for instance, Michael Robartes declares in the prefatory section of *A Vision*, 'The marriage bed is the symbol of the solved antinomy, and were more than symbol could a man there lose and keep his identity, but he falls asleep.'[69] And in *Dramatis Personae, 1896–1902* Yeats suggests that the Irish masses who rioted at *The Countess Cathleen* were guilty of not fully distinguishing the symbolic from the real: '. . . the disturbances were in part my own fault. In using what I considered traditional symbols I forgot that in Ireland they are not symbols but realities.'[70] In the earliest stages of Yeats's career the purpose of the symbol was to draw man upward towards the divine; in the last stages it clatters loudly to earth. As the phase-fifteen dancer turns into an insane girl with a broken knee-cap, the symbolic becomes swallowed in the physical; the metaphoric tenor becomes lost in the metaphoric vehicle:

> Processions that lack high stilts have nothing that catches the eye.
> What if my great-grandad had a pair that were twenty foot high,
> And mine were but fifteen foot, no modern stalks upon higher,
> Some rogue of the world stole them to patch up a fence or a fire.
> Because piebald ponies, led bears, caged lions, make but
> poor shows,
> Because children demand Daddy-long-legs upon his timber toes,
> Because women in the upper storeys demand a face at the pane,
> That patching old heels they may shriek, I take to chisel and plane.
>
> Malachi Stilt-Jack am I, whatever I learned has run wild,
> From collar to collar, from stilt to stilt, from father to child.
> All metaphor, Malachi, stilts and all. A barnacle goose
> Far up in the stretches of night; night splits and the dawn
> breaks loose;
> I, through the terrible novelty of light, stalk on, stalk on;
> Those great sea-horses bare their teeth and laugh at the dawn.[71]

'High Talk' presents the problems of 'The Circus Animals' Desertion' on the historical level instead of the personal; the stilts keep shrinking, not because of the poet's own revelation but because the highest symbolic poetry is impossible in this stage of the historical gyre. The appetite for the grand manner still exists, although it too is much deformed, only ladies wishing to find a voyeur at the window; so the poet quixotically

returns to 'chisel and plane' to make more stilts. It is clearly
futile, for the modern era does not permit the balance, the
aesthetic equilibrium which makes such a delicate feat as stilt-
walking possible: metaphors decay rapidly because there is no
coherent world-view in the twentieth century to give them sub-
stantiality: the 'led bears, caged lions' are all too tame, clois-
tered, regressive, trivial, while the modern poet's craft has 'run
wild'. So in the last four lines the poem tears itself apart: the
Stilt-Jack was a thin fiction for Yeats himself, but it is simultaneously too thin and too fictive; it was an exercise in an out-
moded poetics, so he dismisses it, 'All metaphor, Malachi,
stilts and all', lets the stilt-walker lurch into chaos. And the poem
ends in a wilderness of metaphors which have stiffened into
meaninglessness because they lack referents—an impressive,
calculated incoherence.

'High Talk' and 'The Circus Animals' Desertion' both suggest modes in which the poet can make a new start; but they are
both farewells to art as well. It is always interesting when a
poet says goodbye to his technical art: 'Farewell sweet phrases,
lovely metaphors'. Thus George Herbert resigned himself to
simpler declarations of his love of God as his *Temple* neared
completion. Yeats resigned himself, not to God, but to a world
without artifice, the wild thickness of things:

> Not such as are in Newton's metaphor,
> But actual shells of Rosses' level shore.[72]

But of course the shells mean more because they are contractions
of metaphors than they would have meant if they had been simple
deposits of calcium carbonate. So Yeats finally moved through a
world where all metaphors had collapsed, all flame had become
fuel—where the masks that he had created to speak his poetry
had no recognizable form but that of his own face.

Bibliography

Adams, Hazard. 'Yeats' Country of the Young,' *PMLA*, LXXII (1957), 510–19.

Alspach, Russell K. *Irish Poetry from the English Invasion to 1798*. Philadelphia: University of Pennsylvania Press, 1959.

—. 'Some Sources of Yeats's *The Wanderings of Oisin*,' *PMLA*, LVIII (1943), 849–66.

Bachchan, Harbans Rai. *W. B. Yeats and Occultism*. Delhi: Motilal Banarsidass, 1965.

Berryman, Charles. *W. B. Yeats: Design of Opposites*. New York: Exposition Press, 1967.

Beum, Robert. *The Poetic Art of William Butler Yeats*. New York: Frederick Ungar Publishing Co., 1969.

Blake, William. *The Poetry and Prose of William Blake*, ed. David V. Erdman. Garden City: Doubleday and Co., 1965.

Blavatsky, Helene Petrovna. *Isis Unveiled*. New York: J. W. Bouton, 1877.

Bloom, Harold. *Yeats*. New York: Oxford University Press, 1970.

Bradford, Curtis B. *Yeats at Work*. Carbondale: Southern Illinois University Press, 1965.

—. *Yeats's* Last Poems *Again*. Dublin: The Dolmen Press, 1966

Bridge, Ursula, ed. *W. B. Yeats and T. Sturge Moore, Their Correspondence, 1901–37*. New York: Oxford University Press, 1953.

Clark, David R. 'Poussin and Yeats' "News for the Delphic Oracle,"' *Wascana Review*, 2, i (1967), 33–44.

—. *W. B. Yeats and the Theater of Desolate Reality*. Chester Springs: Dufour Editions, Inc., 1965.

Donoghue, Denis, and J. R. Mulryne, ed. *An Honoured Guest*. London: Edward Arnold, 1965.

Ellmann, Richard. *The Identity of Yeats*. New York: Oxford University Press, 1954.

—. *Yeats: The Man and the Masks*. New York: The Macmillan Co., 1948.

—. 'Yeats without Analogue,' *Kenyon Review*, XXVI (1964), 30–47.

Engelberg, Edward. *The Vast Design: Patterns in W. B. Yeats's Aesthetic.* Toronto: University of Toronto Press, 1964.

Garab, A. M. *Beyond Byzantium: The Last Phase of Yeats's Career.* The Northern Illinois University Press, 1969.

Gregory, I. A. P. *Cuchulain of Muirthemne.* London: John Murray, 1911.

—. *Gods and Fighting Men.* New York: Charles Scribner's Sons, 1904.

—, ed. *Ideals in Ireland.* London: At the Unicorn, 1901.

Gwynn, Stephen, ed. *Scattering Branches.* London: Macmillan & Co. Ltd., 1940.

Hall, James, and Martin Steinmann, ed. *The Permanence of Yeats.* New York: Collier Books, 1961.

Henn, Thomas R. *The Lonely Tower: Studies in the Poetry of W. B. Yeats.* London: Methuen & Co. Ltd., 1965.

Hoare, Dorothy M. *The Works of Morris and of Yeats in Relation to Early Saga Literature.* London: Cambridge University Press, 1937.

Hoffman, Daniel. *Barbarous Knowledge: Myth in the Poetry of Yeats, Graves, and Muir.* New York: Oxford University Press, 1967.

Homer. *The Iliad of Homer,* trans. Richmond Lattimore. Chicago: The University of Chicago Press, 1962.

—. *The Odyssey of Homer,* trans. Richmond Lattimore. New York: Harper and Row, 1965.

Hone, Joseph. *W. B. Yeats 1865–1939.* London: Macmillan & Co. Ltd., 1965.

Jeffares, A. Norman. *A Commentary on the Collected Poems of W. B. Yeats.* London: Macmillan & Co. Ltd., 1968.

—. *W. B. Yeats: Man and Poet.* London: Routledge & Kegan Paul Ltd., 1949.

—, and K. G. W. Cross, ed. *In Excited Reverie.* London: Macmillan & Co. Ltd., 1965.

Johnson, Lionel Pigot. *The Complete Poems of Lionel Johnson,* ed. Iain Fletcher. London: The Unicorn Press, 1953.

Koch, Vivienne. *W. B. Yeats: The Tragic Phase.* Baltimore: The Johns Hopkins Press, 1951.

MacNeice, Louis. *The Poetry of W. B. Yeats.* London: Oxford University Press, 1941.

Melchiori, Giorgio. *The Whole Mystery of Art.* London: Routledge & Kegan Paul Ltd., 1960.

Miller, Joseph Hillis. *Poets of Reality.* Cambridge, Mass.: Belknap Press of Harvard University, 1965.

Miller, Liam, ed. *The Dolmen Press Centenary Papers.* Dublin: The Dolmen Press, 1968.

Milton, John. *Complete Poems and Major Prose,* ed. Merritt Y. Hughes. New York: The Odyssey Press, 1957.

Moore, Virginia. *The Unicorn: William Butler Yeats' Search for Reality*. New York: The Macmillan Co., 1954.

Morris, William. *The Collected Works of William Morris*. 24 vols. London: Longmans Green and Company, 1913.

Nathan, Leonard E. *The Tragic Drama of William Butler Yeats*. New York: Columbia University Press, 1965.

Oshima, Shotaro. *W. B. Yeats and Japan*. Tokyo: The Hokuseido Press, 1965.

Parkinson, Thomas. *W. B. Yeats: The Later Poetry*. Berkeley: University of California Press, 1964.

—. *W. B. Yeats: Self-Critic*. Berkeley: University of California Press, 1951.

Plotinus, *The Enneads*, trans. Stephen MacKenna, revised by B. S. Page. New York: Pantheon Books Inc., 1957.

Pound, Ezra. *The Cantos, 1–95*. New York: New Directions Publishing Corp., 1956.

—. *Drafts and Fragments of Cantos CX–CXVII*. New York: New Directions Publishing Corp., 1968.

Rajan, Balachandra. *W. B. Yeats: A Critical Introduction*. London: Hutchinson University Library, 1965.

Reid, Forrest. *W. B. Yeats: A Critical Study*. London: Martin Secker, 1915.

Rhys, Sir John. *Lectures on the Origin and Growth of Religion as illustrated by Celtic Heathendom*. London: William and Norgate, 1888.

Roberts, The Rev. Alexander, and James Donaldson, ed. *The Ante-Nicene Fathers*. 10 vols. Grand Rapids: Wm. B. Eerdmans Publishing Co.

Rousley, Joseph. *Yeats's Autobiography: Life as Symbolic Pattern*. Cambridge, Mass.: Harvard University Press, 1968.

Saul, George Brandon. *Prolegomena to the Study of Yeats's Poems*. Philadelphia: University of Pennsylvania Press, 1957.

Schopenhauer, Arthur. *The World as Will and Representation*, trans. E. F. J. Payne. 2 vols. New York: Dover Publications, Inc., 1966.

Seiden, Morton Irving. 'A Psychoanalytical Essay on William Butler Yeats,' *Accent*, VI (1946), 178–90.

—. *William Butler Yeats: The Poet as a Mythmaker 1865–1939*. Michigan State University Press, 1962.

Sinnett, A. P. *Esoteric Buddhism*. Boston: Houghton, Mifflin, and Company, 1887.

Skelton, Robin, and Ann Saddlemyer, ed. *The World of W. B. Yeats: Essays in Perspective*. Seattle: University of Washington Press, 1965.

Spenser, Edmund. *The Works of Edmund Spenser*, ed. Edwin Greenlaw, Charles Grosvenor Osgood, and Frederick Morgan Padelford. 6 vols. Baltimore: The Johns Hopkins Press, 1938.

Stallworthy, Jon. *Between the Lines: Yeats's Poetry in the Making*. Oxford at the Clarendon Press, 1963.

—. *Vision and Revision in Yeats's* Last Poems. Oxford at the Clarendon Press, 1969.

Stauffer, Donald A. *The Golden Nightingale*. New York: The Macmillan Co., 1949.

Stevens, Wallace. *The Collected Poems from Wallace Stevens*. New York: Alfred A. Knopf, 1956.

Tennyson, Alfred. *Poems and Plays*. London: Oxford University Press, 1965.

The Ten Principal Upanishads, trans. Shree Purohit Swami and W. B. Yeats. London: Faber and Faber Ltd., 1938.

Torchiana, Donald T. *W. B. Yeats & Georgian Ireland*. Evanston: Northwestern University Press, 1966.

Ure, Peter. *Towards a Mythology: Studies in the Poetry of W. B. Yeats*. London: University Press of Liverpool, 1946.

Vendler, Helen H. 'Yeats's Changing Metaphors for the Other World,' *Modern Drama*, VII (1964), 308–21.

—. *Yeats's Vision and the Later Plays*. Cambridge, Mass.: Harvard University Press, 1963.

Whitaker, Thomas R. *Swan and Shadow: Yeats's Dialogue with History*. Chapel Hill: University of North Carolina Press, 1964.

Wilson, Francis Alexander Charles. *W. B. Yeats and Tradition*. New York: The Macmillan Co., 1958.

—. *Yeats's Iconography*. London: Victor Gollancz Ltd., 1960.

Yeats, William Butler. *Autobiographies*. London: Macmillan & Co. Ltd., 1955.

—. *The Celtic Twilight*. London: A . H. Bullen, 1902.

—. *The Collected Plays of W. B. Yeats*. London: Macmillan & Co. Ltd., 2nd edn., 1952.

—. *The Collected Poems of W. B. Yeats*. London: Macmillan & Co. Ltd., 2nd edn., 1950.

—. *Essays and Introductions*. London: Macmillan & Co. Ltd., 1961.

—. *Explorations*. London: Macmillan & Co. Ltd., 1962.

—. *Irish Fairy & Folk Tales*. London: The Walter Scott Publishing Co. Ltd.

—. *John Sherman & Dhoya*, ed. Richard J. Finneran. Detroit: Wayne State University Press, 1969.

—. *The Letters of W. B. Yeats*, ed. Allan Wade. London: Rupert Hart-Davis Ltd., 1953.

—. *Letters on Poetry from W. B. Yeats to Dorothy Wellesley*. London: Oxford University Press, 1964.

—. *Letters to Katharine Tynan*, ed. Roger McHugh, New York: McMullen Books, Inc., 1953.

—. *Mythologies*. London: Macmillan & Co. Ltd., 1959.

—. *The Secret Rose*. London: Lawrence & Bullen Ltd., 1897.

—. *The Senate Speeches of W. B. Yeats*, ed. Donald R. Pearce. Blooming-ton: Indiana University Press. 1960.

—. *The Tables of the Law; & The Adoration of the Magi*. Stratford-upon-Avon: The Shakespeare Head Press, 1914.

—. *The Variorum Edition of the Plays of W. B. Yeats*, ed. Russell K. Alspach. London: Macmillan & Co. Ltd., 1966.

—. *The Variorum Edition of the Poems of W. B. Yeats*, ed. Peter Allt and Russell K. Alspach. London: Macmillan & Co. Ltd., 1957.

—. *A Vision*. London: Macmillan & Co. Ltd., revised edn., 1962.

—, ed. *The Oxford Book of Modern Verse, 1892–1935*. Oxford at the Clarendon Press, 1936.

Zwerdling, Alex. *Yeats and the Heroic Ideal*. New York: New York University Press, 1965.

Notes

Page references are to the English edition of Yeats's works.

Chapter 1

1 W. B. Yeats, *Autobiographies* (*The Bounty of Sweden*, II), pp. 532–3.

2 *Autobiographies* (*Reveries*, XXIV), p. 87.

3 W. B. Yeats, *Explorations*, p. 300.

4 *The Collected Poems of W. B. Yeats*, p. 218.

5 W. B. Yeats, *Essays and Introductions*, p. 138.

6 W. B. Yeats, *Mythologies*, p. 346.

7 *Essays and Introductions*, p. 394.

8 W. B. Yeats, *A Vision*, p. 24.

9 *Mythologies*, p. 342.

10 *Autobiographies* (*Estrangement*, XLII), pp. 486–7.

11 'Her Vision in the Wood', *Collected Poems*, p. 312.

12 Donald Torchiana, *W. B. Yeats & Georgian Ireland*, p. 306. The passage is part of a discussion of Yeats's source for the episode, Sir Jonah Barrington's *Recollections;* the relevant incident in Barrington is quoted in A. Norman Jeffares, *A Commentary on the Collected Poems of W. B. Yeats*, pp. 259–60.

13 *Mythologies*, p. 26.

14 *Mythologies*, p. 28.

15 *Mythologies*, p. 28.

16 *Mythologies*, p. 23.

17 *Mythologies*, p. 29.

18 *Mythologies*, pp. 24–5.

19 *Mythologies*, p. 25.

20 'Her Vision in the Wood', *Collected Poems*, p. 313.

21 *Mythologies*, p. 28.

22 *Essays and Introductions*, pp. 277–8.

23 'Meditations in Time of Civil War', *Collected Poems*, p. 228.

24 *Explorations*, p. 451.

25 *Explorations*, pp. 24–5.

26 *Collected Poems*, p. 393.

27 Yeats also quotes this line from Nash as an example of beautiful symbolic poetry in 'The Symbolism of Poetry', *Essays and Introductions*, p. 156.

28 *Explorations*, pp. 202–3.

29 *Essays and Introductions*, p. 43.

30 *Essays and Introductions*, pp. 298–9.

31 *Mythologies*, pp. 228–30.

32 *Mythologies*, p. 229.

33 *Mythologies*, p. 230.

34 *Mythologies*, p. 221.

35 *Mythologies*, p. 112.

36 *Mythologies*, p. 337.

37 *Mythologies*, pp. 259–60.

38 *Mythologies*, p. 259.

39 *Mythologies*, pp. 336–7.

40 W. B. Yeats, *The Secret Rose*, p. 139.

41 *Mythologies*, p. 240.

42 *Mythologies*, p. 243.

43 'Under Ben Bulben', *Collected Poems*, p. 400.

44 'The Man and the Echo', *Collected Poems*, p. 394.

45 *Mythologies*, p. 354.

46 *Collected Plays*, p. 291.

47 *Collected Plays*, p. 441.

48 'Vacillation', *Collected Poems*, p. 284.

49 *Collected Poems*, p. 167.

50 'Blood and the Moon', *Collected Poems*, p. 268.

51 *Collected Plays*, p. 143.

52 *Explorations*, p. 20.

53 *Essays and Introductions*, p. 407.

54 *Essays and Introductions*, p. 403.
55 *Essays and Introductions*, p. 406.
56 *Explorations*, p. 320.
57 For example, see *Essays and Introductions*, p. 40.
58 William Blake, *Jerusalem*, 98: 28–36.
59 Quoted in Yeats's note to 'The Tower', *Collected Poems*, p. 533.
60 *Essays and Introductions*, p. 157.
61 *Ante-Nicene Fathers*, ed. the Rev. Alexander Roberts and James Donaldson, vol. I, p. 321.
62 *Collected Poems*, p. 285.
63 *Essays and Introductions*, p. 483.
64 *Explorations*, pp. 353–4.
65 *Explorations*, p. 434.
66 *Autobiographies* (*Dramatis Personae*, xv), p. 435.
67 *W. B. Yeats and T. Sturge Moore, Their Correspondence 1901–1937*, ed. Ursula Bridge, p. 73.
68 *Mythologies*, pp. 354–5.
69 Yeats admitted Schopenhauer's influence—especially that of the third book of *The World as Will and Idea*—in his 1930 Diary (*Explorations*, p. 303): 'Certain abstract thinkers, whose measurements and classifications continually bring me back to concrete reality—the third book of *The World as Will and Idea*, Coleridge at Highgate.'
70 Arthur Schopenhauer, *The World as Will and Representation*, vol. I, pp. 198–9.
71 'Memory', *Collected Poems*, p. 168.
72 *Mythologies*, pp. 359 and 356.
73 *Essays and Introductions*, pp. 394–5.
74 *Mythologies*, p. 359.
75 'Blood and the Moon', *Collected Poems*, p. 269.
76 W. B. Yeats, 'The Literary Movement in Ireland', *Ideals in Ireland*, ed. Lady Gregory, p. 93.
77 *Mythologies*, p. 30.
78 *Essays and Introductions*, p. 291.
79 *Mythologies*, p. 332.
80 *Collected Poems*, p. 45.

Chapter 2

1 'Sunday Morning', *The Collected Poems of Wallace Stevens*, p. 69.
2 See *The Oxford Book of Modern Verse, 1892–1935*, chosen by W. B. Yeats, p. xxxvi
3 *Collected Poems*, p. 218.
4 *Collected Plays*, p. 129.
5 *A Vision*, pp. 273–4.
6 *W. B. Yeats and T. Sturge Moore*, p. 162.
7 *W. B. Yeats and T. Sturge Moore*, p. 164.
8 *Collected Poems*, p. 281.
9 Helen H. Vendler, *Yeats's Vision and the Later Plays*, p. 117.
10 *Explorations*, p. 378.
11 See 'The Delphic Oracle upon Plotinus', *Collected Poems*, p. 306.
12 *Essays and Introductions*, p. 306.
13 *Autobiographies* (*The Death of Synge*, xiii), p. 508.
14 E.g., *W. B. Yeats: Letters to Katharine Tynan*, ed. Roger McHugh, p. 67.
15 E.g., *The Letters of W. B. Yeats*, ed. Allen Wade, p. 798.
16 *Explorations*, pp. 392–3.
17 *Explorations*, p. 400.
18 *Explorations*, pp. 402–3.
19 *W. B. Yeats and T. Sturge Moore*, p. 154.
20 *W. B. Yeats and T. Sturge Moore*, p. 153.
21 *A Vision*, p. 262.
22 *Explorations*, p. 401.
23 *Explorations*, p. 403.
24 Richard Ellmann, *The Identity of Yeats*, p. 19.
25 Thomas R. Whitaker, *Swan and Shadow*, p. 27.
26 *Variorum Poems*, p. 796.
27 *Variorum Plays*, p. 1198.
28 *Variorum Plays*, p. 44.
29 'The Wanderings of Oisin', *Collected Poems*, p. 431.
30 For a discussion of the sources, see Russell K. Alspach's article in *PMLA* 58, p. 850.
31 I quote here from Arthur Symons' elegant mistranslation, which Yeats himself quotes in *Autobiographies* (*The Tragic Generation*, xi), p. 321.
32 W. B. Yeats, *John Sherman & Dhoya*, ed. Richard J. Finneran, pp. 120 and 122.

33 *Explorations*, p. 392.
34 *Variorum Poems*, p. 807.
35 *Variorum Poems*, p. 807.
36 I have quoted from the less obscure 1889 version (see *Variorum Poems*, p. 47).
37 *Collected Poems*, p. 68
38 *Variorum Poems*, p. 177.
39 According to 'He Thinks of his Past Greatness When a Part of the Constellations of Heaven', originally 'Mongan Thinks of his Past Greatness. . . .' (*Variorum Poems*, p. 177).
40 *Variorum Poems*, p. 807.
41 *Collected Poems*, p. 313.
42 *Collected Plays*, pp. 633–4.
43 *Collected Plays*, p. 635.
44 *Collected Plays*, p. 636.
45 *Collected Plays*, p. 638.
46 *Collected Plays*, p. 639.
47 *Collected Plays*, p. 634.
48 *Collected Poems*, p. 293.
49 *Essays and Introductions*, p. 472.
50 *Explorations*, pp. 21–2.
51 This is clear from the passage on Raphael's madonna, cited above, from *Essays and Introductions*, p. 472.
52 From an early draft of the opening lyric, printed in *Letters of W. B. Yeats*, p. 817.
53 *Letters of W. B. Yeats*, p. 817.
54 F. A. C. Wilson, *W. B. Yeats and Tradition*, p. 85.
55 *Letters of W. B. Yeats*, p. 817.
56 *John Sherman & Dhoya*, p. 53.
57 *John Sherman & Dhoya*, pp. 46–7.
58 *Collected Poems*, p. 197.
59 'Demon and Beast', *Collected Poems*, p. 209.
60 *Collected Poems*, p. 135.
61 See *Autobiographies* (*Four Years*, XVIII), p. 171.
62 *Autobiographies* (*Reveries*, IX), p. 47.
63 *Letters to Katharine Tynan*, p. 68.
64 *Explorations*, p. 18.
65 *Collected Poems*, p. 37.
66 *Variorum Plays*, p. 1285.
67 'Demon and Beast', *Collected Poems*, p. 210.
68 *Autobiographies* (*Four Years*, XII), pp. 141–2.
69 *Autobiographies* (*The Tragic Generation*, VI and IX), p. 307, pp. 313–14.

70 Lionel Pigot Johnson, *The Complete Poems of Lionel Johnson*, ed. Iain Fletcher, p. 67, or *The Oxford Book of Modern Verse*, pp. 106–7.
71 *A Vision*, p. 274.
72 *Autobiographies* (*The Tragic Generation*, VIII), pp. 310–11.
73 *Autobiographies* (*The Tragic Generation*, VII), p. 310.
74 See, for example, Richard Ellmann, *Yeats: The Man and the Mask*, p. 50, and the psychoanalytic theory of *The Wanderings of Oisin* posited in Morton I. Seidman's 'A Psychoanalytical Essay on William Butler Yeats', *Accent* VI, pp. 178–90.
75 *Autobiographies* (*The Tragic Generation*, IX), p. 313.
76 The phrase is from a cancelled stanza of 'The Circus Animals' Desertion'; see Stallworthy, *Between the Lines*, p. 221.
77 *Letters to Katharine Tynan*, p. 67.
78 For the source of the bell-branch, see Russell K. Alspach, *PMLA* 58, p. 864.
79 *Variorum Plays*, p. 1286.
80 *Variorum Poems*, p. 794.
81 *Variorum Poems*, p. 795.
82 'The Choice', *Collected Poems*, p. 278.
83 *Collected Plays*, p. 45.
84 Ezra Pound, *Cantos 1–95, The Pisan Cantos*, p. 99.
85 Ezra Pound, *Drafts and Fragments of Cantos CX–CXVII*, p. 23.

Chapter 3

1 'News for the Delphic Oracle', *Collected Poems*, p. 376.
2 *W. B. Yeats and T. Sturge Moore*, p. 143.
3 *W. B. Yeats and Tradition*, pp. 216–23.
4 *The Iliad of Homer*, trans. Richard Lattimore, Book XIV, lines 346–52, p. 303.
5 *Essays and Introductions*, pp. 134–5. Yeats's quotation from Homer is from *Odyssey*, VIII, line 1248.
6 *Essays and Introductions*, p. 194.
7 *Essays and Introductions*, p. 194.
8 'Among School Children', *Collected Poems*, p. 244.

9 *The Letters of W. B. Yeats*, p. 719.

10 *Essays and Introductions*, p. 440–1.

11 H. P. Blavatsky, *Isis Unveiled*, p. xvi.

12 *Collected Poems*, p. 375.

13 *Explorations*, p. 451.

14 *Collected Plays*, pp. 111–12. Yeats probably discovered the idea from a passage in Wilde's 'The Decay of Lying', according to which Greek brides kept a statue of Hermes or Apollo in their bedchamber in order to bear children as lovely as the images on which they gazed.

15 *Explorations*, pp. 434–5.

16 *Explorations*, pp. 435–6.

17 *Explorations*, p. 433.

18 *Autobiographies* (*The Death of Synge*, XL), p. 526.

19 *The Enneads* (Ennead V, Tractate 8), p. 429.

20 *Explorations*, p. 305.

21 *Explorations*, pp. 309–10.

22 *Variorum Poems*, p. 826.

23 *Explorations*, p. 396. The same idea is found in *A Vision*, p. 247, where Yeats says, 'Plotinus thought that every individual had his idea, his eternal counterpart'.

24 *Explorations*, p. 368.

25 *The Enneads*, p. 428.

26 *Explorations*, pp. 397 and 398.

27 *Explorations*, p. 307.

28 *A Vision*, p. 280.

29 *The Enneads*, p. 422.

30 *The Enneads*, p. 423.

31 *The Enneads*, p. 206.

32 *The Enneads*, p. 63.

33 *Autobiographies* (*The Bounty of Sweden*, XIII), p. 555.

34 *Collected Poems*, p. 306.

35 *Explorations*, p. 373.

36 *Explorations*, pp. 449–50.

37 See *A Vision*, p. 232, and *Explorations*, p. 307.

38 *The Enneads* (Ennead III, Tractate 6), p. 209.

39 *Explorations*, p. 438.

40 *Explorations*, p. 440.

41 *Collected Plays*, p. 307.

42 *Mythologies*, p. 270.

43 See *A Vision*, p. 226.

44 *Essays and Introductions*, p. 366.

45 *Essays and Introductions*, p. 370.

46 *Essays and Introductions*, p. 59.

47 William Morris, *The Water of the Wondrous Isles*, *The Collected Works of William Morris*, Vol. XX, p. 90.

48 *Essays and Introductions*, pp. 60–1.

49 *Essays and Introductions*, p. 53.

50 *Essays and Introductions*, p. 63.

51 'Wisdom', *Collected Poems*, p. 246.

52 Cf. 'The soft, domesticated Christ' mentioned in *Explorations*, p. 434.

53 *John Sherman & Dhoya*, p. 102.

54 Thomas R. Henn, *The Lonely Tower*, p. 249.

55 *The Identity of Yeats*, p. 285.

56 *Cantos 1–95, A Draft of XXX Cantos*, p. 77 or *The Oxford Book of Modern Verse*, pp. 244–5.

57 *Cantos 1–95, A Draft of XXX Cantos*, p. 78.

58 *Cantos 1–95, A Draft of XXX Cantos*, p. 76.

59 *The Odyssey of Homer*, trans. Richmond Lattimore, Book XXIV, lines 73–9, 85–92, p. 347.

60 *Collected Poems*, p. 301.

61 *Variorum Poems*, p. 678.

62 *Collected Poems*, pp. 469–70.

Chapter 4

1 *Mythologies*, p. 310.

2 *Explorations*, p. 150.

3 *Explorations*, p. 393.

4 *Variorum Plays*, p. 1158.

5 *Variorum Plays*, pp. 1136–7.

6 *A Vision*, p. 302.

7 *W. B. Yeats and T. Sturge Moore*, p. 86.

8 *A Vision*, p. 300.

9 *Explorations*, p. 311.

10 *Explorations*, p. 312.

11 *Explorations*, pp. 312–3.

12 *Explorations*, p. 336.

13 *Explorations*, p. 437.

14 *Explorations*, p. 404.

15 *Collected Poems*, p. 519.

16 *Explorations*, p. 374.

17 *Explorations*, p. 399.

18 *W. B. Yeats and T. Sturge Moore*, p. 154.

19 *Explorations*, p. 369.

20 'Politics', *Collected Poems*, pp. 392–3.

21 Jon Stallworthy, *Vision and Revision in Yeats's Last Poems*, p. 73.

22 'The Circus Animals' Desertion',
Collected Poems, p. 391.
23 *Variorum Poems*, p. 742.
24 *Variorum Poems*, p. 743.
25 *Collected Poems*, p. 462.
26 *Collected Poems*, p. 460.
27 'The Two Kings', *Collected Poems*,
pp. 508–9.
28 *Collected Poems*, p. 509.
29 'A Bronze Head', *Collected Poems*, p.
382.
30 *Collected Plays*, p. 24.
31 *Collected Plays*, p. 40.
32 *Autobiographies* (*Dramatis Personae*,
xiv), p. 431.
33 *Collected Plays*, p. 17.
34 *Collected Plays*, p. 19.
35 *Collected Plays*, p. 316.
36 *Essays and Introductions*, pp. 271–2.
37 *Autobiographies* (*Estrangement*, xvii),
p. 468.
38 *Explorations*, p. 393.
39 *Collected Plays*, pp. 259 and 260.
40 *Collected Plays*, p. 271.
41 *Collected Plays*, p. 263.
42 *Autobiographies* (*The Death of Synge*,
xxxiv), p. 522.
43 *Explorations*, pp. 153–4.
44 *Explorations*, p. 416.
45 *Collected Plays*, pp. 641–2.
46 See Ellmann, *Yeats: the Man and the
Mask*, p. 79.
47 The story of the poem's development
is told in Curtis B. Bradford's *Yeats
at Work*, p. 154–67, but I quote Jon
Stallworthy's transcription (*Between
the Lines*, p. 221) because I prefer
'un-imaged' to Bradford's 'un-

imagined' for thematic reasons.
48 *Explorations*, p. 425.
49 'The Great Day', *Collected Poems*,
p. 358.
50 'Lapis Lazuli', *Collected Poems*, p. 339.
51 Jon Stallworthy, *Vision and Revision
in Yeats's Last Poems*, pp. 159–60. I
have omitted cancelled lines for the
sake of legibility.
52 'Under Ben Bulben', *Collected Poems*,
p. 399.
53 *Variorum Plays*, p. 1143.
54 'Meru', *Collected Poems*, p. 333.
55 *Essays and Introductions*, p. 521.
56 *Essays and Introductions*, p. 195.
57 *Mythologies*, p. 290.
58 *Autobiographies* (*Hodos Chameliontos*,
ix), p. 272.
59 *Autobiographies* (*Estrangement*,
xxxiii), p. 482.
60 *Mythologies*, p. 366.
61 *A Vision*, p. 84.
62 *Explorations*, p. 290.
63 *Explorations*, p. 377.
64 *Collected Poems*, p. 332.
65 *Autobiographies* (*Dramatis Personae*,
vii), p. 402.
66 *Autobiographies* (*Dramatis Personae*,
xv), p. 435.
67 *Autobiographies* (*Dramatis Personae*,
xiv), p. 431.
68 *Essays and Introductions*, p. 158.
69 *A Vision*, p. 52.
70 *Autobiographies* (*Dramatis Personae*,
x), p. 416.
71 'High Talk', *Collected Poems*, p.385.
72 'At Algeciras—A Meditation upon
Death', *Collected Poems*, p. 278.

Index to the Works of Yeats
mentioned in the Text